Architecture has been incessantly theorised, taught and practiced merely as an art of aestheticised material structures and space. Sarah Robinson presents architecture convincingly and inspiringly as a network of relationships, actions and interactions; buildings reveal, structure and articulate our encounters and relations with the world. Through deftly weaving knowledge from diverse disciplines ranging from philosophy to psychology, anthropology to neuroscience and history to poetics—this book opens up comprehensive and balanced, but truly radical views of the complex phenomenon of architecture. The reader will surely encounter and experience buildings differently after having read this significant book.

—Juhani Pallasmaa, Architect, Professor Emeritus (Aalto University), Writer, Member of the Pritzker Architecture Prize Jury, 2008–2014

A veritable encyclopedia of ideas, all pressing toward one sage insight: good design—far from being an act of technocratic rationality—resides in the poetic, festive, and cultural interplay between self and other, or better, the art of exploring the depth of our visceral engagement with the world. All else is inhumanity.

—Harry Francis Mallgrave, Emeritus Director of Architectural and Theory program at Illinois Institute of Technology and the author of *The Architect's Brain, Architecture and Embodiment* and *From Object to Experience*, among other books

Robinson's clear prose brings hope—stitching together insights from philosophy, existential phenomenology, the cognitive sciences, ethology, psychology, anthropology, architectural and literary history, to shed light on possibilities that are open to designers and architects in our complex world . . . in an intellectual poetics meant to evoke, resonate and make you think.

—Alberto Pérez-Gómez, Director of the History and Architecture Program at McGill University and the author of *Architecture and the Crisis of Modern Science, Built Upon Love* and *Attunement*, among other books

Architecture is a Verb

Architecture is a Verb outlines an approach that shifts the fundamental premises of architectural design and practice in several important ways. First, it acknowledges the centrality of the human organism as an active participant interdependent in its environment. Second, it understands human action in terms of radical embodiment—grounding the range of human activities traditionally attributed to mind and cognition: imagining, thinking, remembering—in the body. Third, it asks what a building *does*—that is, extends the performative functional interpretation of design to interrogate how buildings move and in turn move us, how they shape thought and action. Finally, it is committed to articulating concrete situations by developing a taxonomy of human/building interactions.

Written in engaging prose for students of architecture, interiors and urban design, as well as practicing professionals, Sarah Robinson offers richly illustrated practical examples for a new generation of designers.

Sarah Robinson is an architect practicing in San Francisco and Pavia, Italy. She holds degrees in philosophy and architecture, and was the founding chair of the Frank Lloyd Wright School of Architecture Board of Trustees. Her previous books—*Mind in Architecture: Embodiment, Neuroscience and the Future of Design* with Juhani Pallasmaa (2015) and *Nesting: Body, Dwelling, Mind* (2011)—have been among the first to explore the connections between the cognitive sciences and architecture. She co-founded and edits the journal *Intertwining*, is an adjunct professor at Aalborg University, Denmark and teaches at NAAD / IUAV University of Venice.

Architecture is a Verb

SARAH ROBINSON

Routledge
Taylor & Francis Group

NEW YORK AND LONDON

First published 2021
by Routledge
52 Vanderbilt Avenue, New York, NY 10017

and by Routledge
2 Park Square, Milton Park, Abingdon, Oxon, OX14 4RN

Routledge is an imprint of the Taylor & Francis Group, an informa business

Library of Congress Cataloging-in-Publication Data
Names: Robinson, Sarah (Architect), author.
Title: Architecture is a verb / Sarah Robinson.
Description: New York : Routledge, 2021. | Includes bibliographical
    references and index.
Identifiers: LCCN 2020039862 (print) | LCCN 2020039863 (ebook) |
    ISBN 9780367610371 (hardback) | ISBN 9780367610364 (paperback) |
    ISBN 9781003103004 (ebook)
Subjects: LCSH: Architecture—Human factors.
Classification: LCC NA2542.4 .R62 2021 (print) | LCC NA2542.4 (ebook) |
    DDC 720.1/03—dc23
LC record available at https://lccn.loc.gov/2020039862
LC ebook record available at https://lccn.loc.gov/2020039863

ISBN: 978-0-367-61037-1 (hbk)
ISBN: 978-0-367-61036-4 (pbk)
ISBN: 978-1-003-10300-4 (ebk)

Typeset in Avenir and Dante
by Apex CoVantage, LLC

Contents

Foreword

In this new book, Sarah Robinson adds her poetic and highly erudite voice to a body of work in the history and theory of architecture that has been building over the last 50 years upon a realisation of two fundamental and incontrovertible conditions: (1) the real importance of architecture and the lived environment for human wholesomeness, for psychosomatic health, involving both body and emotional consciousness and (2) the concomitant limitations of an architectural practice driven instead by instrumentalised technological concerns and/or misguided formalist conceits. Robinson takes up the challenge clearly articulated by Dalibor Vesely in his book *Architecture in the Age of Divided Representation*: "Restoring the practical nature of situations as a primary vehicle of design enables us to move away from inconclusive play with abstract form and functions."

Vesely deplored the fact that architecture could no longer be depended upon as the tacit literacy of culture, stating a problem that has been addressed, be it optimistically or pessimistically, by many of his students, students of his students and other like-minded writers, all given due credit in the pages of this book. Robinson's clear prose brings hope, stitching together insights from philosophy, existential phenomenology, the cognitive sciences, ethology, psychology, anthropology, and architectural and literary history, to shed light on possibilities that are open to designers and architects in our complex world.

Starting already in the nineteenth century, once detached from the habits of practical life, often deliberately abdicating its inveterate responsibility to contribute towards a meaningful lifeworld, architectural form was fetishised as an end in itself. Today, as then, architects' still-prevailing fascination with geometries is symptomatic of the same conceptual errors that have long mislead the humanities and natural sciences into believing in their self-referential relevance. The critique of twentieth-century phenomenology went a long way to correct such errors. More recently, building upon new insights in the cognitive and neurosciences that have blurred the sharp lines traditionally drawn between the natural sciences and the humanities, Robinson embraces an enactive understanding of cognition and emotion, positing the body as an 'I can, therefore I am' and leaving behind the old and mistaken Cartesian axiom, 'I think, therefore I am,' thus locating intelligence in the mutual interaction between body, mind and world. Restoring the practical nature of situations in architecture means coming to terms with the full implications of this co-emergence, questioning the valorisation of architecture as an independent aesthetic object (more recently, the fad of "object-oriented ontology") and recognising the fact that human spatiality cannot be reduced to geometric space, as Maurice Merleau-Ponty and Gaston Bachelard, among others, often insisted.

Robinson's approach shifts the fundamental premises of architectural design and practice in several important ways: first, it acknowledges the centrality of the human organism as an active participant interdependent in its environment. Second, it understands human action in terms of radical embodiment—grounding the range of human activities traditionally attributed to mind and cognition: imagining, thinking, remembering—in the body. Third, it asks what a building does—that is, extends the performative functional interpretation of design to interrogate how buildings move and in turn move us, how they shape thought and action. Finally, it is committed to richly articulating practical, concrete situations. To do this, Robinson develops a taxonomy of human/building reciprocities with rich examples, using the second half of her book to take us in a beautifully constructed journey across time and space, in visits that 'demonstrate' its theses.

This book is constructed from sound arguments but it is not a method—it is not a plot, simple to paraphrase—it is an intellectual poetics meant to evoke and resonate, and make you think. For as Robinson summarily puts it: Situated poetics is the skill to cultivate meanings that are already there—it is not so much creation as revelation—in an attitude of tenderness and acts of exquisite care.

Alberto Pérez-Gómez

Preface

My interest in the ways that findings in the cognitive and neurosciences are reshaping our understanding of our interdependence with our environments stems from my work as an architect, but also from my own sense of connectedness to the natural world. I grew up in the woods next to our house, and came home only when I was hungry or it grew too dark. Over the course of my childhood, I watched the woods diminish to the size of a basketball court. Trees were replaced with fake colonials. My building of rafts and forts and climbing in trees was replaced with a jungle gym. Yet even before these disappearances, I despised being in buildings, and it wasn't until I went to live at Frank Lloyd Wright's Taliesin West that I could spend the whole day quite happily inside. The difference was the abundant light, but also something more—the fusion of indoors and out, the proportions, the textures, the thoughtfulness of the details—in the interweaving of all of these qualities, I felt the same nurturing presence that I felt in the woods. And this is what ultimately motivates my interest in learning how our surroundings shape us, to discover ways that we, as designers, can orchestrate that same living presence.

This sense of presence cannot of course be reduced to a style, formula, or an 'ism' of any kind; rehashing the work of the masters will definitely not do, but there are some recurring strategies that have worked in the past and that can be developed to ripen into the future. An approach that integrates the findings of the cognitive sciences in a non-reductive, non-prescriptive and poetic way to the practical task of constructing environments worthy of life has crystallised for me over the last decade or so—and it is one that concentrates on interactions. The old 'problems' of the body/mind, physical/biological, nature/culture, subject/object all seem to wither in the face of interaction. When we consider the interaction of breathing, who exactly is doing the breathing? What is outside becomes inside in the breath; the same could be said for eating, resonating, remembering, thinking, playing, inhabiting and on and on. The title *Architecture is a Verb* comes from this emphasis on action, and asks what architecture *does*. This book is organised in two parts that hinge on what I have called a Taxonomy of Interactions. The first part articulates a theory of embodiment in terms of architectural design, and is my effort to convince you of the validity of interpreting and organising the interactions in the way that I have done. The second half considers practical and poetic design approaches worthy of these interactions. If you do not need theory or convincing, you could jump to the second half of the book, or even read only one chapter. All the parts are integral to and build the whole, yet I have tried to make each one semi-self-sufficient, so if you find overlaps here and there, this explains why.

My organisational metaphor for the Taxonomy of Interactions is Jean Gebser's five structures of consciousness. I discovered Gebser through a chance encounter and have found a clarity and freshness in his work that is remarkably relevant today. I hope to have been able to convey something of his generative approach in these pages. Many of the voices you will hear alongside my own are those that are so interwoven into my own thinking as to be thoroughly incorporated—corporally present in my person. The cast of characters is a promiscuous blend that does not respect categories; poets sometimes converse with scientists, anthropologists with artists, philosophers with ecologists—all in the thread of a single page. I see connections more than I do divisions, and this tendency is the impetus that guides this work.

Acknowledgements

The thinking in these pages developed from the opportunities presented to me over the past five or so years since the publication of the book *Mind in Architecture: Embodiment, Neuroscience and the Future of Design* that I edited with Juhani Pallasmaa. I am grateful for the generous invitations that allowed me to freely explore these themes. I wish to particularly thank Franco Guidi and Lucia Matti at Lombardini22 in Milan, Vittorio Gallese and Alessandro Gattara in Parma, who with Davide Ruzzon is one of my co-editors of the journal *Intertwining*. I also want to acknowledge Davide's untiring dedication to NAAD, the Neuroscience Applied to Architectural Design at IUAV, the University of Venice; Laura Sangiorgi in Varese; Roberta Dall'Ara in Milan; Hannele Jäämeri in Helsinki; Pedro Borges de Araújo in Porto; Zachi Arpad, Vlad Brătuleanu and Roxana Chis in Bucharest; Juanita Botero Lopez in Bogotá; Kim Coventry in Chicago; Deborah Barlow in Boston; Anne Depue in Seattle; Catherine Baumgartner in San Francisco; Michael and Suzanne Johnson in Cave Creek; Aris Georges at Taliesin; and Bob Condia, Wendy Ornelas and David Seamon in Manhattan, Kansas. Bob's insistence that I study the work of Indra Kagis McEwen and Jane Hirshfield proved essential to my project. I am also grateful to Andrea Jelić, Lars Brorson Fich, Tenna Dokter Olsen Tvedebrink, Runa Hellwig and Zakaria Djebbara for their invitation to be an adjunct professor at the University of Aalborg in Denmark, which provided the very first occasion to present this approach. I also wish to thank Klaske Havic for her thoughtful support; Larry Hickman for his help with John Dewey; Krystal Racaniello for her immediate enthusiasm, and both she and Christine Bondira's thorough professionalism at Routledge, as well as the six anonymous reviewers for their insightful comments. I am especially indebted to the lifework, kindness and enduring support of Harry Francis Mallgrave, Alberto Pérez-Gómez and Juhani Pallasmaa. My husband Paolo Bazzurro and our three children are my dearest supporters, and I dedicate all of these efforts to them.

Situated Poetics 1

Where are you right now? At this very moment, what do you touch, smell, taste, hear and see? Are the sounds around you distracting or pleasing? What about the light? Is it soft or harsh? And the air? Is it moving or is it stale? Do you want to breathe it, to bring it inside your body? *How you are* has very much to do with *where you are* and with the particularities of your situation. This is so obvious that we take it for granted—but let us pause for a moment to notice what is so very ordinary. Consider the daily experience of light: the light that makes its way through your window not only warms your skin, it expands the space around you, making both it and you feel a little larger. The light shifts your mood and regulates your hormone levels, tuning your body to seasonal and cosmic rhythms. The light not only enters your space, it enters your imagination, unveiling the hidden, inviting you to trace its path. Without your awareness, your mind begins to fill in the shadows the light has brought newly into relief. The light carries your mind along with it, tugging your attention towards the opening, tempting you to seek the source of this sure and quiet power. In this instance, is it clear where your mind is? Is it in your body, in the window or travelling along with the light? What is outside and what is in? Is it clear where you end and the world begins?

When asked where the mind is, the philosopher John Dewey said if he had to locate it anywhere, he would locate it in the situation.[1] And he used this word in its original sense. The verb *situate* is rooted in the words 'to settle, to dwell, to be at home.' If it seems difficult to imagine your mind being situated in a place that is technically on the other side of your skin, think for a moment again about where you are *sited* at this moment—your position, your posture. The way you are seated right now releases a cascade of physiological shifts in your body; every gesture has its chemical signature that conditions how you feel. And how you feel influences how you think, directs what you notice and ultimately contributes to what you do. So, again, is your mind located in your skull, in the nervous bundle housed inside your spinal cord, in the arch of your posture, in the back of the chair that supports that arch, in the ground that supports the chair—or does it thread through all of these?

Something as simple as experiencing light or positioning your body has important implications for design, whose full import requires that we "not take for granted that life exists more fully in what is commonly thought big than in what is commonly thought small,"[2] as Virginia Woolf insisted. To fully acknowledge the untapped potential of what is so seemingly humble and patently mundane means reevaluating what is appropriate to the enduring practice of architecture. All of our actions are *interactions*. Our actions do not take place in isolation but are influenced and modulated by our situation. "The use of typical situations as a primary vehicle of design is a new departure towards an approach that may be best described as situational or as a new poetics of architecture," wrote Dalibor Vesely. And the proposition of using typical situations as the basis of a new design approach is more remarkable than it might initially seem. We now know that our movements and postures shape the way we think and feel, and that these movements are afforded by concrete situations. Changing the variables of the situation means changing our possible movements and actions. If each of our movements elicits subtle but cumulative shifts and gauges the way we engage in our lives, imagine the impact that the compounding of those changes might have on our moods, behaviours and cultural habits. Our buildings structure, choreograph and sediment our actions to materialise our collective cultural values and social practices. Yet we architects, intoxicated with our grand schemes and overarching plans, have missed the radical potential of what is commonly thought small.

Almost 20 years ago, Vesely clearly articulated the corrective to this neglect: "Restoring the practical nature of situations as a primary vehicle of design enables us to move away from inconclusive play with abstract form and functions."[3] This directive subjects the broadly misinterpreted dictum 'form follows function' to a new level of rigour. Once detached from the concrete fabric of practical life, form was hollowed of meaning and fetishised as an end in itself while function was split from its raison-d'être in the body and relegated to the domain of technological manipulation. Architects' fascination with games of abstraction is symptomatic of the same conceptual errors that mired disciplines in the humanities and natural sciences in fruitless debates pitting mind over matter and nature versus nurture. Yet such disputes have since been laid to rest. New insights in the cognitive and neurosciences have collapsed the lines traditionally drawn between the natural sciences and the humanities, grounding them both in "corporeal matters of fact."[4] Finally giving the body its due has shifted the worn 'I think, therefore I am' that privileged the mind over the body to the engaged 'I can, therefore I am'—locating intelligence in the mutual interaction between body, mind and world. Restoring the practical nature of situations means coming to terms with the full implications of the fact that "inhabited space transcends geometric space,"[5] as Bachelard insisted. The space beyond our skin is a field of possibility— tempered and conditioned by the possibilities it affords for action. Indeed, architectural space is the matrix of situated human action long before it is structured geometrically. It is finally time to accept that architecture is not merely a testing ground for novel forms or arbitrary theories but is and has always been the very fabric of human becoming.

Architecture's Resistance

Though its humanist role has been obscured over the course of the last two centuries, in the long haul of human development, architecture has undoubtedly served as the topological and corporeal ground of interpersonal, cultural and social practices. Here again, let us consider what is most mundane, what is most common to human experience: we are born of the body and we are born incomplete. The fact that the way we move—that we walk upright— had the combined cause and consequence that we are born before we are physiologically prepared and so must complete the last quarter of our gestation outside the womb. Our utter dependence on our surroundings is without parallel in the natural world: most mammals can run, walk and swim within hours of their arrival into the world. While they are protected from their surroundings through the thickness of their skin, our very survival depends on the receptivity and fragility of ours. Our nervous system wraps us outside and in, and our life depends on the sensitivity and integrity of the succession of envelopes in which we are surrounded. This nascent vulnerability—the fact that we simply cannot exist outside a constructed envelope—is, at the same time, the very reason that we have become human in the first place. We become human only in the arms of another. Whether held by human arms or the support of an incubator, human life develops in the nested interactions that take place in a succession of constructed envelopes. To say that we have coevolved with our buildings is to grossly understate the deeply intertwined, developmental nature of our transactions with our surroundings. We are who we are because of the innumerable ways we have mutually shaped and interacted with our dwellings. And I do not mean this in a strictly functional sense—our very existence has depended upon extending ourselves not only physiologically, but also psychologically and socially through the medium of our constructed habitat.

Recognising the profound role that environmental factors play in shaping cognition is the major catalyst bridging disciplines whose knowledge bases were formerly opposed. This research is critically relevant to architectural practice, especially since it is our business to structure the environment in which we now spend 95 percent of our lives—the built environment. And our unique position between the natural sciences and humanities makes it all the more opportune. After all, our position between disciplines underlies our long-standing habit of uncritically adapting theories to suit our needs regardless of the sources or nature of the knowledge. So, it is particularly puzzling why architects have been so slow to integrate this new knowledge base which is actually directly relevant—and potentially revolutionising—to our practice. Perhaps this resistance stems from two interrelated sources that both have to do with architecture's unique capacity to integrate different dimensions of human experience.

At its most profound level, the character of architecture—like that of matter itself—is resistance. Most of the habits of our daily life, which architecture structures and activates, take place at a preconscious level. We take these mundane practicalities for granted. Habit "wears grooves," as Dewey put it, freeing our energies for other pursuits. These patterns of living are deeply resistant to change because they have very concretely shaped who we are. Neither our bodies nor our buildings are merely the accumulation of building blocks, whether we call them cells or bricks, but the dynamic concretion of kinaesthetic capacities and performances. The astronauts of NASA, when freed from the constraints of gravity, still insist on eating around a table, even though food floats from their plates. This configuration stabilises not only their body, but their mental state. This pattern of activity has shaped our body and our appetites and cemented our relationships. Our deep evolutionary history freshly awakens in the present every time we enjoy a meal. "In every culture a series of things is taken for granted and lies fully beyond explicit consciousness of anyone," writes Hans Georg Gadamer, "even the greatest dissolution of traditional forms, mores, customs, the degree to which things held in common still determine everyone is only more concealed."[6] We are largely unaware of our interdependence with our environment for the same reasons that other animals are unaware of theirs—because it operates unconsciously as our extended body. The importance of that which is most vital is disclosed by the fact that it is very literally overlooked. We tend not to notice the mesh that supports us until it is ruptured, just as we do not appreciate the background of good health until we fall ill. The colloquialism 'to fall ill' is very revealing in this regard; we fall from our tacit means of support.

The Possibility of an Integrated Approach

Yet, this richly embodied embedded experience, the formative process of daily life that both gives rise to buildings and is then shaped by them, is not recognised much less attended to because the intentions of architecture are oriented elsewhere. The narrowed contemporary vision of architecture as a profession positioned within and judged according to the criteria of technical disciplines is unequipped to deal with such humble realities. I use the word *humble* here in its etymological sense, as it derives from *humus* and its shared origins in the words *soil*, *human* and *humour*. This loss of humanity has gradually eroded the practice of architecture to the extent that we are now calling for a 'human-centred' architecture. If human beings are not the central interest of our practice, then who—or better, what—is the flash dance of vanity, the production of commodity, the ceaseless fodder that must feed the capitalist machine? We all seem to agree, as Vesely did, "that the goal of architecture is life,"[7] but we fail to fully understood that technology and instrumental rationality are only a means—a means which determines the specific ends which can be effected. Our quasi-religious belief that technology will ultimately save us mistakenly assumes that modern society can and will undergo a technological transformation *in toto*. This totalising vision does not recognise that different levels of reality undergo different rates of change commensurate to their evolutionary histories and constitutions. We assume the wholesale adaptation to the levelling imperatives of technological progress without acknowledging that such means and methods operate on different strata of consciousness at varying rates and in differing ways. Deeply embedded and slowly accreted cultural habits and practices are immune to transformation through technological means alone. The crux of the problem, as Vesely explains, is this:

> That the articulation of cultural life is directly linked with conditions that remain relatively unchanged, while at the same time the path of culture that is open to technological transformation has changed radically, creates tension and eventually a deep void in the very heart of culture itself.[8]

This deep void characterises the curious blend that the profession of architecture has become: in his words, "a mosaic of expert knowledge brought together either as abstract systems or as the intuitive improvisations of personal vision,"[9] neither of which are capable of responding to the complex imperatives of creating and sustaining a more-than-human habitat. The inadequacy of these approaches is even more evident in the fear that integrating this new knowledge will somehow curb personal creativity. Such a fear betrays a deep confusion about the nature of genuine creativity. We have equated creativity with personal freedom, yet taking seriously corporeal matters of fact argues otherwise. Freedom is built upon limits. Freedom is not free rein; it is rather, as Robert Frost insisted, "being easy in your harness."[10] Genuine creativity is a spontaneous process like the open-ended play of nature whose staggering diversity is all the more complex because of its inherent respect for limits. Failing to reckon with the facts of our embodiment for fear that it will dampen creativity trivialises the true role of our vocation and the opportunity to redeem it. After all, "architects determine the nervous makeup of generations,"[11] as Richard Neutra warned more than 70 years ago.

A growing chorus of voices are calling for a new approach to both architectural education and practice, and enough momentum is gathering to finally shift an exhausted paradigm. As Harry Mallgrave has recently written: "The sovereignty of speculative theory over the past six decades has run its course and today has become antiquated by the momentous leaps that have been made in the humanities and natural sciences."[12] The much lamented gulf between these different kinds of knowledge is beginning to heal because both are discovering that their respective disciplines are rooted in the interdependence of body/mind/world. This collective knowledge is reaching a degree of corroboration to finally serve as a source of rapprochement also for us. Dalibor Vesely was at pains to show that the tension that has riddled architectural practice can only be bridged with a new kind of knowledge capable of reconciling genuine creativity with the productive capability of modern science. And again, he lucidly articulated the antidote:

> To preserve its primary identity and humanistic role in the future, architecture must establish credentials on the same level of intelligibility as instrumental thinking, while at the same time it must integrate and subordinate the instrumental knowledge and technical potential of human beings to their praxis.[13]

He uses the term *praxis* here in its classical sense, as a patterning activity fundamental to the constitution of human beings and our concrete situation in the world.

Architecture Is a Verb

Such a reorientation means changing our habits of thought, and as we have seen, the most deeply seated habits are those of which we are least aware. Is it not curious that the prosaic word we use to refer to human artifice—the word *building*—is both a noun and a verb? Builders build buildings. But the hallowed realm of architecture lacks such an option. Why is it that architects do not architect architecture? This detail reveals the hidden presence and absence of the body, its presumed level of engagement and its level of prestige. The builder builds with his body, while the architect projects her 'vision' from her disembodied mind. It would surely be easier to use the word building for this manifesto, yet that would sorely miss the point of this broader concern: architecture's latent capacity to harmonise different levels of experience is compromised when such dualities are left intact. Correlating the profane building with body and static architecture with the almighty mind mutilates the very basis on which the latter could fulfil its conciliatory role.

A chief impediment to imagining this formative capability is the habit of thinking of architecture in terms of the noun *form*, rather than in terms of the verb *forming*. A thoroughgoing interrogation of the noun is necessary to this fundamental reorientation. As the physicist David Bohm points out: "Truly original discoveries in science and in other fields have generally involved such inquiry into old questions, leading to a perception of their inappropriateness, and in this way allowing of the putting forth of new questions."[14] To do this is often very difficult because these presuppositions are deeply hidden in the very structure of thought. The well-known example is the way Einstein was forced to discard the confused presuppositions commonly accepted in the physics of his day before he could arrive at new questions leading to radically different notions. The language of physics is unfit to describe the actual dynamic processes that physics itself studies. "What is . . . is movement," insists Bohm.[15] Even particles which are presumably static are actually "ongoing movements that are mutually dependent because ultimately they merge and interpenetrate."[16]

An obstacle to dynamic thinking is the subject-verb-object structure of sentences which implies that action arises in a subject and is exerted on an object. Why do we say, for example, that it is raining, instead of that rain is happening? To whom, exactly, does 'it' refer? This is but one example of how our language is unable to speak of ongoing processes. Yet in other languages, movement is taken as a primary notion and apparently static things are treated as relatively invariant states of continuing movement. In ancient Hebrew, for example, the verb was primary. The root of all lost Hebrew words is a verb form, while adverbs, adjectives and nouns were obtained by modifying the verbal form with prefixes and suffixes. Even the English words *dwell* and *dwelling*, like the word *building*, are both nouns, verbs and gerunds—their versatility demonstrates that both terms are implicitly connected to ongoing living processes. Calling attention to the movement initiated by the verb serves to correct this centuries-old deficit. This act of reordering attention forces us to reconsider the realities which the verbs describe and opens new possibilities for thinking in terms of active embodied engagement.

Radical Embodiment

John Dewey also complained that language tended to perpetuate and reify divisions rather than articulate continuity and movement. The deep void present in our language dawns in the fact that we lack a unified word to speak about mind and body. "Our language is so permeated with consequences of theories which have divided the body and mind from each other, making separate existential realms out of them, that we lack words to designate the actual existential fact."[17] Like the phenomenologists, he hyphenated words to knit back together false divisions. Admitting that the term body-mind was a half measure, he lamented that "we find it easier to make a conjunction of two inconsistent premises rather than rethink our premises."[18] In the name of rethinking our premises, let us do away with the dash altogether and perform a kind of affirmative action on our understanding of body. Our body is our very basis of knowing and is already a mind. Applying pressure in this way, our understanding might swell and enlarge commensurate with the marvel that is the dynamic body. After all, if it weren't for the body's astonishing sensitivity and deep knowing, we would never have invented words like 'mind' and 'soul.'

The deep-seated and unconscious valuations privileging mind over body, thinking over doing, theory over practice, architecture over building are based on premises that are frankly obsolete. We now know that the precious concepts with which we construct our vertiginous theories are born in bone, muscle and nervous skin, that they originate in the primal movements of play.[19] The dynamic behavioural patterns from which concepts arise have deep evolutionary histories that we share with other animals. And what's more, the so-called external world has shaped our perception. Our well-known preference for the dialectic of prospect and refuge derives from our deep past on the African savannah.[20] Our preference for vertical lines, the calming sense of colonnades, likely originates in our primate experience of swinging through trees.[21] We were shaped by our interpersonal relationships in the natural world and belong to it—it is only in the last two millennia that we have decisively lost contact, which in the time horizon of human evolution is but a brief episode. The undeniable proof of this enduring connection is written in our bodies—in the fact that our hearts beat in synchrony with those near to us,[22] in the fact that our stress hormones decrease when we walk on grass[23] and in the fact that we are cleansed in the bath of the forest.[24]

Alongside John Dewey, the other champion of embodiment whose voice resonates throughout this endeavour is Maurice Merleau-Ponty. A student of Edmund Husserl, the founder of phenomenology, he was committed to restoring the validity of human experience to legitimate inquiry. Our project to restore lost dimensions of life to the legitimate practice of architecture follows his precedent, and the success of our efforts hinges on adopting his particular orientation. Whereas Husserl's protégés, Heidegger among them, tended to emphasise the ontology of the body—that is, they endeavoured to understand what the body is—Husserl's concern was epistemological—that is, how the body knows and in turn how the body makes knowing possible at all. His work was critical in bringing to light how embodied experience is a communal nexus of meaningful situations, expressive gestures and practical actions—the very ground of praxis. This crucial difference in orientation shifts our preoccupation with what a building *is*—a passive form—to a what a building *does* in an active sense, and asks how we know, feel and sense *according to* our buildings, how they afford and reinforce certain gestures and modes of perception while atrophying others. The phenomenologists built the crucial groundwork for such a shift and their work has been corroborated and reinforced by subsequent work in the natural sciences. Long-neglected subjective experience is gradually being legitimised through instrumental methods, and we gain to profit from this alliance. Addressing architecture as a verb—asking not what a building is in an object sense, but what it does in the sense of an ongoing dynamic process—can inform our practice in just this radical way, if by *radical* we mean *radici*, Latin, meaning 'from the roots.'

Situated Poetics

The aim here is not to proffer a new theory to which we append yet another 'ism' or to construct a foolproof system intended to substitute genuine creativity. An approach worthy of honouring architecture's latent capacity to integrate multiple dimensions of human experience can only be poetic. And this approach is called 'poetics' for precisely this reason—poetry distills meaning in few words *to go beyond them*. "The difference between the action of a poem and of an ordinary narrative is physiological,"[25] wrote Paul Valéry. Poetry moves us in a way other than ordinary narrative precisely because it is rooted in the viscera. A word refers not only to a concept; it also evokes an image and *makes* a sound. The fact that a word is also a sound and a shape, that it emerges through the collective embodied processes of history, that it belongs to everyone and no one, is more than a metaphor to guide our efforts. The use of the word *poetic* here has not to do with its strict reference to a literary type, but its deeper kinaesthetic moorings in the body.

In its original sense, poetics refers to a way of making, rooted in the Greek *poeisis*, which in turn derives from the even more ancient Sanskrit word meaning 'building, piling up'—and it is this sense of piling up, accrual and accretion of processes already in motion, that is emphasised here. It was perhaps this sort of primordial condensation of embodied meaning over the long haul of human history to which Valéry was alluding. Even before words are formed into language, there is the sensitive fabric of a living mesh, what Husserl called 'kinaesthetic consciousness' and Merleau-Ponty named 'the Flesh.' This is the kinaesthetic fabric of daily life. In Vesely's words, "the implicit (tacit) level of the pre-reflective world is highly structured but not articulated in a way possible to express in language and thought."[26] This place inaccessible to language is the *prima materia* of architecture. The poetics he outlined at the conclusion of *Architecture in an Age of Divided Representation* was based on a way of making that revealed the richness of this latent world by means consistent with its origin, situated in the communicative space of culture and characterised by a deep respect for the natural world, made manifest in *the rich articulation of typical situations*. And despite its rather ominous title, at the heart of his masterwork is a message of hope:

> The poetic paradigm lingering in the depths of our culture has been overshadowed by the contemporary version of poetics often reduced to technical innovation and aesthetics. Yet we should not therefore conclude that the creative power of the poetic paradigm is lost or dead. It is still alive in many areas of culture, including architecture, and most strongly in the creative conditions and possibilities of practical life.[27]

Yet, when the world is on fire and we are drowning in the consequences of our apocalyptic actions, is it not a luxury to invest our efforts in the rich articulation of typical situations? Again, let us consider that which is commonly thought small—the act of eating. Our life obviously depends on consuming food for nourishment. But eating is far more than a biological fact or even a discrete act. Eating is a process that extends backward and forward through time and is therefore ripe with personal, interpersonal, social, cultural and political consequences and implications. Cooking our food triggered a cascade of consequences that were physiological, leading to enlarged brain size, social, leading to communal group bonding, settlement patterns, and political, leading to the division of labor, consolidated power structures and elaborate cultural expressions[28]—a constellation of consequences blossomed forth from this act—which is not an action per se, but an interaction in a situation whose variables interact and reinforce each other. Eating processed food enacts a chain of consequences not only in our body chemistry but in agricultural and labor practices, leading to fossil fuel dependence, deforestation, etc. It not only matters what you eat but how and *where* you eat. Overeating tends to occur when the occasion of the meal is stripped of interpersonal and social meanings, leading to emotional isolation, depression and obesity. The role of the atmosphere of the meal is as substantial as the food itself.[29] This action/interaction envelops divisions like body/mind/nature/culture. It was perhaps for this reason that John Dewey said that the mark of civilisation is determined by the extent to which its cultural practices unite the actions of the body and mind. Far from being a luxury, these seemingly small adjustments have a major collective impact. And as he insisted, "the integration of mind-body in action is the most practical of all questions that we can ask of our civilisation."[30] Dignifying something as mundane as eating—sourcing food locally, preparing it with care, sharing it attentively in an atmosphere of love—is a poetic act. This kind of enacted poetry triggers a cascade of material, emotional, social, cultural and political consequences that when compounded over populations and across time are by no means trivial.

The approach outlined here shifts the fundamental premises of architectural design and practice in four ways: first, it acknowledges the centrality of the human organism as an active participant interdependent in its environment. Second, it understands human action in terms of radical embodiment—grounding the range of human activities traditionally attributed to mind and cognition: imagining, thinking, remembering—in the body. Third, it asks what a building *does*—that is, extends the performative functional interpretation of design to interrogate how buildings move and in turn move us, how they shape thought and action. Finally, it is committed to richly articulating practical, concrete situations. To do this, we develop a taxonomy of human/building reciprocities—and study them through the mesh of diverse disciplines, asking how interdisciplinary research in the cognitive sciences, ethology, psychology, anthropology, architectural and literary history, film and poetry enrich a multidimensional understanding of how design impacts not only human behaviour—but human becoming.

Paying particular attention to the humble, to that which is commonly thought small, favours practical ground-up interventions to abstract top-down solutions. It builds from the rubble of the ivory tower, rather than denying that it has already fallen. It is not a denial of technology but a more rigorous evaluation of its intended use and outcomes in terms of the complex bio-cultural history of the situation at hand. It positions the architect as a generalist whose professionalism consists in responsibly interpreting, integrating and poetically responding to interdisciplinary facts. Who, rather than dictating a totalising solution, more closely resembles the physician—whose use of the expertise of the physiologist, radiologist and neurologist, combined with carefully attending to the patient—is ultimately the only person who can undertake treatment for the case. Who, like one bound by oath to the art of a practice that considers the complex web of environmental, social and ethical variables, shares the attitude of Hippocrates, who declared: "We cannot understand the body without a knowledge of the whole of things."[31] Situated poetics is the skill to cultivate meanings that are already there. It is not so much creation as revelation—in an attitude of tenderness and acts of exquisite care.

Notes

1. John Dewey, *Experience and Nature* (New York: Dover, 1958), 234.
2. Virginia Woolf, *The Common Reader* (London: Hogarth Press, 1932), 150.
3. Dalibor Vesely, *Architecture in the Age of Divided Representation* (Boston: MIT Press, 2004), 373.
4. Maxine Sheets-Johnstone, *The Primacy of Movement* (Philadelphia: John Benjamin, 1999), 23.
5. Gaston Bachelard, *The Poetics of Space* (New York: Beacon, 1996), 27.
6. H.G. Gadamer, *Truth and Method*, 2nd ed., trans. W. Glen-Doepel, G. Barden and J. Cumming (London: Sheed & Ward, 1975), 82.
7. Vesely, *Architecture in the Age of Divided Representation*, 23.
8. Ibid., 46.
9. Ibid.
10. Robert Frost, *Christian Science Monitor*, Page 13, Column 4, Boston, MA (May 23, 1957).
11. Richard Neutra, *Survival through Design* (Oxford: Oxford University Press, 1954), 15.
12. Harry Francis Mallgrave, *From Object to Experience* (London: Bloomsbury, 2019), 10.
13. Vesely, *Architecture in the Age of Divided Representation*, 384.
14. David Bohm, *Wholeness and the Implicate Order* (New York: Routledge, 1980), 27.
15. Ibid.
16. Ibid.
17. Dewey, *Experience and Nature*, 284.
18. Ibid., 286.
19. Maxine Sheets-Johnstone, "Movement as Way of Knowing," *Scholarpedia* 8, no. 6 (2013), 30375.

20. Jay Appleton, *The Experience of the Landscape* (London: Wiley, 1975).

21. Sarah Robinson, "John Dewey and the Dialogue between Architecture and Neuroscience," *Architectural Research Quarterly* 19, no. 4 (2015).

22. Martina Ardizi, Marta Calbi, Simona Tavaglione, Alessandra Umilitá, and Vittorio Gallese, "Audience Spontaneous Entrainment," *Nature Scientific Reports*, 10 (2020), Article no. 3813.

23. G. Chevalier et al., "Earthing: Health Implications of Reconnecting the Human Body to the Earth's Surface Electrons," *Journal of Environmental and Public Health* (2012), Article no. 291541.

24. Q. Li, K. Morimoto, A. Nakadai, H. Inagaki, M. Katsumata, T. Shimizu, Y. Hirata, K. Hirata, H. Suzuki, Y. Miyazaki, T. Kagawa, Y. Koyama, T. Ohira, N. Takayama, A.M. Krensky, and T. Kawada, "Forest Bathing Enhances Human Natural Killer Activity and Expression of Anti-cancer Proteins," *International Journal Immunopathology Pharmacology* 20, no. 2 (Apr–Jun 2007), 3–8.

25. Paul Valéry, *The Art of Poetry*, trans. Denise Follett (Princeton: Princeton University Press, 2014), 211.

26. Vesely, *Architecture in the Age of Divided Representation*, 83.

27. Ibid., 373.

28. Richard Wrangham, *How Cooking Made Us Human* (New York: Basic Books, 2009).

29. Maria Golam and Abraham Weizman, "Familial Approach to the Treatment of Childhood Obesity: Conceptual Model," *Journal of Nutrition Education* 33, no. 2 (Mar 2001), 102–107.

30. John Dewey, *Philosophy and Civilisation* (New York: Minton Balch, 1931), 299.

31. As quoted in John Dewey, *The Later Works*, Vol. 3 (Evanston: Northwestern, 1953), 27.

From Vitruvius to the Resonant Body

2

If there has been the equivalent of a bible for architects, it was written in the first century BC by Marcus Vitruvius Pollio. His *Ten Books on Architecture* covered the most practical concerns, from site selection; identifying patterns of wind, water and stars; techniques of slaking lime and laying bricks to the aesthetic concerns of proper proportion. Buildings were codified according to their uses and the formulae of their component parts; columns, ornaments, doorways and sound vessels were proportioned according to the classical canon that had been handed down from the ancient Greeks. No clear distinction was made between the practical and the aesthetic. Architecture was ordered according to his eponymous triumvirate of commodity, firmness and delight.

Although Vitruvius was the first to explicitly codify the practices of building, his efforts were not a matter of invention but of transcription. He systematised what was then commonly understood practical knowledge that had been passed from master to apprentice in a craft tradition. The finest buildings of antiquity were scaled according to the Greek canon whose proportions derived from the human body. The body was measure in every sense of the word; early systems of measurement all stemmed from the actions and dimensions of the human body. Thales determined the height of the great Egyptian pyramid by comparing its height to his own shadow. The length of one's stride was the basis of the Roman mile, which equalled 1,000 paces. The size of the earth was understood from the number of strides it took to cross its surface. The vast and the small were measured according to the body. Vestiges of this ancient reliance are still with us today. Even in the 'absolute' metric system, the modern meter is one forty-millionth of the earth's circumference; 40,000 kilometres is very close to 252,000 Roman stades, which were strides.[1] In Vitruvius's rendering of the canon of ideal proportions, finger (digit), palm, foot and cubit were associated with Pythagorean perfect numbers of 6, 10 and 16. Their perfection derived not from a transcendent source, but from the concrete facts of the body: six related to the unit of the foot, which is one-sixth of a man's height; ten because the hands are composed of ten digits, which relates back to the foot, which is 16 digits long. These numbers were understood in terms of the relationship between the part to the whole, and their harmonious relation was understood to reflect a larger harmony between human and cosmic worlds.

The Greek standard of proportions that Vitruvius codified, known as the Polyclitan canon, was not a prescribed system, but was embodied three-dimensionally in the figure of Doryphoros and his counterpart the Amazon. The two most copied sculptures of antiquity, they were understood to represent the ideal proportions of the human form—and their authority reigned unquestioned for two millennia. For the ancient Greeks, movement was innate, and this inner sense of animism emanated from their depictions of the body. As Dewey pointed out, the organic body held a special position in the Greek hierarchy of being. Their "pious attention"[2] to the body is evident in all of their art forms—their sculpture, religion and various forms of recreation. Vitruvius converted the Polyclitan canon from three to two dimensions by imagining him lying flat on the ground, with the point of a compass centred on his navel, his fingers and toes passively outstretched to touch the circle in which they are encompassed. In this move, the ideal man lost not only a dimension, but also his female counterpart and his sense of movement. Circumscribed by the heavenly geometries of the circle and the square, this description was the basis for Leonardo's *homo quadratus* 1,500 years later.

From Source to Subject

It is important to remember that Vitruvius considered architecture to be an imitation of nature and the human body to be nature's most refined expression. The body was a microcosm of a greater macrocosm; there was no discontinuity between them. It was this underlying sense of harmony that made the human body worthy of representing the proportions of the cosmic order; the body was ideally proportioned to mediate between them. The very fact that there was only crude technological mediation between body and building meant that the buildings of antiquity were perforce intimately related to the proportions and capacities of the human body. The limits of the body tempered and constrained every detail of the built environment. Bricks were scaled to the size of the hand and bore fingerprints; terra-cotta tile shingles are flared at the sides to this day because they are shaped by the human thigh, which served as their original formwork. These details belonged to the Ptolemaic world understanding, in which things were nested inside other things. Medieval medicine understood the body in the same way that it understood the cosmos—as a series of nests.[3] Both cities and houses were modelled on the body and were interchangeable metaphors echoing the nested structures that ordered the relationship between macrocosm and microcosm.[4] In these early conceptions, the body was an idealisation, but not yet an abstraction. This sense of protected containment gradually began to lose its coherence as the Renaissance discovery of the perspectival sense of space began to take an increasingly powerful hold.

Leonardo could not have diagrammed his *homo quadratus* without Euclidean geometry. This two-dimensionalisation of the body that started with Vitruvius's description, and came to fruition with Leonardo, introduced an entirely new notion of space. Euclid mathematised and axiomatised space, permitting it to be considered homogeneous, universal and regular—thus providing the decisive condition for a scientific account of space that would

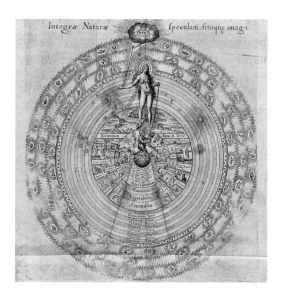

Image 2.1 Robert Fludd, Anima Mundi, 1617

Note: In the world picture of the Ptolemaic cosmos, the body was understood to be nested within in a hierarchy of spheres.

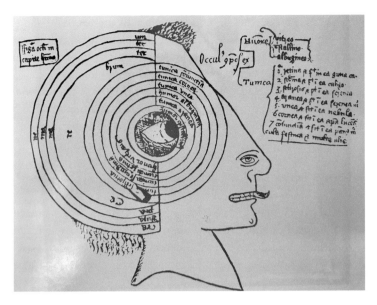

Image 2.2 The microcosm of the eye understood within the concentric circles of the cosmos, MS Sloane 420, from the fourteenth century

Source: The British Library London.

follow 400 years later. The discovery of space in the Renaissance led to mathematisation of space in the Enlightenment. The 'space' that had hitherto supported the body became a meaningless backdrop from which the human was abstracted. The human body that was the very source of geometry became a mere subject of geometry with the rise of the new science. Claude Perrault, who was commissioned by the King of France to translate Vitruvius's treatise from Latin to French, set out to establish his own canon of columnar proportions in an effort to impose a discipline on the incipient wave of neoclassicism. In his studies of renowned classical buildings, Perrault found no rigid and consistent measure to which the columns of those buildings adhered. This led him to make two decisions—moves that, as Harry Francis Mallgrave has stressed, proved to be disastrous to humanist theory.[5] First, he jettisoned the classical canon, and in its place devised his own canon by simply averaging the measurements of the classical buildings he had surveyed. And secondly, he used his authority as a medical doctor to openly declare that canonical proportions were in no way informed by the proportions of the human body. The final severance was executed by his brother Charles, who was instrumental in establishing Cartesian physics in France—when he famously proclaimed that "man has no proportion and no relation with the heavenly bodies infinitely distant from us."[6] This attitude was so prevalent by the eighteenth century that Edmund Burke casually discarded one of the last cornerstones of Renaissance: "The body never supplied the architect with any of his ideas."[7] As the traditional cosmos disintegrated, the relationship between body and building that had been affirmed for millennia had all but dissolved and concern for the body virtually disappeared from architectural discourse.

Qualitative Measure

Understanding the implications of shifting the body from being the source of measure to being the subject of measure might help in restoring meaning to bodily experience and dignity to the essential task of housing the body. For the ancient Greeks, the notion of measure was qualitative—everything in the right measure was the key to the good life. Measure was not considered as it is today as a comparison between a thing and an external standard. Measure had an inner and outer meaning—if something went beyond its proper measure, that did not mean that it no longer conformed to an external standard, but that it was inwardly out of harmony and was therefore bound to lose its integrity and to fall apart. The Latin *mederi*, from which the word *measure* derives, meant to cure and is the root of the word *medicine*. Good health was the consequence of having things in their proper measure. The body and music were understood to share the same harmonic system of measure, and like the sense of measure as related to health, an understanding of measure was essential to understanding harmony in music, which was considered rhythm and right proportion, tonality and intensity. This measure was applied equally to architecture. This qualitative sense of measure went entirely beyond the sense of an external standard and pointed to an underlying order that could be perceived through the senses. By the time of the Enlightenment, measure lost its meaning as a tempering force and indicator of relationships and retained that of being a strictly external standard with an independent existence. Torn from its mesh of broader meaning, in Perrault's codification of proportions, measure was strictly quantitative. This loss of quality was indeed to have devastating consequences—Dewey traces the final unraveling of body from mind whose unity had hitherto been unquestioned to the surrender of quality as a matter of serious study, much less scientific investigation.[8] Quantity which could be objectively measured was considered to be real, while qualities which were immeasurable—but whose existence could not be denied—were relegated to the separate realm of mind and psyche, and were understood to be distinct from the real objects of scientific inquiry: the body and the physical world conceived as objects.

Le Modulor

The introduction of the metric system accomplished the final purging of the body from a legitimate system of measure. For the very first time in human history, the metric system was a system with no relation to corporeal form or common human experience, and Le Corbusier was among the artists in France who rebelled against its institution. He too sought a system of universal quasi-qualitative measure and, much like his predecessors, based his system on the human form and the harmonic scale of music. Developed in the years between 1943 and 1955—an era fascinated with mathematics as a potential source for universal truths—his *modulor* was an attempt to synthesise the Imperial measuring system with its basis in the human form (a foot, a digit, etc.) with the Golden Section, which had been known since classical times but was rediscovered by Leonardo of Pisa in the sixteenth century. With characteristic nerve, Le Corbusier intended his system to be universally applied in both architectural and engineering. Such an ambitious undertaking involved his entire office, who collectively made the arbitrary decision that the ideal human form would be a six-foot-tall man. They allegedly considered basing the modular on the female form, but that idea was quickly dismissed. One of the major flaws with his system was the manner in which he arrived at his so-called absolute numbers. Like his fellow countryman Claude Perrault—who arrived at his canon of column measurements through averaging inputs from diverse sources to arrive at a measure that no actual column from antiquity matched—in reality, very few, if any, actual people conformed to the averaged measurements of the *modulor's* ideal man. Further, his aspiration to base his proportional system on music never came to fruition because though he appreciated music, he had limited technical knowledge of the musical craft. In the end, he interpreted the body as an external, frozen form understood exclusively through vision. Unable to fulfil his humane intention to restore the body to its status as the source of measure, he ended up portraying the body in its most superficial sense: as a measurable container empty of dynamic experience. Despite its worthy intentions, the *modulor* treated the body neither as source, nor subject, but as an abstraction cut off from the processes of life.

No Such Thing as Average

The problem with applying the notion of an average, whether to columns or to human beings, is that it is inevitably an objective measure with no counterpart in actual living, breathing people. Another example of understanding the body not as a complex and dynamic boundary, but as an object among objects specified by its outward quantitative specifications, is the study conducted by the Cleveland School of Medicine in 1943, whose goal was to determine the dimensions of the average or 'normal' woman. In order to do this, they averaged the data gathered on 15,000 young adult women and created the statue named Norma. To their surprise, they found that less than one percent of the actual women came even close to matching even half of Norma's dimensions.[9] Another similar study was carried out seven years later by the US Air Force. In their effort to understand why so many of their fighter jets were crashing—sometimes up to 17 times per day—they surmised that perhaps the cockpits were no longer sized to fit the pilots. In high-speed, fast-acting situations, the cockpit and the pilot demanded a hand-in-glove fit. To test their hypothesis, they conducted a study to find the size of the average pilot. In their analysis of the bodily dimensions of 4,063 men, they found that not a single pilot fit within an average range on all ten dimensions, and less than 3.5 percent were 'average' on only three dimensions.[10] Like the story of Norma before them, they found that not one living, breathing pilot matched the average. But, unlike the Norma study, they did not blame the actual living, breathing women for not matching the ideal. Instead, they innovated. They designed adjustable hand controls, seats, foot pedals—all the features that are now standard equipment not only in cockpits, but in every automobile.

Situated Bodies

Le Corbusier, like the architects of antiquity, believed that architecture had a metaphysical mission to manifest an ideal order on a physical plane expressed through proportion. Yet, it is important to remember that proportion is not a measure in and of itself—but a set of relationships. Proportion gains its meaning in relationship; its system of variables must be understood relative to—that is, in relationship with—each other. When those relationships are torn apart, there is no proportion, only number. If the ideal order is understood to transcend the physical rather than to be immanent within it, such a mission is doomed to failure. The dualism that so tidily categorises the ideal with the unchanging and the intangible—as opposed to the physical, which is changing and tangible—has proven to be untenable by physics and neuroscience alike, yet somehow our imaginations have been unable to widen sufficiently to embrace the possibility that matter may not be dead. To the physicist, the atom is not strictly a unit so much as a pattern of probability. We now know that the human heart produces a bioelectrical field that can be measured from 15 feet away, and that at no point can one delineate where exactly that field ends. From neuroscience, we know that the nervous system extends in energetic layers beyond the surface of skin. So while we inevitably need a degree of standardisation, what hopefully the *modulor* has taught us is that human beings cannot be averaged. Perhaps Le Corbusier and his predecessors were looking for universals in the wrong place. For something to earn the status of being called a human 'universal' means that it can, in principle, be applied to all categories of human experience—and that is a very demanding requirement, indeed. What is universal in human beings is not our dimensions, which change over the course of an individual lifetime, not to mention between different individuals. What earns the status of being called a universal is our openness, our plasticity, our evolutionary transformations in interdependence with our context—all of which condition and scale our inter-actions, our movements and our possibilities.

This sense of the universal is rooted in a mutuality between organism and environment and offers a deeper understanding of proportion. Proportion is here understood to be a relationship between the specific capacities of the organism with the specific features of the environment in which they both mutually coevolved, in a working relationship that is bounded but not fixed. Far from being analogous to a yardstick, or the facsimile of a Platonic ideal, the body is an open process in transformation. It is closer to the way the philosopher Elizabeth Grosz understands the body:

> A concrete, material, animate organisation of flesh, organs, nerves, muscles, and skeletal structure that are given a unity, cohesiveness, and organisation only thorough their psychical and social inscription as the surface and raw materials of an integrated, cohesive totality. The body is, so to speak, organically/biologically/naturally 'incomplete'; it is indeterminate, amorphous, a series of uncoordinated potentialities that require social triggering, ordering, and long-term 'administration.' The body becomes a human body . . . only through the intervention of the (m)other and, ultimately, the Other or Symbolic order (language and rule-governed social order). [11]

This unfinished, continually open, interdependent process is how Dewey understood the body at the turn of the last century: "Every body exists in a natural medium to which it sustains some adaptive connection,"[12] he wrote. Yet, what is so blatantly obvious has been painfully overlooked—our inherited norms, standards and ideals have considered the exterior envelope of the body as a hard, impermeable boundary, cut neatly from its adaptive connections. We now know that bio-cultural boundaries are not discrete, but the sites of intense interactions.

The efficacy of the envelope that surrounds our skin depends on its permeability—on the constant intake of air, water, and physical and emotional nourishment. There is nothing 'hard' about this line. The medium which allows and sustains the body is interpersonal, social, biological, symbolic, cultural and political in its myriad, intertwining and interpenetrating dimensions. Ever the pragmatist, as one interested in clarifying his argument rather than showcasing his intellectual superiority, Dewey liked to use accessible metaphors to make his point:

> In the ultimate analysis, the mystery that the mind should use a body, or that the body should have a mind, is like the mystery that a man cultivating plants should use the soil; or that the soil which grows plants at all should grow those adapted to its own physico-chemical properties and relations.[13]

He even apologises for having to reiterate such obvious statements, but found it necessary to do so because traditional theories have so thoroughly separated life from nature and mind from organic life:

> The thing essential to bear in mind is that living as an empirical affair is not something which goes on below the skin-surface of an organism; it is always an inclusive affair involving connection, interaction of what is in the organic body and what lies outside in space and time, and with higher organisms, far outside.[14]

We are indeed born of the body and are born incomplete. We are nested within our environments; that early sense of protection that the Ptolemaic cosmos intuited in a sense applies to our terrestrial situation. Our bodies and perceptual systems developed in and were shaped by our surroundings, so what is important for proportion is not the vain search for an invariable standard, but the attunement of our body's capacities, endowments and possibilities that enable us to inhabit our habitat in partnership. That is, rather than the imposition of an external standard, the proportioning system emerges from the variables of the situation. We are scaled and potentiated and enhanced by our environment, and in turn that environment is scaled and enhanced by our inhabitation in an immanent mutuality. The ecological psychologist J.J. Gibson suggested this more than 50 years ago: "For perception this nesting is what counts, not the metric dimensions of empty time with its arbitrary instants and durations. Time as such, like space is not perceived."[15] The relative and qualitative dimensions of measure are here restored; *umwelt* and organism are scaled and tempered according to each other.

Space as Medium

And because we are physically and existentially nested, we cannot properly speak about the body without speaking about the space we are *in*. One of the most quoted passages in key texts on embodiment over the last 30 years was written by John Dewey more than a century ago:

> To see the organism *in* nature, the nervous system *in* the organism, the brain *in* the nervous system, the cortex *in* the brain is the answer to the problems which haunt philosophy. And when thus seen to be *in*, not as marbles in a box but as events are *in* history, in a moving, growing, never finished process.[16]

While cognitive scientists have worked to redress "the problems which haunt philosophy," we seemed to have missed the architectural promise implicit in Dewey's spatial metaphor.[17] What if we were to take seriously the meaning of *in*, in just the way he suggests? It is not that we occupy space as a container, but that space *inter*penetrates our very body. The rich body of literature of the nineteenth-century German empathy theorists together with the phenomenologists has seriously refined our sense of space, taking it far from the notion of neutral geometric space or space as passive container. Otto Bollnow developed the notion of *lived-space* in direct response to Eugène Minkowski, who had written a book called *Lived Time*—reminding us that space has qualitatively different locations within it, and these qualities are tied to existential bodily and cosmic happenings and movements. These intuitions about space are being corroborated by cognitive neuroscience. Vittorio Gallese, one of the discoverers of mirror neurons, insists that "the primordial quality turning space, objects and behaviour into intentional objects, that is, into the objects of our perception and thoughts, is their constitution as the potential targets of the motor potentialities that our body expresses."[18] And in fact, Gallese acknowledges his debt to Merleau-Ponty, who wrote that space is not some sort of ether in which all things float . . . the points in space do not stand out as objective positions in relation to the objective positions in relation to the objective position occupied by our body; they mark in our vicinity, the varying range of our *aims* and *gestures*.[19]

The Cartesian dictum 'I think, therefore I am' is replaced with Husserl's 'I can, therefore I am.' Space can either invite, open and extend human possibility, or cripple human potential. The philosopher of atmospheres Gernot Böhme develops a similar argument in his understanding of what he calls the space of bodily presence—a domain not delineated by mathematics but by its existential character:

> Bodily space is the manner in which I myself am here and am aware of what is other than me—that is, the space of actions, moods and perceptions. As a space of actions, the space of my bodily presence comprises my scope for actions and movements. It might be called my *sphaeres activitatis*.[20]

It must be stressed that space is not a neutral backdrop awaiting impregnation by our desires and actions, in a one-way operation. Space possesses a qualitative character of its own, which combines with and modulates our actions; it is not an inert backdrop. We tend to confront space from a frontal perspective, like the one Le Corbusier depicts in his drawings, but space is something in which we are immersed. Replacing the word *space* with its residue of geometric connotations with the word *medium* nudges our thinking towards understanding our surroundings as a kind of support system. The dictionary definition of *medium* in fact includes this definition: 'the substance in which an organism lives or is cultured.' The term *culture* here is interesting because it evokes the meaning of culture in the term *agriculture* (plants can flourish and thrive in certain cultural conditions and not others), while reiterating Dewey's foregoing comparison with the soil. The word *medium* derives from the root *medhyo* meaning 'middle.' The Latin *medius* means 'middle, midst, centre, interval, in-between,' which shares the same root as the words *measure*, *mood* and *health*. Medium is open-ended—but not neutral. It possesses its own particular viscosities and resistances. Think of the way artists use the word *medium* to describe the mode, means and channel of their craft, immediately suggesting possibilities and creative restraints. Medium imparts the idea of space as a plenum or a latency, as something full of potential. Imagine the way in which iron filings array themselves about a magnet—each filament aligns according to the pattern of the governing field. Think too of the way grains of sand pattern themselves according to different frequencies on a resonating plate. The iron filings and the grains of sand move according to the interacting field they enter. "The organism is not just a structure but a characteristic way of interacting."[21] wrote Dewey. Bodies are interdependent entities whose characteristic way of interacting is patterned by the medium in which they are immersed. Merleau-Ponty pointed to this implicitly orienting field as the primordial basis of our being in the world:

> We must not wonder why being is orientated, why existence is spatial . . . and why our coexistence with the world *magnetises* experience and induces a direction in it. The question could be asked only if the facts were fortuitous happenings to a subject and object indifferent to space, whereas perceptual experience shows that they are presupposed in our primordial encounter with being and that being is synonymous with being situated.[22]

So, again here we have a way of considering space in terms not of quantitative distances or Cartesian points in which independent entities act on each other

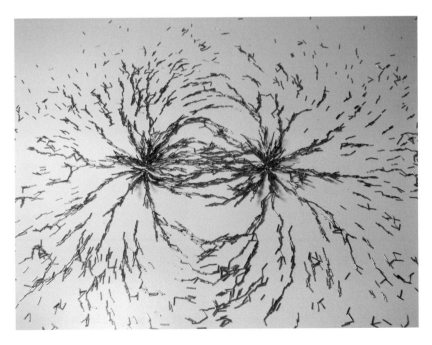

Image 2.3 Iron filings arrayed in a magnetic field
Source: Courtesy of Windell Oskay (Creative Commons).

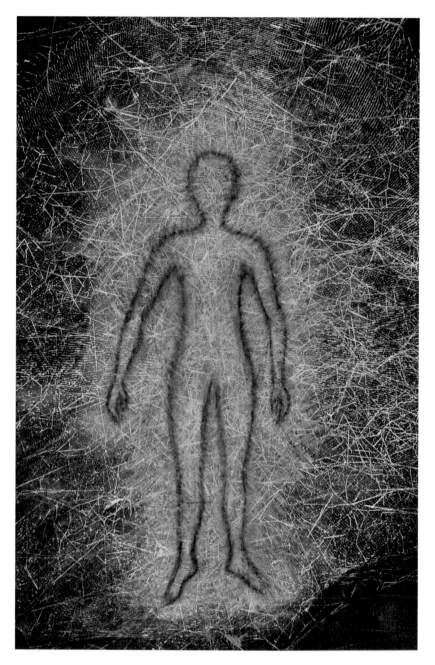

Image 2.4 Resonant body in immersive space

Source: Drawing by Sarah Robinson.

through electromagnetic and gravitative forces but in terms of a dynamic plenum of possibility in which bodies form and are formed by the medium in which they are immersed—suggesting the sense in which our surrounding medium can potentially actualise our latent capacities, meet our inchoate needs and support us in a mutually sustaining fashion.

Resonant Bodies

A real impediment to imagining space as medium in these qualitative terms is our still exclusive reliance on vision as the bearer of ultimate truth. Vision channels our attention to the space in front of us, and this reinforces the illusion that space is not only in front of us, but outside of us. In the world according to vision, the immersive dimension is missing. We are immersed in a medium, and it is very telling that a much more accurate indicator of space tends not to be our sense of vision but our sense of hearing. The philosopher Gernot Böhme directs us to another German thinker, this time from the sixteenth century, Jakob Böhme, who developed a model that might move us in the direction away from emphasis on vision. His treatise *De Signatura* understands everything that is in the world according to the model of the musical instrument. The body is understood to be a resonant body whose shape and materiality generate an attunement—a literal 'tuning' which he calls the signature—the characteristic way in which a thing expresses itself. According to this model, we understand something because we resonate with it. An utterance causes an inner bell in us to vibrate and we sympathise by means of our whole body. Interaction is therefore a phenomena of resonance, and the world discloses itself, not as isolated objects acting on one another through thrust and pressure, but through communication. The world is not conceived as a container in which marbles roll, or a billiard table on which balls clash, but presents itself as a great concert. The resonant body knows through an all-body engagement with a vibrating, pulsing and dynamic world. It is a condition reminiscent of the one John Hull describes in his book *Touching the Rock*, where he records his "descent into blindness" and calls himself a wholebody seer. Or, as Gernot Böhme describes experiencing music:

> Of changing, interpenetrating, emerging and vanishing figures . . . space is experienced affectively: spread-out as heavy and oppressive, the up-rising as lightening and joyous, the splitting-up as funny and so on. Taking both these aspects together, one realises that musical space is, to be exact, bodily space expanded, that is, a feeling-out into space which is shaped and articulated by music.[23]

He suggests that the phenomena of music are exemplary of this body-medium-music intertwining and asks, "Might it be the case that what we call music is our way of participating in this great concert?"[24]

Sphere Activitatis

Thinkers from John Dewey, Merleau-Ponty, Elizabeth Grosz, Jakob and Gernot Böhme, and Vittorio Gallese have worked to reimagine the human body beyond the static Vitruvian ideal. Their efforts can help develop an alternative way not only to represent, but to more fully understand and tangibly design for the living, dynamic, open, emergent, plastic, multi-gendered body-in-process. There is no body without a mind and no mind without a body, nor is there a body without a surrounding medium—that living mind-body-medium is a *sphere activitatis*—affirming Dewey's dramatic insistence that "the integration of the mind-body in action is the most practical of all questions that we can ask of our civilisation."[25] Dewey's remark seems obvious enough, but like many of his statements, it is a distillation of his broader philosophy of embodiment. What is the body if not a body in action, and it is through action that we engage with, take in and integrate our surroundings. From the standpoint of action, if we treat some functions as primarily physical and others primarily mental—digesting, reproducing and moving as conspicuously physical, while thinking, imagining and desiring as distinctly mental—when studied more closely, they can be regarded not as a difference of kind, but of degree and emphasis. If we attempt to draw a sharp line consigning one set of actions to the physical and the other to the mental, we find that the person who eats and digests is the same person who feels joy or sorrow—one eats and digests differently when one is happy or when one is sad. As Dewey puts it:

> The emotional temper of the festal board enters into the allegedly merely physical act of digestion. The eating of bread and drinking of wine have indeed become so integrated with the mental attitudes of multitudes of persons that they have assumed a sacramental, spiritual aspect.[26]

Indeed, biblical stories revolve around shared meals—and the divine enters through the sharing of food. The visitation of Sarah and Abraham occurred during a meal. Christ's forgiveness of his assassin is immortalised in the Last Supper and rehearsed anew in the sacrament of the bread and wine of Communion. Victor Hugo's bishop offers warm food and shelter to a ragged criminal in *Les Misérables*. Offering hospitality to a stranger in the Islamic tradition is tantamount to playing host to God. In Zen Buddhism, mindfully eating is an acknowledgment of interdependence with the cycles of nature and an act of gratitude. Eating is not only prototypical of the way in which an action cannot be reduced to strictly separate dimensions—it also levels the classical hierarchy of the senses.

One's sense of taste, considered among the lowest of the senses, is actually a keenly accurate source of knowing. Tasting is the primary way we come to know the world—our earliest survival depends on distinguishing the sweetness of milk and the warm smell of refuge. All subsequent distinctions depend on this primary sense of taste and smell in what Richard Kearney calls a "carnal hermeneutics."[27] To have good taste is an aesthetic, as well as an ethical talent. To be savvy, or to possess savoir faire, is to be able to conduct oneself skillfully in the ways of the world. Both *savvy* and *savour* come from the Latin *sapienza*, which means 'knowledge of the highest order.' These usages of language disclose the indissolubility of the mind-body-in-action and the rootedness of 'higher order' faculties in the flesh. The call for qualitative measure finds its expression in precisely these humble actions. The *measure* of a civilisation, for Dewey, was the extent to which it succeeded in seamlessly integrating the mind-body-in-action:

> The more human mankind becomes, the more civilised it is, the less there is some behaviour which is merely physical and some other purely mental. So true is this statement that we may use the amount of distance that separates them in our society as a test of the lack of human development in that community.[28]

In a further refinement, think instead of this separation not in terms of linear distance, but in dimensional depth. The highest achievements of civilisation are born of the flesh. Culture forms and reinforces habits, while civilisation in the sense that Dewey speaks of it here is process that *transforms*. And, by attending to and supporting these human actions, we have the possibility to restore these lost dimensions.

Notes

1. Robert Tavernor, *Smoot's Ear: The Measure of Humanity* (New Haven: Yale University Press, 2007), 20.
2. John Dewey, *The Essential Dewey: Pragmatism, Education and Democracy*, eds. Larry A. Hickman and Thomas M. Alexander (Bloomington: Indiana University Press, 1998), 135.

3. Marie-Christine Pouchelle, *The Body and Surgery in the Middle Ages*, trans. Rosemary Morris (New Brunswick, NJ: Rutgers University Press, 1990).
4. Ibid., 127.
5. Harry Francis Mallgrave, *The Architect's Brain* (Chichester: Wiley, 2010), 33.
6. Charles Perrault, *Parallèle des Anciens et des Modernes*, 2nd ed. (Paris: Jean Baptiste Coignard, 1692–1696), 4:46–59.
7. Edmund Burke, *A Philosophical Inquiry into the Sublime and Beautiful* (London: Penguin, 1998), 135.
8. John Dewey, *Experience and Nature* (New York: Dover, 1958), 252.
9. J. Urla and A. Swedlund, "The Anthropometry of Barbie: Unsettling Ideals of the Feminine Body in Popular Culture," in *Feminism and the Body*, ed. L. Schiebinger (New York: Oxford University Press, 2000), 412.
10. Todd Rose, *The End of Average* (New York: Harper Collins, 2016).
11. Elizabeth Grosz, "Bodies-Cities," in *Sexuality and Space*, ed. Beatriz Colomina (Princeton: Princeton Architectural Press, 1997), 243.
12. Dewey, *Experience and Nature*, 277.
13. Ibid.
14. Dewey, *Experience and Nature*, 282.
15. J.J. Gibson, *Reasons for Realism* (Hillsdale, NJ: Lawrence Erlbaum, 1982), 413.
16. Dewey, *Experience and Nature*, 295.
17. I have suggested these points in my essay, "Resonant Bodies in Immersive Space," in *Architectural Design, Neuroarchitecture*, guest-ed. Iain Ritchie (2020).
18. Vittorio Gallese, *Architecture and Empathy* (Helsinki: Peripheral Projects, 2015), 39.
19. Maurice Merleau-Ponty, *Phenomenology of Perception*, trans. Colin Smith (London: Routledge Kegan Paul, 1962), 143.
20. Gernot Böhme, *The Aesthetics of Atmospheres* (London: Routledge, 2017), 117.
21. Dewey, *Experience and Nature*, 292.
22. Merleau-Ponty, *Phenomenology of Perception*, 252. Italics added.
23. Böhme, *The Aesthetics of Atmospheres*, 117.
24. Ibid., 115.
25. John Dewey, *The Collected Works of John Dewey: Later Works*, Vol. 3, 1927–28, ed. JoAnn Boydston (Carbondale: Southern Illinois University Press, 1991), 29.
26. Ibid., 28.
27. Richard Kearney and Brian Treanor, *Carnal Hermeneutics* (Fordham: Fordham University Press, 2015).
28. Dewey, *The Collected Works of John Dewey*, 29.

Extended Organisms— 3
Surrogate Bodies

A brilliant mathematician who was an amateur philosopher—a term used here in its etymological sense: *amateur* comes from the word *amore*, 'love'— Alfred North Whitehead lacked formal training in philosophy. Yet the work in philosophy that he undertook late in his career quickly became so highly regarded that he was offered a professorship in philosophy at Harvard. His Gifford Lectures at the University of Edinburgh initially attracted hundreds. By the end, attendance dwindled to less than a dozen people. Those who endured Whitehead's notoriously difficult communication style witnessed an intellectual breakthrough that would later be published as *Process and Reality*, widely regarded as one of the seminal texts in twentieth-century thought. His role as an outsider was perhaps a precondition for his radically innovative conception of reality. According to Whitehead, the world is not composed of bits of matter or "things-in-themselves" existing independently of one another—but consists of processes defined by their relations with other processes. "There is urgency in coming to see the world as a web of interrelated processes, of which we are integral parts," he passionately argued, "so that all of our choices and actions have consequences for the world around us."[1] His words could hardly be more urgent, and it is indeed time that we fully considered how our design choices and actions impact the world around us. With this in mind, a reconsideration of Whitehead's thought is long overdue.[2]

Philosophy of the Organism

Hailed as the founder of process philosophy, Whitehead did not use that term but called his the *philosophy of the organism*. Rooted in the words *to do*, like the related terms *organ* and *organise*—*organism* suggests coordinated action.

Whitehead's philosophy was grounded in this deeper meaning; not organism as static independent entity, but organism as web of embedded, interrelated, coordinated processes. He wrote:

> It is the accepted doctrine in physical science that a living body is to be interpreted according to what is known of other sections of the physical universe. This is a sound axiom, but it is double-edged. For it carries with it the converse deduction that other sections of the universe are to be interpreted in accordance with what we know of the human body.[3]

Whitehead wanted to show how the mental framework inherited from classical physics prevents this more subtle, rigorous and open-ended understanding. This statement articulates a predicament which continues to plague us to this day; the spectacular successes in physics in the first half of the twentieth century led researchers to interpret the living body according to physical laws, but this understanding has only been applied in one direction. According to Whitehead, we have yet to do the converse—that is, we have not interpreted the universe according to what we know about the human body.

We tend to forget that the self-contained particle of physics is not an entity with an independent significance, but an abstraction of a larger process—and, as Whitehead put it, "an abstraction is nothing less than the omission of part of the truth."[4] To abstract literally means 'to detach'—and is rooted in the words *to draw*, in the sense of drawing a line around one part to the exclusion of the rest. While certain physical laws or patterns of behaviour may be deduced from abstracting the particle from its surrounding mesh, those behaviours change their validity when their larger context is taken into consideration. Whitehead uses an example from genetics to illustrate his point: "When geneticists conceive of genes as the determinants of heredity, the analogy of the old concept of matter sometimes leads them to ignore the influence of the particular animal body in which they are functioning."[5] The old concept of matter, to which he refers, operates according to the container/contained model, which in this particular version interprets genes to contain codes telling them what to do, and those codes are in themselves sufficient to specify inherited traits. Whitehead wrote this passage in 1925, 75 years before the human genome was mapped and 85 years before the hard line drawn between nature and nurture blurred beyond distinction. Now we know that although genes play a critical role, heredity is a complex process involving external and internal variables in a dynamic situational interplay in which no one factor can be considered definitively determinant.

The problem with the 'old concept of matter' is that it obscures three undeniable facts: firstly, it minimises the primacy of change; secondly, it diminishes the importance of relations; and finally, it does not acknowledge, much less account for, the creativity of life processes. For Whitehead, change is fundamental and not secondary. That is, thinking of any material thing, whether a brick or a person, as being in essence the same through time— while the changes it endures are secondary to that essential nature—fails to account for the active and experiential nature of the most basic elements, or simply for the fact that 'all things flow.' The terms *matter* and *form*, according to Whitehead, were abstractions, but not irreducible building blocks. Form is not a container for dead matter. Matter flows and *form* is a verb. To assume that enduring entities are the most real and fundamental things in the universe is to mistake the abstract for the concrete—a conceptual error he called "the fallacy of misplaced concreteness."[6] What *is* concrete are the processes of dynamic becoming rather than static being. The notion of changeless 'essences' are abstractions from such interrelated events. The most concrete reality is the fact of change—as we saw with the body, the sole universal is openness and interdependence. Reality is a perpetual becoming, "It makes or remakes itself," wrote Henri Bergson, "but is never something made."[7]

The Biological and the Physical: Where Do We Draw the Line?

Whitehead upset the basic categories that normally guide our thinking. The obvious difference between biology and the physical sciences—physics, geology, chemistry, etc.—is that the former presumably studies the living or animate world, while the latter studies the inanimate. Yet such a division is only obvious in the Latin sense of the word *obvius*, which means 'in the way' and evolved into the modern usage: 'evident without reasoning or observation.' But in fact, when subjected to closer inspection, the crucial difference between disciplines is not one of kind—that one studies the living, while the other studies the dead—but a difference in scale: "Biology is the study of larger organisms; whereas physics is the study of smaller organisms,"[8] Whitehead insisted. A difference in scale is not merely scale in a spatial sense, but a difference in degrees of complexity commensurate with an increase in scale. The larger the organisms, the greater number and intricacy of relationships and connections, and the greater their complexity. And, true to the etymological meaning of *organism* as organised activity—an organism, whether a molecule or a human heart, was what he called a society—that is, a group of individuals—engaged collectively in organised activity. Their important difference is their degree of complexity; their commonality is that both are abstractions of a larger process.

In *Process and Reality*, Whitehead openly acknowledged his gratitude to three philosophers: Henri Bergson, William James and John Dewey, the first thinkers to seriously reckon with the implications of Darwin's discoveries. Whitehead's philosophy of the organism continued this task—and taking seriously the implications of Darwin's work indeed necessitates one to challenge categories assumed to be 'obvious.' While the *Origin of Species* and the *Descent of Man* have radically shaped the course of Western thought, what is less appreciated was Darwin's preoccupation with the emotional lives of animals and the formative activities of earthworms. Most of those who profess allegiance to Darwin have overemphasized competition as the operative mechanism of evolution, a bias which rests, according to Whitehead, on misconstruing the environment in its role as a selective sorter, rather than acknowledging that, as he put it, "the other side of evolutionary machinery, the neglected side, is expressed by the word creativeness. *The organisms can create their own environment.*"[9] Evolution is not only a process of genetic sorting through competition but more pervasively a process of slow, deliberate plodding in which organism and environment cooperate in each other's co-creation. Darwin recognised that small obstinate changes yield major effects over time. Perhaps nowhere is this more appreciated than in his final book, *The Formation of Vegetable Mould, Through the Action of Worms*,[10] which turned out to be a runaway best seller. There could scarcely be a more convincing example of the value in taking seriously the ordinary and respecting what is commonly thought small. Two words in the title—*formation* and *action*—betray the broader relevance and unplumbed significance of his humble investigation. Originally a student of geology, Darwin wanted to understand how something as ostensibly inert and stable as geologic strata transformed over the course of eons. Darwin decided to turn his attention to the smaller-scale changes he noticed in the agricultural fields surrounding his home and suspected that the compounded actions of earthworms were causing topsoil to dissipate and disappear over time. After years of patient observation, Darwin noticed that in the course of their daily habits, worms literally move the earth—their movements aerate the soil and the natural chemistry of their guts renders soil and plant matter into fertile pellets. In this cycle of activity, worms deposit new soil on the surface causing that which is above it to slowly submerge. He was not exaggerating when he declared, "It may be doubted if there are any other animals which have played such an important part in the history of the world as these lowly organised creatures."[11] Earthworms move eight tons of earth in a year over a single acre of cultivated land, producing a mineral-rich layer of earth two inches thick. At this rate, entire edifices may be buried over a period of decades. In this transformation of the earth's surface, the organism integrates its internal substances with the surrounding soil, patterning and chemically modifying the local topography. Where does one draw the line between internal and external in this case—or, for that matter, where does one draw the line between the living and the dead?

Extended Organisms

"Where does my body end and the external world begin?" Whitehead asks. "The breath as it passes in and out of my lungs from my mouth and throat fluctuates in its bodily relationship. Undoubtedly the body is very vaguely distinguishable from external nature."[12] Our life depends on the constant interchange of air. Breathing momentarily erases the boundary between outside and in. As Darwin's worms condition their terroir through the filter of their bodies, we too condition our surrounding atmosphere with our breath. And this interchange, as Whitehead stressed, is not solely an asymmetric affair—it is not that worms adapt to a found environment—the two organisms, the soil and the worm, are mutually implicated and transformed in the process. The soil is an extension of the worm's physiology—serving as an accessory kidney, an organ that balances water and filters out toxins. In his book *The Extended Organism*,[13] J. Scott Turner illustrates how the environment has a physiology that extends beyond the conventionally defined boundaries of the organism. He understands the structures built by animals not as examples of 'frozen behaviour'—that is, as artefacts that can be used to probe the past or devices exploited by the genes to project their influence beyond the surface of their skin—but rather as external physiological organs of the animals themselves. Coral reefs, the bodies of sponges, tunnels dug by insects in marine muds, aquatic cocoons that serve as gills and lungs, the trumpet-shaped burrows of mole crickets that amplify their mating calls, the spectacular mound nests of African termites that house not only the colony but serve as gas-exchange systems allowing them to adapt to a wide range of environmental conditions—all exemplify how effectively animals extend their physiology in the structures they build. And this extension is not strictly physiological; researchers in animal cognition study how animals perceive, attend and learn in concert with their surroundings.

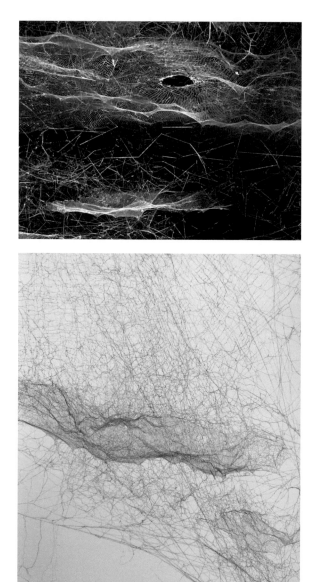

Images 3.1 and **3.2** Spider Webs, Tomás Saraceno, *Aria* Palazzo Strozzi, Florence, 2020

Source: Photo Sarah Robinson.

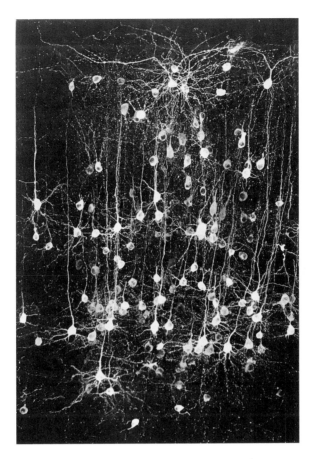

Image 3.3 Convergence of inputs into single neuron in the mouse cortex

Spiders are perhaps the paradigmatic case of extending cognition through the action of weaving. The orbs, cobs, sheets and even single-line webs that spiders create from the silk spun of their own bodies are not so much extensions of their perceptual systems as they are members of their body proper. Spiders detect movements through the vibrations on their webs and are known to manipulate thread tension and thickness on particular chords to increase the amplitude of certain frequencies while lowering others in order to better capture their prey.[14] Spiders tune their webs in an interactive process that truly confounds categories of inner/outer, body/mind and organism/ environment. The artist Tomás Saraceno studies arachnids with a Darwinian sense of patience and dedication, and the collection of 300 arachnids that he houses in his studio in Berlin are the subjects of artistic and scientific collaboration that also confound interdisciplinary categorisation. Learning from spiders, he has developed pioneering digital techniques for visualising complex three-dimensional webs. This experimental work opens new ways to imagine how the worlds we spin become our extended bodies. To do so requires thinking with Whitehead—that is, interpreting the physical universe according to what we know about the human body.

The Primacy of Movement

Understanding the environment as an extended body—as an interweaving of organism/medium/movement—is wonderfully illustrated by the work of two Greek brothers who are fluid dynamicists at MIT. In their effort to resolve the long-standing issue of how fish are able to swim at incredible speeds, which could not be explained by the anatomy and musculature of their bodies alone, they turned their attention to the way the fish moves. In doing so, they noticed that the fish flips its tail to recapture the kinetic energy in its wake, recovering the energy from vortices that spin off their own bodies. They achieve their remarkable speeds by sensing naturally occurring currents and creating additional vortices with their tails to propel them faster than their strictly physiological capabilities alone would allow. "The real 'swimming machine,'" writes the cognitive scientist Andy Clark, "is not the tuna alone, but the tuna in its 'proper context'—the tuna, plus the water, plus the vortices it creates and exploits."[15] The finely tuned movements of the tuna belong to and are inseparable from the medium and the historic process from which those movements emerged. What is prior or more fundamental in this instance: the tuna, the water, the movement—or the dynamic process which subsumes such distinctions?

When the brothers privileged one of the variables, the form and mass of the tuna's body, their problem was irresolvable. Only when they considered the process of swimming—that is, until they ventured to understand not merely the organism's structure, but its characteristic way of interacting in its surrounding medium—were they able to solve the problem. Another long-standing issue from the field of child development was resolved using a similar approach. Unable to figure out why the stepping gestures that newborns make when they are held upright vanishes at about two months of age, only to reappear during the latter half of the first year, researchers generally attributed this disappearance and reappearance to brain development. They assumed that the vanished gesture reappeared when the baby's brain achieved a certain level of maturity. Yet, by closely studying movement, Esther Thelen and Linda Smith showed that it was not brain development, but rather the muscular capacity and coordination of the baby's legs that were the decisive factors. Babies coordinate their muscles and tendons on the job, learning by doing rather than by obeying some sort of preprogrammed behaviour that automatically springs forth when their brain has reached a certain level of maturity. Through the playful exploration of their bodily possibilities and movements, babies develop a highly personal understanding of their worlds. Their developing skills are grounded in the rhythms and pace of their own body in concert with the constraints and affordances of their surroundings. As Thelen and Smith put it: "Development does not happen because internal maturational processes tell the system how to develop. Rather, development happens through and because of the activity of the system itself."[16]

Another study illustrating the mutually determining interplay between form and action is one that the psychologist Louise Barrett recounts in her book *Beyond the Brain*.[17] Neurobiological research with rats revealed that the complex behaviour of baby rats was based on some very basic rules: until they are seven days old, the rule is to 'stay in contact with a vertical surface,' which results in wall-following behaviour known as thigmotaxis[18] and 'to move towards warm objects.' At ten days, a new rule emerges, which is to 'do what your litter mates are doing.' In another unrelated experiment, robots were made that approximated the simple shape of living rats, with tapered noses in the front and no internal computer program. The researchers discovered that the robotic rats behaved remarkably similarly to the real rat pups. When the 'roborat' contacted a wall, its pointed nose caused it to slide along in the direction determined by the angle at which it encountered the wall. Other kinds of movement were constrained by this contact, which resulted in the wall-hugging behaviour.[19] Encountering a corner limited its ability to move forward even further, so in this case its only option was to move backward. Yet when encountered by other robots while in this position, this option was prevented. As the other robots crammed in from the sides, the classic huddling and corner-burrowing behaviours shown by real rats then emerged. These robotic rats were not following a set of programmed rules, nor were they oriented towards a goal—their 'behaviour' resulted from their interactions with the environment. These actions, which appeared to be organised and goal oriented, were in fact the consequence of their movements, the shape of their bodies, and the configuration and constraints of their surroundings.[20]

Huddling and corner-burrowing behaviour clearly have evolutionary advantages—using a wall or a fellow creature to trap and share heat confers thermodynamic benefits while decreasing one's risk to predation. The role of the shape of the animal's body in allowing and easing movements that condition the likelihood of certain behaviours is scarcely considered, but a powerful dimension of the evolutionary process—and this interactive shaping tends to be reciprocal. Consider the fact that for a primate, it takes more neural activity to move a single finger than it does to move the whole hand.[21] This sort of energetic economy makes sense only when one considers the historical process and actions that gave rise to the hand. Primate bodies were adapted to swinging through trees, an activity requiring coordinated grasping of the entire hand. This gesture exploits the mechanical properties of the tissues in the hands, creating synergies between muscles and tendons—the mind of the hand—saving on the more elaborate and energetically expensive involvement of the central nervous system. In this instance again, movement is both cause and consequence of morphology, and mind emerges from and is situated within a particular field of interacting events. Our bodies, our perceptual and cognitive systems, evolved in the deep history of our situational milieu and our actions are potentiated, tuned and reinforced by features in the environment.

As Thelen and Smith's work makes evident, development is not an inevitable march toward maturity but a process textured with patterns of dynamic stability that appear, disappear and reappear and capacities that evolve and dissolve over time. In this rich temporal weave, the impetus of change is not a genetic program—but a venturing of movement and discovering patterns, an adjusting and readjusting, and an expanding of one's bodily capacities according to the opportunities and constraints available in the situation at hand. Development is a not a linear succession of stages, but an emergent shaping process tempered by myriad internal and external dimensions. Movement is constrained by but also moulds morphology, a word itself which suggests change—'to morph.' Many compounded movements, like the activity of earthworms, change the shape and generate the conditions that then go back to reshape. Once the baby is able to step, that stepping elicits a cascade of chemical changes through the whole organism. This interactive engagement happens at every stage of the life process. The postures we habitually assume possess chemical signatures that cascade through the body. The psychologist Amy Cuddy has shown that power position of standing with feet firmly grounded, posture upright and shoulders squared in a gesture of self-possession (aka the Wonder Woman pose) releases higher levels of testosterone.[22] The gesture elicits a chemical wash that adjusts our mood, muscles, expectations and outcomes.[23] "We feel because we do,"[24] declares the cognitive neuro-scientist Colin Ellard.

In stressing the primacy of movement—placing importance on the historical unfolding of the growth process—Thelen and Smith's work helped overcome two more dualisms stemming from the 'old concept of matter.' One version interprets matter as shell and mind as animator, the 'container and contained' model that manifests in the contemporary notion that the brain is the command centre controlling an otherwise brute body. Another, albeit more subtle version interprets mind to be latent in matter and the changes endured in the developmental process to actualise an inner essence. In the contemporary rendition of this teleology, the baby's early actions and personal experiences are inconsequential to the eventual functioning of the genetically programmed brain. Both of these versions ignore both Dewey's and Whitehead's insistence that the enduring fact is the *creative unfolding of the growth process* itself. Mind is, as Dewey insisted, "more than a bare essence . . . it is a property of a particular field of interacting events."[25] Dewey used the terms *action* and *formation* as Darwin employed them in the title of his last book—*form* is a verb, an achievement, a fluorescence of compounded, organised movements.

The philosopher/dancer/biologist Maxine Sheets-Johnstone has long argued that movement is the matrix of cognition. We all enter this world as babies, and all learning begins kinetically. As we have seen, for babies, stepping is a process of discovery from which practical skills and concepts are born. As Sheets-Johnstone puts it:

> Infant movement is the generative source of fundamental human concepts . . . corporeal concepts such as hard and soft, jagged and pointed, weak and strong, open and closed and so on . . . human infants are not pre-linguistic; language is post-kinetic.[26]

The spatial, temporal and energetic concepts that grow from our direct bodily engagement with our surroundings form the basis of verbal language.[27] And the kind of thinking that emerges in movement differs from thinking in words or thinking in images precisely because it accesses these formative bodily engagements that lie at the origin of language. Sheets-Johnstone has shown that such concepts are the basis of what Husserl called the "two-fold articulation"[28] of movement and perception. Again, complementing this research, neither language nor behaviour is a static acquisition pre-programmed in strict terms of culture or biology, but emerges in a dynamic unfolding of movement-perception-cognition generated and articulated within a particular situation.

Primordial Techne

From the matrix of early movements, we form our bodies, our skills, our basic concepts, our sense of possibility—and ultimately our repertoire of 'I cans.' This repertoire then serves as the basis of our future engagements and determinations of value. Merleau-Ponty recognised this early experience as the primal ground on which knowledge is built. "Our bodily experience of movement is not a particular case of knowledge; it provides us with a way to access the world and the object, with a *'praktognosia'* which has to be recognised as original and perhaps as primary."[29] Like Dewey, Merleau-Ponty's philosophy was informed by the best experimental science of his time. The term *praktognosia*, which he borrowed from the neurophysiologist A. A. Grünbaum, is the German amalgam of the Greek *praxis*—meaning 'habitually repeated action' and *gnosis*, the Greek term for knowledge gained through experience. Husserl earlier referred to this kinaesthetic meshwork as primordial techne.[30] Taken together, these two terms precisely describe the dynamic and indissoluble character of embodied knowledge. These evocative terms radically undermine anachronistic separations of knowledge and practice and delving into their meaning returns us to our opening question of why *building* and *dwelling* are both verbs and *architecture* is not.

Techne has a storied pedigree as the root of the term *technology* and originally meant 'productive action' and referred to art and craft. In ancient Greece, *techne* was more closely associated with the term *episteme*—another term for knowledge. While *techne* referred to practical knowledge—knowing how to do something through the experience of repeatedly doing it—*episteme* was knowledge that could be generalised into rules and mathematic principles. Greek science was modelled upon this kind of epistemic knowledge that emphasised the logic of mathematical proof at the expense of the value of practical discovery. As Dewey points out:

> The early meanings that Greek philosophers associated with *techne* were nested within an epistemological hierarchy in which the universal (in the case of Plato) and the individual essences (in the case of Aristotle) prevailed as the ultimate arbiters of ontological and practical value.[31]

Shorn of its moorings in embodied experience, abstract mathematical knowledge was not understood as derivative of practical knowledge but was deified as an end in itself. So crucial was this kind of knowledge, Plato declared that no one could enter his republic without knowledge of geometry.

The other Greek term for knowledge, *gnosis*, which referred to knowledge gained from intimate experience, more aptly describes the sensuous, visceral accrual of knowledge that takes place in the unfolding development of every human life. Embodied experience is primary and generative, not derivative; even Plato affirmed that technical skill was the basis of geometry. And this tension is present in the original meaning of *praxis*, in which there is no clear-cut separation between the mental and the physical. More than static, absolute knowledge, *gnosis* is perhaps closer to the word *understanding*, which suggests knowing from below, from standing *under*, from the ground rather than from a detached position surveying from above. Truly understanding something comes through experience, from learning by doing, as Dewey put it: "Understanding has to be in terms of how things work and how to do things. Understanding by its very nature is related to action."[32] The rich, multilayered terms *practognosis* and *primordial techne* describe the articulated field of abilities and possibilities from which the designations body, mind and space are but abstractions. In Whitehead's sense of the term, they each refer only to part of the reality in question.

Inhabiting—The Matrix of Habitual Action

"The body is not a thing, it is a situation: it is our grasp of the world, and the sketch of our project,"[33] insisted Simone de Beauvoir. Husserl understood the body as a "system of possible actions" and Merleau-Ponty called the body-space continuum a "matrix of habitual action."[34] The kinaesthetic field of experience richly textured with our capacities, expectations and possibilities can be articulated more precisely in terms of weaving, fabric, matrices and fluid threads than in terms of hard building blocks. The philosopher Edward Casey used such an analogy: "The tie, the knot, between body and place is so thickly Gordian that it cannot be severed at any point."[35] Antoine de Saint-Exupéry used the same analogy when he declared: "I am a knot into which relationships are tied." Knotting and weaving are central operatives for the architectural historian Indra Kagis McEwen, the anthropologist Tim Ingold and the architect Gottfried Semper, whose work we will discuss in a later chapter. This phase of our inquiry began with Whitehead's insistence that we interpret the physical world according to what we understand of the human body—and hopefully we have come somewhat closer to understanding the body not as a discrete thing but as a situated knot of possible actions. Once rid of the 'old concept of matter,' three facts become undeniable: the primacy of movement and change, the interdependent reciprocity of relations and the ongoing creativity of life processes.

Our habitat is never just given, it is perpetually made. Animals—like earthworms, spiders, termites, birds—do not find ready-made environments. They create and re-create, tune and re-tune their habitats. Their habitat, the place they create, is a matrix of habitual actions, an expression and concretion of habit. Habit has an inner and outer meaning, and refers both to deep-seated and unconscious actions, as well as to clothing—nuns and monks are vested in their habits to this day. Habits were central to Dewey's thinking. For him there was no fixed human nature—human culture and society were the accretion of habits that took shape in actions, artefacts and ideas. And habits were not atomistic; they were both born of and constituted context. "The medium of habit filters all the material that reaches our perception and thought. The filter is not, however, chemically pure."[36] This multidimensional meaning is an entry into understanding how architecture serves as a surrogate body that very concretely shapes us. The inhalations and exhalations of breathing condition the atmosphere within and without; the act of eating is a folding and unfolding of substance; clothing is the first layer of habitat that touches the skin, succeeded by nested layers of the constructed envelopes of shelter. Habitation is this process of inhaling, exhaling, folding, unfolding, clothing, sheltering, shaping and re-shaping. As the philosopher Algis Mickunas writes:

> Phenomenologically speaking, the social space, the architectonics of the lived world is not a distant reality or an opposing system but an analogue of our abilities, a completion of our disabilities or weaknesses and an extension of our activities. At the corporeal level it is not separate from who we are and what we can *do*. To speak metaphorically, we are in constant dialogue with our lived world; the latter is an inter-corporeal world of abilities, tasks, mutual supports and corporeal extensions. Such an environment can be either wholesome, supportive, completing or disruptive, unsupportive, diminishing our abilities or limiting our tasks. One thing is certain, it is our design and in our power to compose it in harmony with our being.[37]

Notes

1. C. Robert Mesle, *Process-Relational Philosophy: An Introduction to Alfred North Whitehead* (West Conshohocken: Templeton Foundation, 2009), 9.

2 Isabelle Stenger's *Thinking with Whitehead: A Free and Wild Creation of Concepts* (Cambridge, MA: Harvard University Press, 2011), has been instrumental in demonstrating the implications of Whitehead's often impenetrable work.

3. Alfred North Whitehead, *Process and Reality*, 2nd ed. (New York: Free Press, 1979), 119.

4. Alfred North Whitehead, *Modes of Thought* (New York: Free Press, 1968), 189.

5. Ibid.

6. Alfred North Whitehead, *Science in the Modern World* (New York: Free Press, 1967), 51.

7. Henri Bergson, *Creative Evolution: Humanity's Natural Creative Impulse*, trans. Arthur Mitchell (New York: Henry Holt, 1911), 272.

8. Whitehead, *Science in the Modern World*, 150.

9. Ibid., 138.

10. Charles Darwin, *The Formation of Vegetable Mould, Through the Action of Worms* (New York: D. Appleton, 1882), 313.

11. Ibid., 313.

12. Whitehead, *Modes of Thought*, 155–156.

13. J. Scott Turner, *The Extended Organism* (Cambridge, MA: Harvard University Press, 2000).

14. Michael D. Breed and Janice Moore, *Animal Behaviour* (Burlington, MA: Academic Press, 2010), 231.

15. Andy Clark, *Mindware: An Introduction to Cognitive Science* (Oxford: Oxford University Press, 2001), 35.

16. Linda B. Smith and Esther Thelen, *A Dynamic Systems Approach to the Development of Cognition and Action* (Cambridge, MA: MIT Press, 1994), 305.

17. Louise Barrett, *Beyond the Brain: How Body and Environment Shape Animal and Human Minds* (Princeton: Princeton University Press, 2011), 161.

18. Ann Sussman and Justin B. Hollander, *Cognitive Architecture* (New York: Routledge, 2015), See chapter 2, for their thorough study of the design implications of thigmotaxis.

19. Barrett, *Beyond the Brain*, 162.

20. Ibid.

21. Ibid., 165.

22. Amy Cuddy's viral TED Talk can be found at: www.ted.com/talks/amy_cuddy_your_body_language_may_shape_who_you_are?language=en

23. D.R. Carney et al., "Power Posing: Brief Nonverbal Displays Affect Neuroendocrine Levels and Risk Tolerance," *Psychological Science* 21, no. 10 (2010), 1363–1368.

24. Colin Ellard, *Places of the Heart: The Psychogeography of Everyday Life* (New York: Bellevue Literary Press), 23.

25. John Dewey, *The Later Works, 1925–1953*, ed. JoAnn Boydston (Evanston: Northwestern, 1981), 201.

26. Maxine Sheets-Johnstone, "Movement as a Way of Knowing," *Scholarpedia* 8, no. 6 (2013), 30375.

27. Maxine Sheets-Johnstone, "The Silence of Movement: A Beginning Empirical-Phenomenological Exposition of the Powers of Corporeal Semiotics," *The American Journal of Semiotics* 35, no. 1–2 (2019), 33–54.

28. Maxine Sheets-Johnstone, "Kinesthesia: An Extended Critical Overview and a Beginning Phenomenology of Learning," *Continental Philosophy Review* 52 (2019), 143–169.

29. Maurice Merleau-Ponty, *Phenomenology of Perception*, trans. Colin Smith (London: Routledge Kegan Paul, 1962), 98.

30. Edmund Husserl, *Nachlass*, Bd. I.21.I.1932. (Belgium: Husserl Archives Leuven).

31. John Dewey, *Reconstruction in Philosophy* (Boston: Beacon Press, 1957), 110.

32. John Dewey, "The Challenge of Democracy to Education," in *Problems of Men* (New York: Philosophical Library, 1946), 49.

33. Simone de Beauvoir, *The Second Sex*, trans. Constance Borde (New York: Vintage, 2009), 44.

34. See Maxine Sheets-Johnstone, "In Praise of Phenomenology," *Phenomenology & Practice* 11 (2017), 5–17.

35. Edward Casey, *The Fate of Place: A Philosophical History* (Berkeley: University of California Press, 1997), 235.

36. John Dewey, *Human Nature and Conduct: An Introduction to Social Psychology* (New York: Henry Holt, 1922), Part 1, Section 2.

37. Algis Mickunas, "The Vital Connection," in *Analecta Husserliana: The Yearbook of Phenomenological Research*, Vol. 22, ed. A. T. Tymieniecka (Dordrecht: Springer, 1987), 53.

Questioning Perception   **4**

In the middle of the last century, the urban planner Charles Abrahams lamented that zoo architects understand their subjects far more accurately than architects understand theirs—it is unthinkable to extract an animal from its habitat and then expect that animal to flourish, yet this is exactly the error we continue to make with ourselves. It is really only in the last two centuries that we have begun to spend 95 percent of our time indoors[1]—in a fraction of evolutionary time, we have transitioned to indoor settings built with little awareness of how our perceptual systems shape and are shaped by those environments. Thinking of a habitat as the concretion of habitual living patterns seems obvious when thinking in terms of animal habitats—yet we seem unable to apply the implications of this same connective logic to ourselves. And this tendency reveals the persistence of our inherited habits of thought. Habits apply not only to behaviours and gestures, but also to ways of thinking and to what we consider valuable. Ideas are not spontaneously generated—as Dewey insisted, "there is no immaculate conception of meanings or purposes."[2] William James also stressed that every perception is an acquired perception. As we have learned with infant development, concepts emerge experientially from embodied situations and are inherited and elaborated within the broadening contexts of interpersonal, cultural and social interactions. The mental frameworks operating within each of our cultural milieux tend to do so preconsciously. The conceptual legacy that has guided Western culture—the privileging of mind over body in the work of Descartes, Locke, Hume, Kant and almost every other modern philosopher one can name[3]—went virtually unchallenged until the twentieth century. The overwhelming tendency to ignore embodiment and situation was only questioned when forced to come to terms with the findings of the natural sciences.

It is difficult to overstate the paradigm-eroding catalyst that Darwin's theory of evolution really was. The proposition that nature changes plastically over time radically challenged the model of mechanically moving planets and immutable forms. And the idea that animals and humans share the same developmental continuum meant there was no essential division between them. So intently was the lens of early science focused on the transcendent heavens, there was little concern to study what actually happened here on Earth. The study of life escaped disciplined attention so thoroughly, there did not seem to be a need to speak about our relationship with our surroundings. The now taken-for-granted term 'environment' was not even coined until the nineteenth century,[4] at around the same time that biology became a legitimate discipline. The term *environment* originated with Goethe, whose studies of plants were further developed by Alexander von Humboldt, who was the first to study them in terms of their surrounding context. Von Humboldt surmised that the patterns of plants—the shape of their leaves, their branching configurations and growth habits—were generated by geographic, climatic, geologic and social factors, anticipating the guiding principle of modern ecology. Humboldt insisted that everything is interconnected, interactive and reciprocal.[5] Studying life required very different conceptual categories and terms than the ones available through physics—and we still struggle to develop a vocabulary sophisticated enough to articulate the creative and mutually shaping adaptive character of inhabiting.

Umwelt and Affordances

At the ecological scale, an animal's world is a rich interplay of acoustic, optical, vibrational and pheromonal fluxes and patterns partially generated by the movement and presence of the animal itself. This interdependence cannot be explained in terms of the equilibrium world of Newtonian physics or classical thermodynamics. The term *environment* describes an animal's surroundings, but there still is no English word to describe the environment in terms of interaction—to do so, we have to employ the term *umwelt*,[6] the German words for 'life' and 'world' joined together into one. The Estonian biologist Jakob von Uexküll coined the word to express how an animal cannot be understood apart from its particular environment. While many animals share the same habitat, each is tuned to that habitat in its own particular way. The spider is sensitive to the forces and features of the habitat relevant to its own particular needs, and to truly understand the spider's lifeworld, we would have to experience that world the way a spider does. One cannot even begin to understand an animal apart from the environment in which that animal evolved and to whose features its perceptual systems adapted. Von Uexküll stressed that animals not only change over time, they change in creative interplay with their environment and their *umwelt* serves as an extended body in both physiological and perceptual terms. He was the first to propose that what an animal perceives depends on what that animal values—which entails that perception is a search for meaning specific to the animal's unique capacities. Up until that time, perception was conceived as a passive intake of sensory data operating in a one-way relationship. He showed too, that perception is intricately tuned and adaptive—the whole body is engaged in discerning a value-laden world unique to each creature. The bee's ultraviolet vision is tuned to discerning colours meaningful to pollination. The bee perceives what humans cannot— their entire body, the way they see, move and behave is geared towards detecting nectar.[7] Also for the worm, the entire body is a unified perceptual organ exquisitely tuned to darkness, vibration and smell aligned with their role in making soil.[8] The term *fitness* refers exactly to this: the reciprocal fit between animal and lifeworld in which matter and meaning are seamlessly bound.

Von Uexküll's work was the precursor to modern neurobiology. The titles of its foundational texts, C. S. Sherrington's *Integrative Action of the Nervous System* in 1920 and Kurt Goldstein's *The Organism* in 1934 both suggest their emphasis on the integration of the senses and the coupling of environmental with internal variables. Goldstein argued that acts of perception are whole-organism events engaging the full range of sensory modalities encompassing mood and muscle in adaptive concert with their lifeworlds.[9] This sense of active, meaningful perception was elaborated 30 years later in the ecological psychology developed by James and Eleanor Gibson. The Gibsons also argued that perception is a multisensory affair not solely reliant on individual organs, but more accurately understood in terms of nested systems—the haptic, auditory, tasting and smelling, visual and basic orienting systems. Perception is coloured with meaning—animals perceive according to what is valuable to them by means of their own repertoire of skills and bodily-experiential possibilities. Gibson's theory of affordances is based on the meaning-motivated action orientation of these systems. Gibson defined an affordance quite broadly as a possibility for action in the environment that refers "to both the environment and the animal in a way that no existing term does. It implies the complementarity of the animal and the environment."[10] Affordances refined and textured Von Uexküll's *umwelt* by articulating the concrete and specific features of the lifeworld that constrain or afford behaviour, which then modulates and changes both organism and environment in a complementary manner.

Niche Construction

Darwin understood behaviour within a complementary field of action and ecological resources—an orientation which becomes particularly clear in another undervalued aspect of his oeuvre, his experimental research in animal psychology. In decades of keenly observing earthworms, Darwin noticed that they developed an array of behavioural strategies to protect their very sensitive skin. An earthworm's entire epidermis is its unitary sensory and motor organ and as such, is exceedingly sensitive to heat and evaporation. To maintain its function and ensure survival, the skin must remain supple and moist. In order to do this, the earthworms make use of available resources in the soil and air to preserve moisture in the design of their burrows.[11] Darwin observed that worms dig burrows that are slightly oblique at the top ending with a basket shape at the bottom lined with seeds and pebbles that are dampened with excreted soil along the way.

> The lining thus formed becomes very compact and smooth when nearly dry, and closely fits the worm's body. The minute reflexed bristles which project in rows on all sides form to the body, thus have excellent points of support: the burrow is rendered well adapted for the rapid movement of the animal.[12]

With "noteworthy skill" the earthworms selected only materials soft to their bodies, and were even able to modify and use materials Darwin brought in from foreign sites in ways that protected and nourished their skin. This pattern of flexible regulation enables them to finely tune the variables of local circumstances to afford comfortable and safe passage with a high level of functional specificity. Worms "exhibit some degree of intelligence instead of a mere blind instinctive impulse in their manner of plugging up the mouths of their burrows," concluded Darwin. They clearly possess significant agency despite not having a brain.[13]

The psychologist Edward Reed insisted that their regulated actions involve a level of awareness, and that worms organise and regulate their actions in terms of the affordances in their environments.[14] Their awareness is not necessarily conscious or self-conscious or a belief about the world, but they possess acute powers of discrimination. This kind of awareness allows many animals to reliably choose places to safely rest, live and nest; to choose among different types of food; and to discern danger. This example illustrates the complementarity between the resources an environment offers and that animal's capacity to perceive and utilise those resources. Affordances do not cause behaviour but make it possible—the serrated tip of a leaf for an earthworm affords pulling, an action which leads to lining a nest, which then leads to somatic thermal and evaporative regulation. Reed collaborated with the Gibsons and together argued that the proliferation and agglomeration of specific affordances creates a 'field of promoted action,' engendering new practices, innovations and sociocultural interactions. Through design, that is, through the modification of their environments, organisms pass on their ecological inheritance—including the built and the given—to their offspring. The auto-catalytic effect that Darwin witnessed in the behaviour of his earthworms is now the subject of niche construction, a discipline that emerged within eco-logical psychology in the 1980s dedicated to studying the way animals modify their environment to influence the processes of natural selection. Their early work on animals and their physical habitats has today broadened to include the role that cultural constructions, including architecture, play in altering human living patterns. Research in niche construction is increasingly applied to fields of the social sciences, archaeology, anthropology and psychology.

Niche is rooted in the word for 'shell,' and related to the word *nest*. Nesting is an activity common to most animals—the nest is truly an extended, surro-gate body that has served a critical role in the evolution of life. The biologist E. O. Wilson has argued that the nest was a critical precursor for enabling

Image 4.1 Collection of bird's nests
Source: Photo Sarah Robinson.

social cohesion. All animals that achieved coordinated social networks without exception had nests.[15] Indeed, niche construction systematically favours some behaviours while inhibiting others and therefore contributes to shaping the course of evolutionary processes. The rapid increase in genetic changes—some biologists suggest that as much as ten percent of the human genome may have been modified over the last several thousand years[16]—has been correlated with the intensification of the built environment. These changes are far faster than earlier genetic models predicted, suggesting the role of culture to be the decisive factor in bringing about these genetic alterations. Humans are born into a constructed legacy of cities, farms and houses built over the course of many generations. These extensions constitute the ecological inheritance so critical to the process of human evolution.[17]

Research in niche construction baffles the neat distinction between natural and cultural realms. The organised behaviour of worms—the modification of their environment to ensure their flourishing—can be called the culture of the earthworm. A word we normally restrict to the circumscribed province of human activity, the word *culture* has much more earthy origins. The Latin *cultura* means 'caring' and 'honoring,' and was originally used in reference to agriculture. *Agriculture* originally meant 'to tend and guard the earth.' Cultivation was a set of practices that developed in a spirit of care and reverence and was prior to and a necessary condition for the harvest. The term 'to cultivate' in an intellectual sense—cultivation through education and refinement of the mind—did not appear until the sixteenth century, and the sense of culture as a collective intellectual achievements of a people did not appear until several centuries later. Culture is not immaculately conceived but a web of actions and processes, practices, attitudes, dispositions and valuations compounded and reenacted over time. This sense of the word *culture* comes through in the work of the psychologist and philosopher Susan Oyama, whose developmental systems theory provided the most compelling challenge to the nature and nurture dichotomy. She completely reframed the terms of the debate, arguing that nature is not a static genetic code imposing its deterministic order, but is itself the web of developmental interactions we call nurture.[18] Human development is not confined to the strict categories of genes or environment, but a process of constructive interactions that together produce, sustain and change living beings over both developmental and evolutionary time.

> What is transmitted between generations is not traits or blueprints or symbolic representations of traits, but developmental means. These include genes, the cellular machinery necessary for their functioning and the larger developmental context, which may include the maternal

reproductive system, parental interaction and other conspecifics as well as relations with other aspects of the animate and inanimate worlds.[19]

Human caring and nurturing relationships are therefore essential factors in the web of the developmental process. Like Dewey, Oyama dismisses notions of a fixed human nature, suggesting instead that the career and destiny of human beings is perpetually open-ended and co-created.

Building further on Oyama's work, the anthropologist Tim Ingold insists that we are not passive subjects prefigured by genes or available cultural forces, but "organism-persons" engaged inextricably in our environment through our movements. We are each endowed with certain skills within a field of social relations, and these skills are not transmitted solely through cultural conditioning or training, but are reenacted in each generation and thus incarnated in the *modus operandi* of the developing organism in the performance of particular tasks. Culture, he suggests, is not a discrete field of transmission but the enaction of skills reincarnated in each succeeding generation. These skills are not only specific techniques one learns with one's body—they are, in Gibsonian terms, "the capabilities of action and perception of the whole organic being (indissolubly mind and body) situated in a richly structured environment."[20] Cultural phenomena are none other than a fine-tuning of the ecological perceptual system through continuous practice actively forged in the sinews of the body.

Neural Plasticity and Epigenetic Change

The 'noteworthy skill' exhibited by the earthworms in crafting their burrows, and the incarnation of culture within the flesh of each new generation, corroborates one of John Dewey's key insights:

> Use reshapes the prior materials so as to adapt them more freely and efficiently to the uses to which they are put, [it] is not a problem to be solved: it is an expression of the common fact that *anything changes according to the interacting field it enters.*[21]

Indeed, architects organise and create the field that gives rise to culture, education and individuality. Such fields serve to enable some behaviours while impoverishing others, sedimenting and reinforcing habit patterns and providing the framework for the visceral enactment of culture. Education was a central concern for Dewey precisely because it structures habit formation.

His observation was an early statement of Hebb's law, commonly described as neurons that fire together, wire together—or, in other words, use it or lose it. In 1949, the biologist Donald Hebb defined a pivotal moment in twentieth-century science when he showed that when two neurons fire together through a synapse, protein grows within the synapse to strengthen the connection. As the bond grows stronger with each synaptic firing, so too does the probability that these two neurons will fire together in response to a similar stimulus in the future. And if this bond is not reinforced by continued firings, the synaptic connections will eventually atrophy or disassemble. This process of neuroplasticity was long known to be the case with children, but now we know it also applies to all phases of the life process. Further reinforcing the biological basis of consciousness and culture, the neurobiologist Gerald Edelman argues that we are born with a 'primary repertoire' of neural circuits that are modified by subsequent experiential selection, and that this experience or incarnation of skill builds a 'secondary repertoire' that reinforces or disintegrates the primary one based on activities experienced within an either rich or deprived environment. This then leads to the third stage, which he calls 'reentrant mapping,' in which specialised functional groups dedicated to emotions, sensory modalities and skills such as language are elaborately synchronised in connections from which higher-level consciousness occurs.[22] Consciousness is thus a dynamic, interdependent process. As Whitehead insisted: "It is a false dichotomy to think of Nature and Man. Mankind is a factor in Nature which exhibits in its most intense form the plasticity of Nature."[23]

Corroborating Ingold's notion of skill, and Dewey's insistence that bodily movements "wear grooves,"[24] neuroimaging studies on musicians have shown that musical training enhances the synaptic complexity in the auditory cortex and the cerebellum. In the case of violinists and cellists, for example, the motor cortex that controls the movement of the fingers on the left hand becomes synaptically enlarged, and conversely, if they quit their training, those connections atrophy.[25] It is well documented that learning to play an instrument at any level of proficiency positively structures synaptic connections that enhance a range of cognitive capacities, from language to mathematics.[26] This brings to mind Frank Lloyd Wright, who was raised in a family of progressive educators who insisted that he learn to play the piano and famously gave him Froebel blocks to play with in his crib. The consequences of these neuronal modifications are not only effected on an individual level—through what is known as epigenetic change; processes that transmit brain capacities and cognitive abilities acquired during a single human lifetime are transmitted to the next generation. This process is called 'epigenetic' precisely because it does not depend on alterations in the actual DNA within the genes, but on factors which influence what is expressed by that same DNA. As Dewey intuited a century ago, the use of certain cell functions during one's lifetime actually alters the structure of the cell, leading to what is known as cell memory. This process is not dissimilar to what we saw with the reinforcement of synaptic connections promoting preferential use of that same connection in the future, which through repeated use over a period of time underlies the phenomena of memory. Cultural developments can be passed onto succeeding generations through genetic mechanisms.[27] As the neurobiologist A. G. Lumsden writes:

> The relationship resembles one of reciprocating interaction, in which culture is generated and shaped by biological operatives while the course of genetic evolution shifts in response to cultural innovations . . . [epigenetic rules may] predispose mental development to take certain specific directions in the presence of certain kinds of cultural information.[28]

Knowledge Is External

One of the central tenets in Don Norman's classic text *The Design of Everyday Things* is that knowledge is external. He arrived at this conviction in a wonderful illustration of interdisciplinary cross-pollination. During a sabbatical at Cambridge, Norman met the psychologist David Rubin who at the time was studying the recall of epic poetry. It was Rubin who showed him that the prodigious acts of memory in which itinerant poets sing tales for hours on end are not strictly feats of memory; at least memory as it is commonly understood. Much of the information needed for retelling the tales did not reside in the poet's head, but out in the world. The poems themselves are structured to organise experience in memorable forms; the lyric sound of the voice incorporates speaker and audience in a live performance that is situational and improvisational rather than a matter of abstract recall. The tales are not memorised so much as they are re-created according to the multiple constraints designed into the poem and the cultural and rhythmic parameters of its performance. The notion of rote memorisation is a modern phenomenon, but the fact that we have integrated mnemonic devices into our daily lives is hardly a subject of debate—the loss of our phone or our computer can render us helpless. The efficacy of such props is even more poignant in communities which struggle with the deterioration of their memory. Some who suffer from Alzheimer's disease, for example, are able to maintain a surprisingly high level of functioning and to live independently at a level which does not correlate with the debilitating effects of their disease. Their remarkable success can be explained only when they are observed in their home settings where an array of props—such as labels, photos, diaries and other concrete memory strategies—serve important cognitive functions. Their increased reliance on these props and strategies operates as a 'field of promoted action' that compensates for their neurological deficit. Both the recall of the 'singer of tales' and the recall of the Alzheimer's sufferer relies on cultural formulas and external devices that exceed or compensate for cognitive limitations in the biological system. As Andy Clark puts it:

> Certain aspects of the external world . . . may be so integral to our cognitive routines as to count as part of the cognitive machinery itself (just as the whorls and vortices are, in a sense, part of the swimming machinery of the Tuna).

Our interdependence with our cognitive props "is as important and intimate as that of the spider and her web."[29]

The cultural formulas and external devices that both Don Norman and Andy Clark describe can be understood as a kind of cognitive scaffolding that concretely extends and distributes mental activities and helps explain the drastically different worlds that animals and humans inhabit. While it is now accepted that animals and humans share homologous neurobiological structures, it remains difficult to account for their vastly different cognitive abilities; the important differences cannot be explained in terms of our genetic repertoire, the vast majority of which we share. Instead, these differences are, according to the psychologist Michael Tomasello, the consequence of synchronised cultural factors that join together to cause the "ratchet effect"[30] of cumulative cultural development. What distinguishes humans from other animals is not the possession of culture per se, but rather the way that culture is organised to lead to the accumulation of knowledge. The ratchet effect characterises our highly developed ability to pool cognitive resources and to engage in mimetic, instructed and collaborative learning. When an invention is made, for example, it is shared with others and subsequently refined and perfected, thus accelerating the pace of change and technological development. This inheritance evolves with each generation under the tutelage of adults, afforded and facilitated by our disproportionately long period of immaturity. Our prolonged adolescence, according to Tomasello, arose precisely to extend this collaborative process of learning. Cumulative culture has led to the important cognitive products, processes and extensions that cannot be directly accounted for by specialised biological adaptations.

Reprogramming Sensory Life

Returning to the concern with which we opened this chapter—endeavouring to understand how perception is shaped by the interplay of myriad biological, cultural and social factors—we can now turn our attention to the way in which each new technology reprograms sensory life[31] as Marshall McLuhan insisted. McLuhan argued that every technology—the printing press, the novel, the computer—reorders perception according to the means of those technologies. Working in the 1960s, McLuhan studied how the transition from print to the electronic media of telephone, radio and television shifted patterns of perception subtly but indelibly over time. New media does not replace the content of the old media but reshapes the way it is conveyed—and the way it is conveyed reshapes and reprioritises our senses. Communicating the daily news transitioned from paper, to radio, to television and now to the internet, and each transition changes not only the content of the news according to the vessel of its transmission, but in the process reorders perception. Although controversial at the time, McLuhan's argument becomes all the more convincing in light of what we know about neural plasticity. Numerous studies suggest that different technologies restructure synaptic connections in differing ways.[32] In addition to the social and interpersonal changes enacted by intensified computer and cell phone use, these technologies have physiological consequences impacting sleeping patterns, stress levels, overeating and weight gain, energy and physical coordination, musculoskeletal discomfort and posture—making it clear that "children growing up in media-rich environments literally have brains wired differently from those who did not come to maturity under those conditions."[33]

McLuhan was strongly influenced by Eric Havelock, the Greek classicist whose work on Homer's epics was the basis of the research informing Don Norman's proclamation that "knowledge is external."[34] Havelock broke radically with the long tradition that understood Greek history as an unbroken monolithic tradition, when he noticed a decisive change in the literature from the fifth century onwards, and argued that Western thought was shaped by the profound change resulting from the shift from an oral to a literate form. In his *Preface to Plato*, Havelock argued that Plato's philosophy was not only revolutionary in content but revolutionised the way information was organised and communicated. Plato was a pivotal figure in the larger cultural perceptual shift taking place in Greece catalysed by introduction of the phonetic alphabet. The alphabet, Havelock argued, was a precondition for Plato's philosophy of ideas, and the Greek achievement of abstracting sound into visual equivalents was a critical basis of their overall analytic orientation—one that has shaped Western thinking to this day. The written word created an environment entirely unlike the one that preceded it—the practical wisdom embodied and memorised in epic poetry in a communally shared corporeal realm became frozen on the page, locked inside books and accessed primarily through vision by the privileged few. The new environment was in fact an anti-environment; receding from its reliance on external cues, it turned radically inward.

The implications of this momentous shift were the focus of Havelock's colleague Walter Ong's studies of orality and literacy. Ong showed how the pressures on the respective perceptual systems have psychosocial implications—oral language tends to be aggregative and connecting rather than analytical and dissecting, participatory and empathetic rather than objectively distanced, and situational rather than abstract. In oral cultures, the word is not an object; it is an event. Objects can be solidified and possessed, and events are shared and temporal. Ong argued that:

> Primary orality fosters personality structures that in certain ways are more communal and externalised, and less introspective than those common among literates. Oral culture unites people in groups. Writing and reading are solitary activities that throw the psyche back on itself.[35]

These divergent perceptual modes also contribute to different kinds of knowledge. Knowledge in oral cultures tends to be unifying and strives for harmony, whereas in literate cultures knowledge is proprietary, hierarchically valued and divisive. Ong's colleague, the anthropologist Edmund Carpenter, made pivotal contributions in understanding the cultural implications of perceptual biases in his close association with the Inuit in Canada. The atmospheric and ecological conditions of their Arctic environment make vision a less reliable sense, forcing them to rely on their highly refined acoustic awareness. Carpenter showed how their finely tuned haptic and acoustic perception manifests in their art, language, mechanical skill and spatial sense.

> The senses aren't mere input channels: they make their own worlds of spaces and relations. Every sense has its own paradigm of pleasure and pain, creates its own time and space—is, in fact, a unique environment, produces its effects. Media interpenetrate and interplay with one another, much as senses do . . . Media, like art forms, are models of sensory programming.[36]

The perceptual shifts caused by the cataclysmic shift from orality to literacy have been importantly elaborated by the psychiatrist and literary scholar Iain McGilchrist, who has argued that the ascendance of the left hemisphere of the brain, which specialises in the analytical skills that literacy demands, has sacrificed the skills associated with the right hemisphere. The aptitudes and abilities of empathy, motor skill and peripheral vision once called upon in oral culture are in a process of atrophy, because they are unsupported by today's cultural habits, technologies and values.[37]

Technology is a mode of organising experience, and the impact of the most pervasive technology of our daily lives—the buildings we inhabit—on our sensory systems was most persuasively addressed by Juhani Pallasmaa in his critique of ocular centrism in *The Eyes of the Skin*. The perceptual restructuring resulting from the cultural-technological transitions from orality to literacy emphasised vision to the overwhelming exclusion of the other senses. Vision's 'paradigm of pleasure and pain' favours the objectively distanced and abstract and has created architecture that does the same. "The inhumanity of contemporary architecture and cities can be understood as the consequence of the negligence of the body and the senses, and the imbalance in our sensory system,"[38] he writes. Cut off from the tacit wisdom and tempering force of the body, the architecture of focused vision has resulted in a loss of plasticity, an obsession with form as an end in itself, a contrived absence of depth very literally out of touch with the richness of human experience. Pallasmaa has been instrumental in drawing attention to the need to rebalance our atrophied sensory worlds through deliberately involving our senses of sound, silence, touching and feeling, memory and imagination, and restoring focal vision to its peripheral field. It is important to remember that these critiques of sensory biases are not anachronistic arguments against technology; they are critical assessments of the ways in which every technological shift restructures perception. "The use of technology can enrich the human psyche, enlarge the human spirit, intensify its interior life," writes Walter Ong, "but in order to have this effect each technology must be honestly faced."[39]

Architectural Affordances

"Environments are not passive wrappings but active processes," declared McLuhan. To understand how to concretely work with the perceptual coupling between organism and environment, Gibson's notion of affordances holds a promising key. He opened his talk at a symposium on "Perception in Architecture" in 1976 with the observation and question: "Architecture and design do not have a satisfactory theoretical basis. Can an ecological approach to the psychology of the perception and behavior provide it?"[40] Gibson directly addressed the concerns of architecture by showing how affordances could provide a foundation for a reinvigorated theory of design. "The hypothesis that things have affordances, and that we perceive or learn to perceive them, is very promising, radical, but not yet elaborated."[41] There has been considerable work done in elaborating affordances in design, cognitive science, architecture[42] and dynamic systems theory[43] that we can build upon in this effort. But for now, let's take Gibson's words directly:

> Things will look as they do because they afford what they do . . . Herein lies the possibility for a new theory of design. We modify the substances and surfaces of our environment for the sake of what they will afford, not for the sake of creating good forms as such, abstract forms, mathematic and elegant forms, aesthetically pleasing forms. The forms of Euclid and his geometry, abstracted by Plato to the immaterial level, have to be rooted in substances and surfaces and layouts that constrain locomotion and permit or prevent our actions.[44]

To design things for the sake of what they will afford, not for how they look, but for what they do, would go far beyond the dictum that form follows function, to imply that form itself is a verb—form *forms*. The shape of things, shape our movements, invite or disclose possibilities—are worn and grooved by the shape of our habits. Here Gibson intends form as Whitehead does, not as solely outward and fixed, but form as process. As Paul Klee put it: "Form is the end, death, form-giving is life."[45]

According to Gibson, architects have misunderstood form because they have been taught form as a graphic exercise, treating form as a painter would treat it. In this way, "no one is ever going to understand 'form' . . . the use of the term only promotes confusion."[46] Indeed, how many architecture schools still engage in formal exercises—carving styrofoam solids—and manipulating the cube may have its value as playful, creative experiments, but it perpetuates the obsolete notion that the goal of architecture is to dress up and hollow out a Platonic solid, failing to realise that treating form as an end in itself is, as Klee insisted, death. "What architects are concerned about," said Gibson, "is the layout of surfaces."[47] And to consider surfaces in the way that Gibson intended—that is, trading the word *layout* for 'formal arrangement' and reserving the word *form* for use only in its verbal sense—would be radical indeed. And going a step further, what if we understood surfaces not for what they are, but for what they *do*? Treating surfaces as boundaries that are, like we must now understand the boundary of our skin—not as things but as processes—surfaces as the site of intense interactions.

Several architectural thinkers have unwittingly defined affordances with impressive accuracy—in one of his poems, John Hedjuk wrote: "The rocking chair is the soul of the porch, remove it and all you have left is white pine for the carpenter ants."[48] While the white pine may be food according to the perceptual world of the carpenter ant, for us, it gains it meaning in the way it involves our bodies and imaginations in the act of rocking. The rocking chair is the soul of the porch because its uses and pleasures are personally experienced and culturally known. This is as true with furnishings as it is with larger scale configurations. Building arrangements must mesh with our habits, beliefs and expectations, "for once such 'meshing' is achieved, buildings and activities tend to reinforce each other, for besides the sheer convenience of 'fit,' buildings go on to reassure their users by reinforcing their beliefs and intentions, substantiating their world,"[49] insisted Peter Blundell Jones. The detail of a door handle announces its perceptible function in terms of our bodily potentials, setting in motion an elaborate web of expectations and affordances that work together in concert with a building's broader psychological and cultural purpose. The door handles designed by Alvar Aalto and Gunnar Asplund welcome the hand and encourage grasping, while

> others can be sharp and geometrical, sacrificing ergonomic comfort for visual display. But if we were to see a handle covered in grease, wreathed in barbed wire, or visibly wired to a high voltage source, the avoidance is visceral, for we imagine the experience in an empathetic, emotional manner.[50]

The way that affordances are nested in a field of promoted action is exemplified in scaling up the door handle to the multiple meanings of the door in theatre design. The stage door plays a very different role than the main entrance and is encrusted with its own repertoire of behavioural habits and expectations. The actor's door is carefully placed away in a side street policed by a porter, in order to remain literally and figuratively behind the scenes. The public entrance concretises the ceremonial nature of the event in serving as a threshold to elaborately welcome the audience, while simultaneously holding a place in the imagination of the town. Its grandeur welcomes on multiple dimensions—on one it affords the behaviour commensurate with its ceremonial stature—that is, it engages the audience in the act of also playing dress-up. The phrase 'going to the theatre' already triggers an image of formal dress and the pageantry of display. The spatial configuration and ornamentation control the relations between actors and audience, while also defining the audience to itself. The actions and behaviours associated with the various entrances of the theatre serve to define the broader public perception that contributes to the theatrical event. Once one begins understanding spatial arrangements in this way, examples are endless, and when architectural form is considered as a verb, we begin to understand its power to shape perception.

Notes

1. The metric that Americans spend 95 percent of their time indoors comes from The National Human Activity Pattern Survey (NHAPS): A resource for Assessing Exposure to Environmental Pollutants led by Neil E. Kepeis, and published by the Lawrence Berkeley National Laboratory in 2001.
2. John Dewey, "Morality is Social," in *Human Nature and Conduct: An Introduction to Social Psychology* (New York: Modern Library, 1922), 31.
3. Shaun Gallagher, "Philosophical Antecedents to Situated Cognition," in *Cambridge Handbook of Situated Cognition*, eds. P. Robbins and M. Aydede (Cambridge: Cambridge University Press, 2008), 35–52.
4. The term 'environment' was first used in 1828 and is an English translation of Goethe's *umgebung* by Thomas Carlyle.
5. Detleff Doherr, "Alexander von Humboldt's Idea of Interconnectedness and its Relationship to Interdisciplinarity and Communication," *Journal on Systemics, Cybernetics and Informatics* 13 (2015), 47.
6. Jakob von Uexküll, *A Foray into the Worlds of Animals and Humans: With a Theory of Meaning* (Minneapolis: University of Minnesota Press , 2010), 1.
7. Karl von Frisch, *The Dancing Bees: An Account of the Life and Senses of the Honey Bee* (New York: Harvest Books, 1953).
8. Charles Darwin, *The Formation of Vegetable Mould through the Actions of Worms, with Observation on their Habits* (London: John Murray, 1881).
9. Kurt Goldstein, *The Organism: Holistic Approach to Biology Derived form Pathological Data in Man* (New York: Zone Books, 2000), 210 and 214.
10. J. J. Gibson, *Ecological Approach to Visual Perception* (New York: Psychology Press, 1979), 127.
11. Darwin, *The Formation of Vegetable Mould.*
12. Ibid., 112–113.
13. Ibid.
14. Edward Reed, *Encountering the World: Toward an Ecological Psychology* (New York: Oxford University Press, 1996), 24.
15. Edward O. Wilson, *The Social Conquest of the Earth* (New York: Liveright, 2014).
16. Scott Williamson et al., "Localizing Recent Adaptive Evolution in the Human Genome," *PLoS Genetics* 3, no. 6 (2007), 90.
17. F. John Odling-Smee et al., *Niche Construction: The Neglected Process in Evolution* (Princeton, NJ: Princeton University Press, 2003), 241.
18. Susan Oyama, *Evolution's Eye: A System's View of the Biology-Culture Divide* (Durham: Duke University Press, 2000), 48.
19. Ibid., 29.

20. Tim Ingold, *The Perception of the Environment: Essays on Livelihood, Dwelling and Skill* (London: Routledge, 2000), 5.
21. John Dewey, *Experience and Nature* (New York: Dover, 1958), 285.
22. Gerald Edelman elaborates his model in a number of books: see *Wider than the Sky: the Phenomenal Gift of Consciousness* (New Haven: Yale University Press, 2004) and *Second Nature: Brain Science and Human Knowledge* (New Haven: Yale University Press, 2006).
23. Alfred North Whitehead, *Adventures in Ideas* (New York: Free Press, 1967), 99.
24. Dewey, *Experience and Nature*, 280.
25. See Gottfried Schlaug, "Increased Corpus Collosum Size in Musicians," *Neuropsychologia* 33, no. 8 (1995), 1047–1055; Christian Gaser and Gottfried Schlaug, "Brain Structures Differ Between Musicians and Non-Musicians," *Journal of Neuroscience* 23, no. 27 (2003), 9240–9245.
26. Glenn Schellenberg, "Music Lessons Enhance IQ," *Psychological Science* 15, no. 8 (2004), 511–514.
27. Iain McGilchrist, *The Master and his Emissary* (New Haven: Yale University Press, 2009), 246.
28. Ibid.
29. Andy Clark, *Being There: Putting Brain, Body and World Together Again* (Cambridge, MA: MIT Press, 1997), 24.
30. Michael Tomasello, *Origins of Human Communication* (Cambridge, MA: Harvard University Press, 1999), 5.
31. Marshall McLuhan, *Understanding Media: The Extensions of Man* (Toronto: McGraw Hill, 1964).
32. F. Gottschalk, "Impacts of Technology Use on Children: Exploring Literature on the Brain, Cognition and Well-being," *OECD Education Working Papers*, no. 195 (Paris: OECD Publishing, 2019).
33. Katherine N. Hayles, "Deep and Hyper Attention: The Generational Divide in Cognitive Modes," *Profession* (2007), 187–199.
34. Donald A. Norman, *The Design of Everyday Things*, 2nd ed. (New York: Basic Books, 2002), 54.
35. Walter Ong, *Orality and Literacy* (London and New York: Routledge, 2002), 67.
36. Edmund Carpenter, *They Became What They Beheld* (New York: Ballantine, 1970).
37. Iain McGilchrist, *The Master and His Emissary* (New Haven: Yale University Press, 2010).
38. Juhani Pallasmaa, *The Eyes of the Skin* (London: Wiley, 1996), 19.
39. Ong, *Orality and Literacy*, 82.
40. J. J. Gibson, *Reasons for Realism* (Hillsdale, NJ: Lawrence Erlbaum Associates, 1982), 413.
41. J. J. Gibson, *The Senses Considered as Perceptual Systems* (New York: Houghlin Mifflin, 1966), 285.
42. See Norman, *The Design of Everyday Things*.
43. See the work of Eric and Ronald Rietveld at: www.raaaf.nl
44. Gibson, *Reasons for Realism*, 413.
45. Paul Klee, *Notebooks, Volume 2: The Nature of Nature* (London: Lund Humphries, 1973), 269.
46. Gibson, *Reasons for Realism*, 413.
47. Ibid.
48. John Hejduk, *Such Places as Memory: Poems, 1953–1996* (Cambridge, MA: MIT Press, 1998), 39.
49. Peter Blundell Jones, *Architecture and Ritual: How Buildings Shape Society* (London: Bloomsbury, 2016), 5.
50. Ibid.

Constructing Consciousness

5

From the Colosseum's colossal ellipse, across the Palatine's ruin-shot hills—the broad sweep of the infinitely ancient nested among the constant new—this vision of Rome is how Sigmund Freud imagined the unconscious.[1] For him, consciousness was an archaeology in which the new was anchored in the deep gravity of the past. The Imperial, Medieval, Renaissance and Modern were layers of consciousness that decomposed, but never entirely disappeared—their distant voices continue to echo in the present. The philosopher Gaston Bachelard used a similar analogy to visualise the history of scientific progress. Like Freud's dimensions of consciousness, science itself does not build on a blank slate or an empty lot, but is akin to a half-renovated city where non-Euclidean curvatures rub against post-war apartment blocks. Both Freud and Bachelard argued that not only artefacts, but also ideas and mental states, have a past. Both of their images portray mind on the move, restlessly building and leaving its outgrown productions in its wake. The perpetual parade of changes in architectural styles over time, they would seem to suggest, are outward manifestations of internal shifts of mind. Here consciousness is known by what it produces—and while its products may be solid, consciousness is not analogous to something chopped up in bits, like bricks in a wall or links on a chain. "Such words as 'chain' or 'train' do not describe it fitly as it presents itself," William James famously wrote. Consciousness "is nothing jointed; it flows. A 'river' or a 'stream' are the metaphors by which it is most naturally described. *In talking of it hereafter, let us call it a stream of thought, of consciousness or of subjective life.*"[2]

Staying true to James's stream-of-consciousness metaphor, we can recognise that no river flows smoothly, at the same pace or homogeneously over time. A river's flow is determined by the shape of its bed, the confines of its banks—and from source to delta, is itself a process of gradual accumulation and redistribution. Slowing in the depths and speeding in the shallows—if a river is impeded—its languid surface issues the white froth of resistance. And if dammed, it swallows its surrounding banks. Like a river, consciousness not only flows, but does so in varying intensities and pulses according to the variables of the shifting situation. Consciousness glides along effortlessly until we are faced with a situation which forces us to summon our energies. Confronting uncertainties, like having to orient oneself in an unknown city, quickens consciousness—the unknown generates resistance like a rock creates rapids in a stream, and the rapids image is appropriate: "Consciousness is always in rapid change . . . It is the continuous readjustment of the self and the world in experience. Consciousness is the more acute and intense in the degree of the adjustments that are demanded,"[3] wrote Dewey. And though we may describe the qualities of consciousness in these liquid ways, we can never step outside of consciousness to explain it or measure it against something else. It is important to bear in mind that Freud, Bachelard, James and Dewey described the qualities of consciousness, but they did not pretend to explain it.

Consciousness Is Rhythmic

For William James, consciousness was not only a steady stream, its flow could also be characterised by distinctive moments and patterned with rhythmic qualities:

> The novel states of consciousness that emerge can be identified and individualised. They seem to crack the stream of consciousness if we consider them as independent units. In fact, they are discrete units and exhibit a character of discontinuity. However, the flow of consciousness persists; distinctness does not break the continuous, ongoing activity of consciousness. A silence may be broken by a thunder-clap, and we may be stunned and confused for a moment by the shock as to give no instant account to ourselves of what has happened. But the very confusion is a mental state, and a state that passes us straight over from the silence to the sound. The transition between the thought of one object and the *thought* of another is no more a break in the thought than a joint in a bamboo is a break in the wood. It is a part of the *consciousness* as much as the joint is a part of the bamboo.[4]

His description of the fluidity of consciousness, is, in his words

> vastly different from that dry universe constructed by the philosophers with elements that are clear-cut and well-arranged, where each part is not only linked to another part, as experience shows us, but also, as our reason would have it, is *coordinated to the whole*.[5]

We now know that consciousness not only streams, but does so in rhythmic pulses of oscillating waves. In 1924 the psychiatrist Hans Berger discovered rhythmic electrical currents that could be measured on the scalp. These brain waves were subsequently catalogued according to various bodily states: gamma waves with heightened perception and problem-solving, beta waves with alert and active thinking, alpha waves with physically and mentally relaxed states, theta waves with daydreaming and meditation, and delta waves with sleeping and dreaming. Researchers found that amplitude and phase of the waves varies according to situational events, just as Dewey surmised.

And it is now understood that these modulations do not occur only in a one-way flow. The idea that brain waves follow events, like a wake fans out at the back of a boat—the larger waves, the larger boat—is giving way to the theory that brain waves may contribute to facilitating those very perceptual and cognitive events. That is, the oscillating waves that can be measured with an electroencephalogram not only index those experiences but may act to modulate and pattern them. In other words, our experience of the world pulsates rhythmically just as our consciousness does. When asked to detect a subtle event, such as a slight change in a visual scene, our perceptual sensitivity is not continuous but oscillates several times a second in a rhythmic pattern that correlates with the electrical rhythms of the brain. The brain does not impose a pattern on the ongoing experience, but rather experience and rhythmic patterning mutually occur, entraining and conditioning one another. Imagine viewing a pine forest veiled in a thick fog, a scene like those shown in Chinese watercolour scrolls. Each tree's distinct form oscillates with the constantly shifting fog, alternating in turns of transparency and opacity. According to recent research, this rhythmic shifting is the way we perceive the world—but rather than the fog causing the oscillations, it is the brain waves that pattern them. Brain waves are not only rhythmic, but perception is rhythmic as well.[6] The rhythms of music, speech, sound, colour and light that pattern our surroundings draw neural oscillations into their tempo, effectively synchronising our brain's rhythms in the weave of their broader, interpenetrating rhythms. What this suggests is that though our conscious experience seems to flow continuously, the rhythmic pulses are actually quantised, and are perhaps more akin to what Whitehead called "drops of experience."[7] Bachelard also suspected that "of all the different energies of life, that of the mind must . . . be closest to quantum and wave energy."[8] Rather than a constantly flowing stream, it would be more accurate to imagine mental experience as distinct waves of thought, perception and consciousness, situated in the larger context of the daily, monthly and yearly rhythms that organise our lives.

The Natural History of Consciousness

"We cannot understand consciousness without understanding its natural history," declares Maxine Sheets-Johnstone. Thinking of consciousness in terms of situated rhythms takes consciousness out of the brain into the world and removes its exclusive claims to humans. After all, "we cannot separate organic life and mind from physical nature without separating nature from life and mind,"[9] wrote Dewey. Darwin's homologies between the emotional and cognitive lives of animals and humans[10] suggested this understanding of consciousness more than a century ago. The notion that higher-level cognition is rooted in the more ancient capacity to feel and respond appropriately to the situation at hand is the basis of the affective science pioneered by Jaak Panksepp, Antonio Damasio, Frans de Waal and Giovanna Colombetti. Considering the evolution of consciousness the way an archaeologist considers layers of sedimentary strata,[11] they argue that emotional systems are central to understanding the evolution of the human mind. According to Panksepp, humans share some primordial affective systems with all other vertebrates such as instinctual drives like fight or flight and homeostatic balance, which heavily influences the secondary layer that we share with other mammals, which includes primary emotions such as fear, lust, care, play, rage, seeking, panic and the specific neural electrochemical pathways and behavioural patterns that accompany them.[12] This secondary layer includes social emotions such as care, play and grief and is sculpted by learning and conditioning. These layers of emotion are "largely unconscious, and even when we are regulating them, we do not have clear introspective conscious access to their functioning."[13] Above these is the layer of mind that concerns psychologists and philosophers—the cognitive powers of the neocortex reinforced by language and symbolic systems. What is critical to remember is that although this tertiary layer can regulate emotion, it is not independent of those deeper layers. Like the roots of a tree that underpin its crown, the foundational layers infiltrate and animate the higher layers, in a process that is not strictly neural but embodied, embedded and sociocultural.

Speaking of functions with spatial terms such as 'higher' and 'lower' makes it difficult to imagine the degree of interaction and interdependence that actually take place in the brain. Although it is generally accepted that the brain is organised according to functionally specific regions, there is little consent about the extent to which this actually occurs. Any given brain region and neural network is involved in a wide variety of tasks depending on the context in which those tasks take place. As Luiz Pessoa reminds us, mapping cognitive functions onto the brain by attributing the activations of particular brain areas to nodes of neural networks in a one-to-one correspondence is unsupported by the evidence.[14] Again, context is critical. Cognition is not something that takes place only in the head; the human brain is a thoroughly social and cultural brain. The psychologist and neuroanthropologist Merlin Donald argues that our brains are unable to develop and function properly as cognitive organs unless embedded in the larger environment of symbolic culture. Donald identifies three levels of basic conscious capacity: first, basic awareness and perceptual unity; second, short-term working memory, which extends the reach of awareness over time; and the third level, intermediate-term governance, which lengthens into long-term memory and introduces what he calls a metacognitive or evaluative dimension, which allows the mind to detach from the immediacy of the situation to supervise its own operations. This distinctly human consciousness is contingent on four properties: pronounced neuroplasticity, executive function, expanded working memory and brain-culture symbiosis which he calls 'deep enculturation.' Biological memory systems and cultural memory systems like books and computers together comprise a hybrid cognitive system. Cultural materials and processes are so inextricably intertwined with the brain's development and functioning that they function as a necessary constituent of consciousness and cognition. This unique evolutionary strategy relies on off-loading crucial replicative information into our collective memory systems; cultural mind-sharing is our distinguishing trait. The human brain is unexceptional in its basic design; its distinguishing characteristic is that it relies on the cognitive scaffolding of culture to ensure its full development. Donald writes:

> The ultimate irony of human existence is that we are supreme individualists, whose individualism depends almost entirely on culture for its realisation. It came at the price of giving up the isolationism, or cognitive solipsism, of all other species and entering into a collectivity of the mind.[15]

In *Origins of the Modern Mind*, he proposes a three-stage unfolding of the progression of deep enculturation that is cumulative, conservative and constructed.[16] The earlier stages of cognitive development are operative in and integral to the more recent developments. He places the emergence of symbolic capacity with the acquisition of mimetic skill. Rhythmic mimesis, the capacity to rehearse and refine the body's movements in a voluntary and systematic way, was built on a primate foundation, and formed the basis for the arts of music, dance and other social rituals. These enacted rituals served to strengthen group structures leading to the specialisation of roles and stabilised social hierarchies. These events in turn formed the basis for the second, mythic stage of development whose achievement was the acquisition of speech and the advent of symbols, more sophisticated tools and the emergence of language. This inchoate capacity for symbolism blossomed in the birth of oral languages and narratives built upon mimetic songs, dance and rituals. Mythic forms of cultural expression both drew upon and then reinforced the newly emergent capacity for allegory and metaphor. In the context of mythic culture, the itinerant poets sang their epics and were able to do so because the rhythmic composition and improvisation of the epics structured their memory recall. Their consciousness was patterned and entrained by the epics themselves.

The transition to written artefacts extended memory storage even further, detaching it from the situated bodily encounters of spoken language, laying the foundation for the third stage, which Donald calls theoretic culture. This technologically supported cognitive ecology, which relies on the external memory storage that reading and writing permit, catalysed a rewiring of the prefrontal cortex. This development was not due to an increase in brain size but to the increased amount of connections activated by this revolution in human culture. Echoing Whitehead's insight that humans are nature in its most plastic expression, Donald argues that the quickening of cognitive evolution by supplanting memory with the cultural resources available through drawings, books and computers led to superplasticity. "Only a complex culture can generate the kind of expanding cognitive universe that rewards superplasticity," writes Donald.

> But it also raises the developmental stakes because each child must be crafted to fit the ever changing mould of culture. To achieve this, the human brain has evolved a maximally flexible, self-constructive developmental strategy which can track a moving cultural target.[17]

What started out as initially very gradual, with the invention of the first symbolic symbols, accelerated exponentially with the introduction of written artefacts, and in a ratchet-effect has altered not only how we use our biologically inherited cognitive resources, but has altered those resources themselves. "The human cognitive system, *down to the level of its internal modular organization*, is affected not only by its genetic inheritance, but also by its own peculiar cultural history."[18]

Art Structures Consciousness

Art is universal to all societies and in its capacity to order behaviour and consciousness is a patterning force of a paradigmatic kind. "All art is cognitive engineering,"[19] insists Merlin Donald. Art is a cultural resource that alters not only how we use our biological, inherited cognitive abilities, but alters those very abilities. The role of art in human development is so central that it cannot be understood only in terms of its products, but is characteristic of the way the mind works. Ellen Dissanayake was the first to uncover art's evolutionary importance, but rather than emphasising its role in terms of cognitive engineering, she understands it as a technology of love and care. Locating the ontogenic origins of art in the mutuality between mother and infant, she argues that these early experiences pattern phylogenetic cultural outcomes. Informed by her work with the infant psychologist Colwyn Trevarthen, whose focus is mother-infant bonding, her book *Art and Intimacy* argues that human infants come into the world with sensitivities and predispositions tuned to emotional communication with others that are later elaborated upon in the rhythms and modes of adult love and art.[20] The early envelope of skin, touch, sound and nourishment—the rhythmic signature of new life—patterns the temporal unfolding of subsequent form-making. These rhythmic sensitivities are then elaborated in practices that instil a sense of belonging, social cohesion and psychological well-being.[21]

Discerning patterns is a fundamental characteristic of our biological inheritance and gave rise to the ritual and ceremonies that perform critical cultural functions. Pattern is rooted in the word 'protect,' and that deeper meaning underlies the ceremonial marking of transitional life phases such as birth, puberty, death and healing. Art and ritual were bound together as an effective means to assimilate moments of great uncertainty and anxiety. Dance, song, storytelling and the altered states of consciousness they induce served to reinforce the interpersonal web of relations and to temper otherwise emotionally intolerable experiences.[22] Making art was a powerful way to exert control over unknown circumstances and give shape to the untidy material of daily life. Art emerged as a way to transform ordinary experience into the extraordinary. Creating a bowl from mud and engraving it with patterns and figures lifts it from the ordinary by distinguishing it with an added degree of care. This 'making special' opens a dimension of reality that at once ennobles daily life while providing a buffer from the forces of nature that are indifferent to it. Dissanayake's approach is complementary to the one John Dewey advocates in *Art as Experience*. A crucial overlap between them is Dewey's insistence on the status of rhythm as "a common pattern of art."[23] The need to make art is "rooted deep in the world itself"[24] and emerged as a means to cope with natural change—the function of the arts was to regulate, entrain and synchronise the nested rhythms of cosmic, seasonal and daily rhythms. And these larger rhythms are manifest in the rhythms of consciousness. "Underneath the rhythm of every art and of every work of art there lies, as a substratum in the depths of the subconsciousness, the basic pattern of the relations of the live creature to his environment,"[25] Dewey wrote. The rhythms inherent in early infant-parent bonding that form the basis for elaborating art exemplifies Dewey's insight that "rhythm is an essential property of form."[26] Form is not superimposed upon a material but a crystallisation of the rhythms of experience. Poetry, painting, architecture and music are manifestations of the rhythms which express and exteriorise these "basic patterns."[27] The artist is distinguished by her finely tuned sensitivities to the rhythms of existence. And, like Dissanayake's impulse to make moments of life special, Dewey insisted that "works of art are the most energetic means of aiding individuals to share in the arts of living."[28]

Art structures the rhythms of consciousness—our heartbeat, the soft patterns of speaking, the loving care necessary to incipient life are nested within larger cycles of rhythms. Both Dissanayake's and Dewey's study of rhythm corroborates what we are now learning about the rhythmic nature of consciousness, cognitive and perceptual experience. Edward T. Hall also approached anthropology in terms of cross-cultural rhythms and argued that music is the rhythmic consensus of a given culture.

> Before the Renaissance, God was conceived as a sound or vibration. This is understandable because the rhythm of a people may yet prove to be the most binding of all the forces that hold human beings together. As a matter of fact, I have come to the conclusion that the human species lives in a sea of rhythm, ineffable to some, but quite tangible to others. This explains why some composers seem able to tap into that sea and express for the people the rhythms that are felt but not yet expressed as music.[29]

Gaston Bachelard drew upon the rhythms expressed in music in proposing the method he called "rhythmanalysis"[30] and proposed studying rhythms to understand urban structures. Henri Lefebvre took up Bachelard's suggestion and developed rhythmanalysis as a way to understand urban experiences and the patterns of behaviour that take place in everyday life.[31]

The Future Enters Through the Work of Art

Art not only orders experience, it is uniquely suited to be a cipher of the future's unfolding. The overwhelming tendency to allow experimentation only to science laboratories misunderstands the artist's critical cultural role. Artists open new fields of experience, and their ability to reveal unforeseen dimensions in the familiar is in large part due to their open experimental method. Dewey wrote:

> Because the artist is a lover of unalloyed experience, he shuns objects that are already saturated, he is therefore on the growing edge of things. By the nature of the case, he is as unsatisfied with what is established as is a geographic explorer or a scientific inquirer. The 'classic' when it was produced bore the marks of adventure.[32]

He insisted that experience precedes artistic expression, and this intensely individualised experience seeks an outlet through means and materials common to the public world. As E. T. Hall noticed with certain composers in tune with rhythms that go unnoticed by others, the artist is compelled by the internal pressure to express her experience. And the value of the artistic work lies in its capacity to open dimensions of consciousness that are not apparent to the rest of us. Artists are probes, as McLuhan insisted, and art is advanced knowledge. Merlin Donald insists that artists have always served as a society's early-warning device. Jean Gebser called artists seismographers of consciousness. Dewey was interested in the development of technique in the history of art because it was a tangible indication of the primacy of experience demanding expression. The breakthroughs in Renaissance painting were not directly connected with solving problems in the craftsmanship of painting itself, but emerged in response to the limits of the old form that were superseded by experience. What brought about the change in technique was the advent of new perceptual experience.

Fifty years before the Eiffel Tower was built, Roland Barthes pointed out that the nineteenth-century novel imagined the bird's-eye perspective that the technology of the tower would eventually afford. Victor Hugo's *The Hunchback of Notre Dame* saw the panorama of Paris open beneath him from his steeple, and Jules Michelet's *Tableau Chronologique* opened a panoramic view of France. These comprehensive visions were complete breaks from the travel books of the time that chronicled the teeming bustle of the street and for the first time offered panoramas of the abstracted whole. "It is frequently the function of the great books to achieve in advance what technology will merely put into execution,"[33] Barthes noted. Similarly, the novelist William Gass called the novel a container of consciousness whose role was to enlarge and enrich consciousness. Art materialises a new perception and makes new realms of experience available to those who come into its orbit. Paul Cézanne's struggle to overcome the fixity of perspective grew out of his intense desire to depict matter in the process of taking form. He wanted to show the stable things we see and the shifting way they appear to us—all at once. And this desire fuelled his discovery of techniques that succeeded in depicting the perception of an emerging order. We not only see the work, we see the world *according to* the work, as Merleau-Ponty insisted. And as Gass affirms, "If I alter any reader's consciousness it is because I have constructed a consciousness of which others may wish to become aware, or even for a short time, share."[34]

In another example from literary history, prior to Barthes, Owen Barfield noticed that Romantic poetry had the effect of shifting his consciousness. While reading Shelley's invitation to "make me thy lyre," he noticed that the poem had an invigorating effect on him. The lyre was not a 'mere metaphor.' He began thinking and feeling *according to* the poem; it functioned as an epistemic filter that shifted the way he perceived the world around him. This experience led to his book *History in English Words*, in which he traces how language in earlier ages was metaphoric and figurative and becomes more literal as we move towards the present. He argues that metaphoric language grew out of a completely different mentality, and these different layers of consciousness lay manifest in the etymology of common words. Take the word *electricity*, for example, whose contemporary definition—'a form of energy'—is abstract. When tugged at more deeply, the word is found to be rooted in the Greek *electron*, which means 'amber.' And rubbing fur on amber, as the ancients once did, ignites sparks of static electricity. Their language described this direct experience. Like we saw with electricity, every word carries its traces, its origin. In earlier eras, poetry was not a distinct literary form but a way of experiencing the world, and a natural expression of lived experience. The linguist Jean Gebser noticed a similar effect in Rainer Maria Rilke's poetry. His language was not the linear prose of the Enlightenment. It preserved the vitality of the Romantic while adding something entirely new—a sense of simultaneity. Gebser noticed the same phenomena in other art forms and scientific breakthroughs, and thought he was witnessing firsthand the unfolding of a new dimension of awareness emerging through the mind of the poet.

Laminated Consciousness

The shifts in consciousness, manifest in the evolution of language, have been since corroborated in George Lakoff and Mark Johnson's work on the cognitive science of metaphor. Their *Philosophy in the Flesh* shows that the capacity for abstract reason is grounded in and makes use of the perceptual and motor inference present in 'lower' animals.

> Reason is not completely conscious, but mostly unconscious. Reason is not purely literal, but largely metaphorical and imaginative. Reason is not dispassionate, but emotionally engaged . . . since reason is shaped by the body, it is not radically free, because the possible human conceptual systems and the possible forms of reason are limited. In addition, once we have learned a conceptual system, it is neurally instantiated in our brains and we are not free to think just anything.[35]

Despite the fact that Lakoff and Johnson's work has been amply corroborated in the decades since its publication, we still have not quite reckoned with its implications. That our proudest achievements are rooted in biological soil and potentiated in the web of cultural scaffolding opens both profound potential and grave consequences for design. If reason is indeed an evolving capacity, it must be potentiated in a broader field of collective engagement. The capacity of reason, like a musical talent, must be exercised and continually tested and honed in daily life.

Gaston Bachelard studied the evolution of reason in the context of the history of science. Scientific thinking, according to him, is the progression from animism through realism to positivist rationalism, to dialectical rationalism, and scientific knowledge is a movement through these stages of consciousness in the order indicated. A child understands mass as something determined in terms of size; this is the level of animism. The next level links mass with the use of a scale; this is realism from which one can begin to deduce laws. The theory of relativity connects mass with energy; this is complex realism. Reason is structured by categories, yet the efficacy of these categories is rarely questioned. "Western science simply appropriates concepts such as space, nature, force," notes Maxine Sheets-Johnstone, "without explicating where these concepts come from, how we come to think in such terms, and why those terms are so central to our lives."[36] In his *Philosophy of No*, Bachelard traces the evolution of these concepts by adopting an inductive logic that moves from the particulars to a general theory, rather than from an overarching theory that tries to fit phenomena into categories prescribed by those theories. The inductive approach does not superimpose, but juxtaposes. The Latin *iuxta* means 'closely connected.' To juxtapose means to place them side by side. Consider the coexisting particle and wave theories of light, for example: both are true and each phenomena has a body of rationality to explain it. This rational pluralism, as Bachelard called it, allows two theories to oppose each other, while remaining valid within their own body of reason. Rather than a deductive form of knowing that reduces to component parts, this is a way of knowing that is indicative—that is, it points out, demonstrates, shows and is synthetic. In this approach, the mind must widen to contain both possibilities simultaneously.

> The truly logical synthesis of two originally irreconcilable theories which have nothing but their intrinsic coherence to guarantee their validity requires us to make some deep modifications to our thinking . . . either preserve mental unity and regard divergent theories as contradictory . . . or else unify the opposed theories, making appropriate modifications in the rules of elementary reasoning which seem to have become part and parcel of an invariant and fundamental structure of the mind.[37]

Bachelard showed that scientific breakthroughs are not only breakthroughs in those particular fields but necessitate a renovation of our mental structures.[38] Like the Renaissance painters who were forced by experience to discover new means of expression, in order for scientific knowledge to advance, the mind must be

> transformed down to its very roots in order to produce the like results in its buds. The very condition of the unity of life of the mind demands a variation of the life of the mind, a profound mutation of the human being.[39]

Rather than reason informing science, the findings of science force one to recognise the limits of reason. "Reason must obey science . . . the traditional doctrine of an absolute unchanging reason is only one philosophy and it is an obsolete philosophy."[40]

Where Bachelard showed that scientific knowledge is a movement through these stages of consciousness beginning with animism, Juhani Pallasmaa suggests that artistic thinking aspires in the opposite direction—in a movement away from rationalism back towards a mythical and animistic understanding of the world. Ways of knowing in science and art slide past each other on a shared continuum of thought. "Whereas scientific thought progresses and differentiates, artistic thought seeks to return to a de-differentiated and experientially encompassing understanding of the world. Artistic imagination seeks expressions that are capable of mediating the entire complexity of human existential experience,"[41] he writes. The strata of mind underpinning scientific thinking—and revealed, expressed and developed in the artistic—are mirrored in the evolving nature of language. In Greek, *ruin* is a word which means 'to flow.' In Latin, it changes to 'to fall' and by the time it reaches sixteenth-century English, the meaning 'fall' and 'collapse' have separated completely to refer to 'a heap of fallen bricks.' What began as an ongoing movement transitioned to a *fait accompli*. What was once verb solidified to a noun—shorn of the traces of its becoming. Freud eventually rejected the metaphor of the unconscious as the various stages of Rome's ruin. Buildings could be destroyed, but modes of consciousness survived all of the ages. He famously surrounded himself with Egyptian, Greek and Roman antiquities. Freud wanted his own consciousness to mingle in the milieu of ideas and objects infinitely more ancient than he could imagine, and, from the echo of their distant voices, to know at the same time that everything is in motion.

Notes

1. Sigmund Freud, *Civilization and its Discontents* (New York: W.W. Norton, 1989), 70.
2. William James, *Principles of Psychology*, Vol. 1 (New York: Dover, 1950), 239.
3. John Dewey, *Art as Experience* (New York: Perigee, 1934), 266.
4. James, *Principles of Psychology*, 240.
5. Ibid., Italics added.
6. Gregory Hickok, Haleh Farahbod, and Kourosh Saberi, "The Rhythm of Perception: Entrainment to Acoustic Rhythms Induces Subsequent Perceptual Oscillation," *Psychological Science* 26 no. 7 (2015), 1006–1013.
7. Alfred North Whitehead, *Process and Reality*, 2nd ed. (New York: Free Press, 1979), 18.
8. Gaston Bachelard, *Dialectics of Duration* (Manchester: Clinamen Press, 2000), 131.
9. John Dewey, *Nature and Experience* (New York: Dover, 1958), 296.
10. Charles Darwin, *Descent of Man, and Selection in Relation to Sex* (London: John Murray, 1871); Charles Darwin, *Expression of the Emotions in Man and Animals* (London: John Murray, 1872).
11. Stephen T. Asma, *The Emotional Mind: The Affective Roots of Culture and Cognition* (Cambridge, MA: Harvard University Press, 2019).

12. Jaak Panksepp, "Cross-Species Affective Neuroscience Decoding of the Primal Affective Experiences of Humans and Related Animals," *PLoS One* 6, no. 8 (2011).

13. http://philosophyofbrains.com/2020/02/16/the-emotional-mind-the-affective-roots-of-culture-and-cognition.aspx#_ftn7

14. Michael L. Anderson, Josh Kinnison and Luiz Pessoa, "Describing Functional Diversity of Brain Regions," *Neuroimage* 73 (2013), 50–58.

15. Merlin Donald, *A Mind So Rare: The Evolution of Human Consciousness* (New York: W.W. Norton, 2001), 12.

16. Merlin Donald, *Origins of the Modern Mind* (Cambridge, MA: Harvard University Press, 1993).

17. Donald, *A Mind So Rare*, 211.

18. Merlin Donald, "The Mind Considered from a Historical Perspective: Human Cognitive Phylogenesis and the Possibility of Continuing Cognitive Evolution," in *The Future of the Cognitive Revolution*, eds. D. Johnson and C. Ermeling (New York: Oxford University Press, 1997), 362–363.

19. Donald, *A Mind So Rare*, 19.

20. Ellen Dissanayake, *Art and Intimacy: How the Arts Began* (Seattle: University of Washington Press, 2000), 6.

21. Ibid., 140.

22. Ellen Dissanayake, *What is Art For?* (Seattle: University of Washington Press, 1988), 114.

23. Dewey, *Art as Experience*, 150.

24. Ibid., 153.

25. Ibid., 150.

26. Ibid., 153.

27. Ibid., 147.

28. Ibid., 336.

29. Edward T. Hall, *The Dance of Life: The Other Dimension of Time* (Garden City, NJ: Anchor Press, 1983), 81.

30. The term originates with Portugese philosopher Lúcio Alberto Pinheiro dos Santos who developed a theory of rhythm from the perspective of modern wave physics, medical science and psychology in his 1931 book *Rhythmanalysis*, which influenced Gaston Bachelard who in turn had a great impact on Henri Lefebvre. Bachelard's interpretation of rhythmanalysis was published in *The Dialectic of Duration* of 1936 where he defines rhythm as dialectical phenomenon apparent in myriad aspects of life, thus exceeding dos Santos's strictly scientific approach.

31. Henri Lefebvre, *Rhythmanalysis: Space, Time and Everyday Life* (London: Continuum, 2004).

32. Dewey, *Art as Experience*, 144.

33. Roland Barthes, *The Eiffel Tower* (Berkeley: University of California Press, 1964), 3–22.

34. William Gass, *Finding a Form* (New York: Knopf, 1996), 47.

35. George Lakoff and Mark Johnson, *Philosophy in the Flesh: The Embodied Mind and its Challenge to Western Thought* (New York: Basic Books, 1999), 4–5.

36. Maxine Sheets-Johnstone, *The Primacy of Movement*, 2nd ed. (New York: John Benjamins, 2011), 156.

37. Gaston Bachelard, *The Philosophy of No: A Philosophy of the New Scientific Method* (New York: Orion), 121.

38. Ibid., 122.

39. Ibid.

40. Ibid., 123.

41. Juhani Pallasmaa, "The Space of Time: Mental Time in Architecture," *Antwerp Design Sciences Cahiers*, no. 17 (2007).

Taxonomy of Interactions **6**

We are born of the body to be completed by the world and the task is never finished. Our restless plasticity—the fact that we can seemingly adapt to anything, together with a habit of seeing things in their separation and an imaginative capacity allowing us to transcend the immediacy of our situation—underlie our tendency to believe our surroundings are of little import. Yet, at the same time, our ability to adapt depends on the strength of our interconnections, and our imaginative capacity is constituted by the very places we inhabit. Our sense of invincibility is finally giving way to our sense of interdependence—and this coming to terms with the myriad ways in which we are woven into the world places all the more responsibility on those whose business it is to do the weaving. The burgeoning awareness that context—a word which originally meant 'to weave'—not only matters, but matters crucially, has finally filtered into architectural practice. The seminal 1984 experiment[1] finding that patients in hospital rooms with views towards a natural setting were released sooner, required less pain medication and experienced fewer complications than those without such views contributed to changing the way hospitals are designed. The benefits of integrating gardens into even the most challenging circumstances defies categories of quality and quantity. And while it is true that qualitative shifts have very clear quantitative consequences, enduring less pain and experiencing a sense of delight in our most vulnerable moments does far more than bolster the bottom line. Asking how we heal changes what may have seemed obvious but remained unspoken and brought it into the design brief. We are beginning to ask more subtle questions having to do with quality, rather than merely quantity, of such things as classrooms, parking spaces and hospital beds to question how architecture can foster the full measure of human experience. Questioning perception, we are beginning to understand how our settings shift consciousness, not only in an individual lifetime, but across collective lifetimes. Asking what architecture can actively *do* shifts the emphasis and opens a whole new level of rigour to the design process. Once we begin to identify the processes and characteristics of our interactions in the supportive field of our surroundings, we can apply this more refined awareness in a direction which enhances life. This shift towards interaction can enrich a multilayered approach to design worthy of the complexity and gravity of the task at hand.

Identifying a taxonomy of interactions to inform this kind of approach is a beginning, and is intended as a generative sketch with inexhaustible variations. *Taxonomy* comes from the Greek *taxis*, is rooted in the word *tact*, touch, tactile, *taktikè*, and originally meant 'the art of arrangement'. Taxonomy shares a function as old as language itself—the power to name phenomena and experience in order to bring it into broader awareness. The earliest taxonomy can be traced to 3000 BC and was developed to classify plants used in Chinese medicine. Aristotle's taxonomy did not appear until 30 BC and it was not until the discovery of optics in thirteenth century and the scientific expeditions of the eighteenth century that enough detail and complexity made it necessary to supersede the Greek works. Carl Linnaeus's *Systema Naturae* established the basic structure we take for granted today and transformed botany and zoology into legitimate matters for scientific investigation, which until that time had been fringe subjects of practical medicine. Lamarck was the first to categorise according to hereditary relationships, anticipating Darwin's full-fledged theory of evolution. This Taxonomy of Interactions shares the twin aspirations of these historic precedents—the power to name and to identify developmental relationships. Natural science taxonomies tend to be laid flat like a map of a tree, descendants emerging from a common ancestral trunk. This one is not modelled like a branching diagram showing evolutionary relationships spatially distributed, but models them like the brain where they are functionally intermeshed, in which antecedent structures are preserved and integrated in the successive ones. This organisational structure acknowledges that some interactions are more primordial than others—like the rhythms of breathing and the mutuality of touch—the ground of animacy at the heart of speaking, imagining and thinking. The developmental relationships here reflect the structures of consciousness outlined by the cultural philosopher Jean Gebser. His structures of consciousness serve as an organising metaphor around which human actions/bodily couplings with our habitat are constellated and can be more fully articulated. The perceptual relationships and patterns he discerned in the course of his broad and methodical study provide a schematic design for a Taxonomy of Interactions that gradually builds upon, integrates, informs and enriches successive layers. Gebser was emphatic that his intention was not to systematise, but to elucidate—that is, to bring living and working interrelationships into awareness—and this taxonomy aspires to do the same.

Structures of Consciousness

We will approach Gebser's structures of consciousness as he himself did, as a working hypothesis, continually open to feedback, revision and amendment. His major thesis that human consciousness is a process in transition was unlike that of his neo-Hegelian contemporaries—for him consciousness was not a metaphysical notion or a universal mind developing itself through history. Gebser understood consciousness not as a private consciousness but rather as a structure in which human beings understand themselves and find meaning. Consciousness was not set apart, nor essentially different from the world, but very concretely manifest in perceptual biases, physical and mental dispositions and rhythms expressed through various modalities such as literature, music, visual arts, architecture, philosophy, religion, jurisprudence, physics and the natural sciences. He correlated historical shifts in linguistic grammar and metaphors, expressions of art and architecture, social organisations and physiological attitudes with changes in underlying patterns of shared consciousness and named these patterns 'structures of consciousness.'

His major work, published as *Ursprung und Gegenwart* in various editions from 1949 to 1953, was not translated into English until 1984 as *The Ever-Present Origin*. To describe these patterns of shared consciousness, the original text uses the German word *gestalten*, which has no exact English equivalent, but was translated as 'structures of consciousness.' Yet the original term adds a degree of precision closer to our purposes here—*gestalten* is a verb meaning 'forming and shaping' and was first used by psychologists to describe the organised field of perception. Structures of consciousness are patterning fields in this very active sense. Although when translated as a noun, the word *structure* loses this formative dimension, Gebser intended it in its verbal sense, deliberately avoiding the terms *level*, *stratum*, *stage* and *position* because of their spatiotemporal fixity and implicit hierarchy of values. Like Merleau-Ponty, he was careful not to employ the very modes of thought that he was trying to undermine—so he replaced the terms of Newtonian isolated points and distances with a language of dimensions, thicknesses and depth.

Born in Poland at the turn of the last century, Gebser witnessed two world wars and understood the chaotic period he lived through as the breakdown of an outworn conscious structure and the incipience of a new order, and questioned whether such dramatic shifts had happened at previous pivotal points in history. Decades before Thomas Kuhn's work on paradigm shifts and Merlin Donald's theory of emergent stages of cognitive evolution, Gebser noticed that changes in consciousness structures do not progress linearly, but occur in discontinuous leaps and breakthroughs and argued that transitions in consciousness do not emerge through continuous evolution, but through qualitative mutations. These mutations are not expansions, but *intensifications* that restructure mental and physical habits. "The manifestation of this mutational process should not be construed as a mere succession of events, a progress or historicised course," he argued. "It is, rather, a manifestation of inherent predispositions of consciousness."[2] Rather than using the term *evolution* to articulate these gradual changes, he preferred to describe the process as one of unfolding. And, though it appears that the structures unfold chronologically, they are simultaneously present and operative in us today. Consciousness integrates the antecedent structures, just as the evolution of the brain builds upon preceding structures in a tendency towards increasing complexity.

Gebser's lifelong study was informed and inspired by his close friendships with the leading cultural figures of his time such as Federico Garcia Lorca, Rainer Maria Rilke, Paul Éluard, André Malraux, Pablo Picasso, Carl Jung, D. T. Suzuki, Adolf Portmann, Werner Heisenberg, Sri Aurobindo, Henry Corbin, Károly Kerényi and Walter Gropius. He did not arrive at his structures of consciousness through constructing a theory and imposing it upon phenomena. His approach presumed Husserl's phenomenology, which meant that he did not take for granted that life exists more fully in what is commonly thought big—and paid attention to the intimate particulars and allowed them to unfold according to their own inner logic. Through his close reading of Rilke, Gebser noticed a loosening of fixed grammatical relationships that opened a new way of perceiving multiple dimensions simultaneously. And in this detail, he witnessed the future entering through the work of art. This method of working from the nuance of specifics is the inductive approach that Bachelard advocated in the history of science—one that begins from concrete details to trace their broader implications. And, where Bachelard argued that empirical evidence demands new mental habits for its interpretation, for Gebser, reading Rilke's poetry both embodied and foretold of a new way of perceiving.

Gebser identified five unfolding, interpenetrating structures of consciousness, beginning with the archaic and followed by the magic, the mythic and the mental and finally the integral structure. Gebser correlated each structure of consciousness with a perceptual organ, and identified their respective relationships to space and time, forms of realisation and thought, and social emphases. Every emergent structure of consciousness is latent in germ within the previous one. "For each unfolding of consciousness there is a corresponding unfolding of dimensions. An increase in the one corresponds to an increase of the other; the emergence of consciousness and the dimensioning imply and govern each other,"[3] he wrote. The paradigmatic example is the way in which Renaissance perspective opened three-dimensional space not only through the technique of painting, but in a larger perceptual shift that it made possible, and was further reinforced by the invention of the telescope that triggered a cascade of philosophical and cultural consequences. Experience preceded expression. Technology is stretched to accommodate experience and goes on to shape, pattern and transform subsequent experiences.

The pattern of emergence in Gebser's structures of consciousness can be compared with the transition from infant, toddler, child, adolescent to adult to illustrate the way in which earlier developmental phases are absorbed and integrated. "Just as the unborn in utero recapitulates the phylogenesis at least in principle, so the growing individual traverses the ancestral structures of consciousness, gradually adding them to his or her repertoire of responsiveness to self and world,"[4] noted Georg Feuerstein. Like the maturation process of any individual, certain relational capacities that were the focus of attention at one stage inevitably fade into the background in a subsequent phase. And while adults clearly possess mental and physical capabilities that children lack and modern cultures possess scientific and technological capabilities unknown to indigenous cultures, few adults possess the imagination and spontaneous creativity common to children and most modern cultures can only long for the intimate bond with the natural world that is the very basis of indigenous cultures. The emergent pattern of consciousness is built on the raw material of the old and no one structure was better or worse than another—each has its effective and defective manifestations and inherent capacities and limits. Because the new is inextricably rooted in and constituted of the old, the previous structure does not lose its value, but only its claim to exclusive validity. The failure to integrate the newly opened dimension with the previous structure led to a disintegration untethered from the ballast of depth. "We must consciously retain and presentiate the past,"[5] wrote Gebser.

Archaic Consciousness

The structure closest to human origins, Gebser called 'archaic consciousness,' which is rooted in the Greek *archē*—*archaic* here means 'inception' and 'origin.' This consciousness is zero-dimensional, prespatial and pretemporal—and refers to a time when humans were fused to completion with their surroundings. While Gebser did not suggest an organ emphasis as he did for the others, I will correlate the archaic structure with the skin—our largest organ and our earliest surface of contact with the world. In the skin envelope of early infancy, the distinction between self and other does not yet exist. To describe this period, Gebser refers to Chuang Tzu's statement: "Dreamlessly the true men of earlier times slept."[6] This consciousness is suggestive of the deep sleep of early infancy and the autonomic functioning and presentiment akin to animals. This autonomic consciousness should not be mistaken as a state of unconsciousness. Gebser deliberately avoided the term *unconscious*, and held that consciousness structures have differing patterns, tendencies and rhythms but did not admit dualities such as conscious and unconscious in the Freudian sense.

To even begin to imagine this kind of bond, it is helpful to reflect on the rhythm of breathing. The division between inner and outer that collapses in the breath and the practice of breathing is central to the ancient religions of Hinduism and Buddhism. This early unity is present in the chromatic symbolism of one of the oldest extant texts, the I Ching, which dates from 1000 BC. And, as Richard Wilhelm observed in his translation of the text, "at that time blue and green are not yet differentiated. The common word Ch'ing is used for both the colour of the sky, as well as for the sprouting plant."[7] This ancient tradition did not refer to early humans as primitive in a derogatory sense but understood them rather as 'true men.' Chuang Tzu proclaimed that "true men breathe [even] with their heels, the mass of men breathe [only] with their throats."[8] This further suggests the indivisibility of sky and earth; breathing through the soles of one's feet is the most primal grounding in a complete reversal of our Western habits of thinking. The fusion of blue and green suggests synesthesia as a perceptual orientation. Deriving from the Greek, *syn* meaning 'together' and *aisthesis*, which means 'sense perception'—synesthesia is a condition in which one sensory modality is simultaneously experienced by another. Hearing certain tones of music makes some people see and taste colour; letters and numbers are seen simultaneously in various colours, seeing someone being touched, one can feel touched in the same place. Until four months of age, all babies are synesthetic.[9] The emphasis on the organ of the skin correlates with Merleau-Ponty's philosophy of 'the flesh,' a zero-point

Radial diagram (partial, lower-right quadrant). Reading from the centre outward:

Inner ring (categories):
- MAGICAL
- ARCHAIC

Second ring:
- Imagining
- Making
- Dancing
- Resonating
- Touching
- Resistance
- Breathing

Third ring (concepts):
- Animistic
- Physiology of the Imagination
- Complementarity
- Suspension
- Bodying Forth Form
- Homo Faber
- Mechanisms of Mutuality
- Kinaesthetic Awareness
- Choros
- Sound as a Building Material
- Buildings as Musical Instruments
- Origins of Music
- Haptic Perception
- Sensory Training
- Mindful Physical Presence
- Lungs of the City
- Interconnection
- Strength in Vulnerability
- Cultures of Breathing
- Epistemology of the Skin
- Entrainment
- Empathy
- Affirming the Breath

Outer labels (checkbox items), reading around:

- Tension/Delay
- Mirroring/Epiphany
- Subtle bodies
- Interdependent opposites
- Ambivalence/polyvalence
- Reciprocal meanings
- Organ is the psyche
- Negative capability
- Open-ended
- Nonlinear dreamtime
- Nowhere is there a dead thing
- Threshold between inner and outer
- Demolish hylomorphic model
- Intervening in fields of force
- Itinerant, improvisational, rhythmic
- Weaving architecture
- Making as a way of knowing
- Listening to materials
- Historic precedents
- Situated dance
- Elaborating, manipulation and delay
- Healing and social bonding
- Mimic processes of ritualization
- Formalization, repetition, exaggeration
- Identity of place and dance
- Tone made visible
- Unthawing frozen music
- Multimedia performance work
- Space interpenetrates the body
- Acoustic capacities of materials
- Acoustic acumen of ancients
- Situated music
- Context-dependency of sound/tone
- Coextensive with emotions
- Restorative of psychic balance
- Technology of bonding
- Mediated by vibrations
- Role of past experience
- Feedback of resistance
- Carnal hermeneutics
- Sensory symphonies
- Touching/being touched
- Touching
- Friction
- Slowing down
- Green roofs, walls, towers
- Urban forests
- Restore migration corridors
- Forests, wetlands, mangroves
- Adaptive not mitigative
- Social/interpersonal
- Openings
- Sensitivity to pain
- Density of connections
- Bio-cultural thermal devices
- Integrated vernacular strategies
- Minimise refrigerants
- Sensorimotor communicative
- Layered porosity
- Inner/outer
- Synchrony
- Eurhythmy
- Proportioning
- Actual movement
- Traces of movement
- Motor resonance
- Rhythms
- Visibility
- Poetics

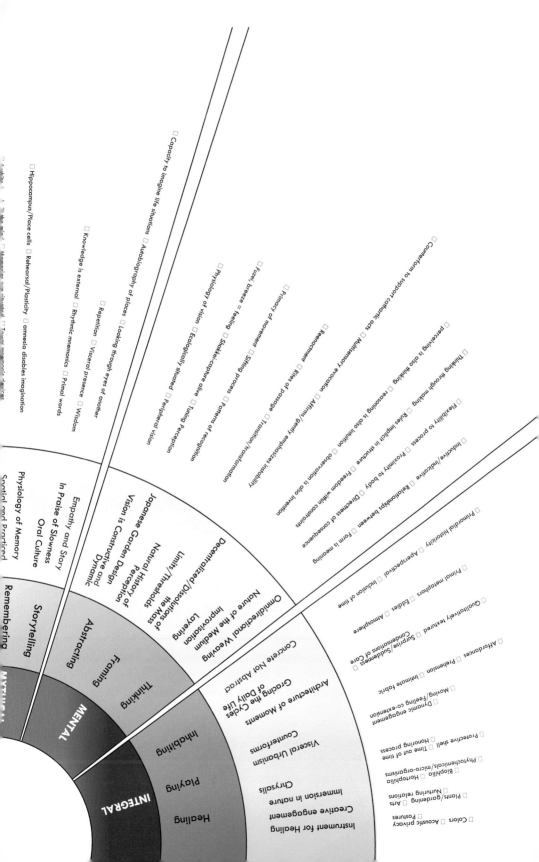

intertwining the inner and outer at once. The flesh is the original matrix that makes perceiving possible; it is the basis of what the philosopher David Abram calls "our interbeing with the earth."[10] The constellation of interactions in this structure reflects the functions of the skin, whose porous envelope is our primary opening towards the world in breathing, resisting and touching.

Magic Consciousness

From the undifferentiated unity of the archaic awakens emergent powers of action. This period is marked by instinct, emotion, sympathy and heightened sensory perception. Here humans are vitally potent; their entire body "forms a seamless transition to the flux of things and nature with which it is merged."[11] This structure is not yet in human beings, but rests in the world. Emotion is not a solely internalised affair but situated in the world of events. This is how Dewey understood emotion—as a coextensive intensity uniting organism and world. Here the human copes with natural events through the use of magic. The root of magic is the same as for the verb 'to make' and this period marks the emergence of *homo faber*—man the maker. The polymodal art forms of this period are tools of sympathetic attunement. Gebser correlated magical consciousness with the cavernous, labyrinthine ear, and there could hardly be a more fitting analogy for gaining some insight into the oldest known human artefacts. No art has since been able to capture the living presence of animals more persuasively and sympathetically than the paintings on the Paleolithic cave walls, precisely because they were created within a cohesive vital fabric in which individuals are not yet distinct. These paintings were part of an elaborate ritual involving journeying into the constricted body of a cave, dancing, fire, sound—imagery that simultaneously engaged the entire organism to enact their magical effects. And today, few art forms are more emotionally and physically gripping than music. Dewey called the ear the 'emotional sense.' The neurobiologist Walter Freeman has argued that the power of music derives from the fact that music evolved as a technology that reinforced emotional bonding.

Gebser located the magic structure of consciousness in the historical period when statues lacked a mouth—the absence of which indicates the extent to which the sounds of nature and spoken words predominated. This kind of consciousness can be experienced today when one is spellbound by music, theatre or an athletic performance. Communication takes place through sympathetic participation, entrainment and resonance and the performers themselves are operating at a subconscious level of synchrony with one another, like a flock of birds that changes direction in a single gesture of flight. This psychic attunement with the collective ego is also evident in advertising and political campaigns, and herein lies the danger—hearing in this phase is without ego or responsibility because responsibility presupposes separateness. As Gebser put it: "The operative principle of magic consciousness though lucidly receptive, is blind, and due to its blindness is destructive."[12] Magic operating in this deficient mode is evident in the crowds that are swept up in the rhetoric of Hitler, Mussolini and the demagogues of today.

If the archaic is analogous with the consciousness of early infancy, the magic is analogous with the awakening of personal agency that occurs in early childhood. As Freud observed, young children have difficulty neatly distinguishing between their own body and emotions and those of the environment. Between the ages of 6 and 12, children experience themselves gradually emerging into a dynamic relationship with the outside world and begin to recognise themselves as separate individuals in a world of natural processes. The psychologist Edith Cobb spent decades studying the autobiographies of geniuses from diverse cultures and eras and found that creative thinkers recollect this period of childhood to renew their imaginative powers.[13] This kind of full-body engagement evokes the sympathetic participation characteristic of magical consciousness in its efficient mode of operation. And Cobb's correlation of this sympathetic identification and the creative powers of children later accessed by adult artists parallels the significance of the act of making. All making, whether spell-casting or modern technology, externalises inner powers and conditions. As Gebser presciently put it: "Every tool, every instrument and machine is only a practical application . . . of the laws of one's own body rediscovered externally."[14] This primal impulse to extend one's body outward in the act of making is the very origin of techne. Dalibor Vesely referred to this impulse as a "deep ordering energy"[15] and similarly traced the origins of techne to the mimetic making of ritual. The skills developed in the making of rituals parallel Merlin Donald's stage of mimetic culture. The watershed adaptation leading to symbolic culture is rooted in the motor skills required to rehearse and refine bodily movements repeatedly in dance, ritual and craft. The character of this consciousness structure therefore suggests the constellation of interactions of resonating, dancing and making.

Mythical Consciousness

The magic and mythic structures overlap around the third millennium BC, according to Gebser, which roughly correlates with Merlin Donald's emergence of mimetic culture. Where magical consciousness expresses one-dimensional unity and merging with nature, mythic consciousness introduces two-dimensional relationships. It is an ambivalent structure of polarities that are not dualistic but complementary; light and dark, silence and sound, life and death, male and female, speaking and listening are all perceived through a world of symbol, ritual, religious feeling, social sentiment and agricultural fertility. The dominant sensory organ is the mouth, a word which is rooted in the word *mythos* and originally meant 'speech, word, report.' Here humans awaken in myth, articulating the world through representing and making audible. Where magic had the stamp of emotion, the mythic period bears the imprimatur of the psyche. Here the persona becomes individuated. *Person* derives from the Latin *per suonare*, meaning 'to sound forth.' This marks the advent of personal experience in which one shares their story—*storia*, meaning 'history.' This sharing is consummated through listening and empathy, as opposed to the sympathy and bodily attunement of the magical phase. Imagination developed with the emergence of mythical consciousness, and through empathic listening we can understand the heart of another speaking human being. In our rationally dominated worldview, however, we need to allow ourselves release from the grip of the cognitive so we can enter polar attunement with another—communication depends as much on silence as it does on what is said.

This is the birth of oral culture epitomized in Homer's epics and may be imagined as Walter Ong suggests:

> The child of today probably passes through stage something like that of the old oral culture . . . but the stage is only something like the old, for it remains the child's stage and cannot be protracted into adulthood. The old oral world was not a world of children but of adults, who had children of their own.[16]

The art of storytelling is a way to affiliate our modern selves with the mythic world present in our everyday actions. Myths of journey, of great discoveries and adventures from Odysseus to Star Wars are as Gebser says, "the collective dreams of the nations formed into words."[17] The mythical period predates the Greek alphabet that shifted the mnemonic rhythms of speech and culture to written texts and the cognitive, cultural and political consequences. Speech is simultaneous, embedded and local, while written communication is linear, atomised and abstract. In oral culture, a word is a sound, an image and an event. Literate culture traps words on the page to be deciphered in the privacy of one's mind. Leonard Shlain has argued that the alphabet changed the way the nervous system developed, which in turn profoundly impacted gender relations. "Misogyny and patriarchy rise and fall with the fortunes of the alphabetic written word,"[18] he writes. The mythic period is the consciousness structure of oral culture whose relationship with language depends upon and reinforces the capacities of empathy. These are skills that involve both hemispheres of the brain: "Nonverbal clues, concrete gestalts, music, inflection, spontaneity, simultaneity, aesthetics, emotion, slips of the tongue, gesticulation and peripheral vision . . . are hemispheric activities requiring a large amount of traffic in both directions across the corpus callosum,"[19] notes Shlain. The imagination that emerged in the advent of myth relies on the images and metaphors of language that are perceived synthetically and all at once, while reading individual words is serial and linear. With its emphasis on empathy and mirrored pairs, the mythic period is characterised by the interactions of imagining, remembering and storytelling.

Mental-Rational Consciousness

Gebser locates the definitive reorganisation of consciousness framing the entire intellectual attitude of the modern age with the discovery of perspective during the Renaissance. This structure is the stepping out of the sheltering, two-dimensional circle and its confines into three-dimensional space. This discovery as fully realised by Leonardo da Vinci not only made technical drawing possible, it made available a formerly latent dimension of the human imagination that irrevocably changed our relationship to the world. Once stretched by new experience, the mind can no longer return to its original dimensions. The projection that began on the canvas catapulted man out of the protected confines of the Ptolemaic cosmos to become the basic axiom of an entire epoch. The basis of the perspectival world is the visual pyramid, in which two lines project from the eyes to intersect at the object viewed, summarised by Piero della Francesca: "The first is the eye that sees; the second the object seen; the third, the distance between one and the other."[20] These three points become the coordinates of the Newtonian worldview—the newly introduced duality between subject and object separated by empty space not to be fused with the sympathetic attunement of the magical consciousness, or harmonised with the empathy of the mythic, but observed with detached vision. *Observe* means 'to stand against,' and this opposition becomes the signature posture of an entire epoch.

The word *perspective* comes from the Latin word 'perspicere,' which means 'to see through' or 'seeing clearly'—this incipient clarity, besides illuminating space, makes humans newly visible to themselves. This emergence of the individual ego is further exacerbated by developments in language. Gebser traces the first emergence of the mental-rational consciousness structure to around 7500 BC with the rise of cities coming to full flower in 500 BC and 1500 AD reaching its zenith in the Enlightenment. The Greek alphabet that externalised and abstracted communication sedimented the transition from orality to literacy and its attendant emphasis on vision and directed, discursive thought. This shift to written communication objectified language, projecting it beyond the situated complementarity of speaker and listener. Once language was projected outside the confines of the body, it could be appropriated to political ends. The anthropologist Claude Lévi-Strauss was among the first to be wary of the consequences of literacy:

> There is one fact that can be established: the only phenomenon which, always and in all parts of the world, seems to be linked with the appearance of writing . . . is the establishment of hierarchical societies, consisting of masters and slaves, and where one part of the population is made to work for the other part.[21]

This period coincides with Merlin Donald's theoretic culture, the externalised memory store made available in written texts intensified with computer media. The new capacity to objectify led to quantitative measurement, abstraction, anthropocentrism, dualistic not polar tension of complements which interdepend, such as speaker and listener, loved and beloved; instead we have narcissism, the hypertrophic ego, mind-body, right-wrong, rational-emotional, etc. One side must always exclude the other. Listening is seen as passive; the goal is to convert the sinners with 'missionary zeal' where everyone must be told how the world is. Complementarities hardened into oppositions.

Other attributes of the mental-rational structure are obsession with time as unit, the future and unlimited progress. At the same time, space is conquered; anxiety arises about loss of time; there is intoxication with conquest; Copernicus ruptures the confines of the Ptolemaic universe; Columbus conquers the encompassing oceans; Vesalius, the first anatomist, burst the confines of the human body to discover bodily space; Harvey reveals the circulatory system; Kepler overthrows antiquity's world image of circular and flat surfaces; and even fabric is punctured with the invention of lace. Horizons expanded while vision was increasingly narrowed. Perspectival vision locates and determines the observer as well as the observed. And, as Gebser cautioned:

> The positive result is the concretion of man in space, the negative result is the restriction of man to a limited segment where he perceives only

one sector of reality. Like Petrarch, who separated landscape from land, man separates the whole from the part which his view can encompass, and forgets the sectors that lie adjacent, beyond, or even behind.[22]

And since perspectival vision cannot deal with wholes, it mistakes the part for the whole and totalises it; this is the basic impetus behind totalitarianism in all its guises. This period inaugurates a new individualistic and rational understanding of nature, which lays the groundwork for modern science and technology. Once nature has been othered, it can be dissected, exploited and fracked. This expulsion from the situated relational dynamics to stand outside as a detached observer has reached its apotheosis in the communication of our time—conversations that once took place face-to-face are now mediated by extraterrestrial satellites. The spatial breakthrough continues to penetrate seemingly endless horizons.

Integral Consciousness

Gebser witnessed the inherent fragmentation in the mental structure reaching its deficient stage and was gravely concerned with its severe imbalance: "an increase in technological feasibility inversely proportional to man's sense of responsibility."[23] He was convinced that technocratic rationality could not transform living conditions for the same reason that Einstein insisted that one cannot solve a problem using the same level of consciousness at which it was created. Gebser noticed that the indications heralding a transformation in consciousness shared a common tendency towards integration rather than separation. Just as the determining factor in mental consciousness was perspectivity, the incipient consciousness could be characterised by its aperspectivity. The two terms were not set in opposition or in negation to one another—rather, the Greek prefix 'a' has a liberating character, suggesting a release from the exclusive validity of fixed perspective. Where perspectival consciousness sought to conquer space, aperspectivity promised to humanise and concretise time. Developments in physics were discovering the simultaneity of past, present and future that echoed Rilke's poetic language. In painting, Picasso incorporated time by showing all aspects of the subject at once. In these developments, Gebser noticed the irruption of the fourth dimension in which time is not spatialised sequentially but integrated as thickness and depth and experienced not as duration but as an intensity. The way to concretise time was to recapitulate all the former consciousness structures in their fullness, and in his friend Picasso, Gebser recognised a paradigmatic case. Drawing on his primitive magical inheritance, mythical and his classicist, rationally accentuated formalist phases, Picasso condensed deep history into the present. "All the temporal structures of the past latent in himself (and in each of us) during the course of his preceding thirty years of painting in a variety of earlier styles,"[24] Gebser wrote.

Architecture, according to Gebser, is a "pre-eminently sociological art,"[25] one that concretely structures practical individual and communal life. And because of its role in patterning the habits of daily life, the history of architectural transformations embody shifts in human consciousness over time. Architecture was such an important index of consciousness, Gebser insisted that

> the transformation of European sensitivity to, and comprehension of the world is nowhere more clearly discernible than in painting and architecture. Only our insight into this transformation can lead to a proper understanding of the nature and meaning of new styles and forms of expression.[26]

He understood the spatial and formal breakthroughs of Frank Lloyd Wright, Le Corbusier and the Bauhaus as indications of this aperspectival shift. Modernism's concern with interpenetrating interior and exterior space, enlivening static space with dynamic time, fixed relations yielding to flexible ones and the open plan in both architecture and city planning all as indications of an emergent consciousness. If it is true, as Gadamer and Ricoeur have maintained, that the value of a theory is determined by how much it enriches the cultural milieu upon entering it, Gebser's notion of aperspectivity has not yet been granted the recognition it deserves. Sigfried Giedion's influential *Space, Time and Architecture* essentially summarises Gebser's cultural critique.[27] Hans Scharoun acknowledged his debt to Gebser's notion of apersectivity in his design of the Berlin Philharmonic.[28] The traditional configuration of the theater with its proscenium stage was a manifestation of fixed perspective, one that so thoroughly dominates the spectator's spatial experience as to undermine the suspension of disbelief critical to the theatrical performance. Scharoun's asymmetrically planned auditorium, with a vaguely defined stage area and no proscenium, and unfocused seating facing a variety of directions, results in a perceptual elusiveness that changes shape and size as one moves through it. The ambiguity of the space affords the festive atmosphere synonymous with theatre's larger cultural role.

This decentreing is characteristic of aperspectival consciousness. In the rational structure, everything is oriented to a centre, and in the new structure, the focal point that was once sought externally in consolidated power structures is found within the individual. The centrifugal thrust of the integral structure need not succumb to the fragmented alienation typical of the rational. Individuation is a constructive achievement but not an end in itself, and would simply not be possible in isolation. Particularity is the consequence of hard-earned struggle—one can only, very literally, become human in the arms of another. The 'other' is not approached as a threat or a project for eventual conversion and domination, but is the very source and possibility of our becoming. Individuality is only recognisable through difference; it does not strive for fusion or uniformity but a multidimensional awareness of the multiple modes of consciousness that simultaneously and meaningfully constitute our world. The aperspectival does not strive to transcend, as the urge for transcendence is unique to the mental-rational mode, but grows and develops *in* and *through* experience. This sense of the individual resonates with the dawning awareness that characterises Nietzsche's *Übermensch*—someone who is, by definition, responsible for making their world. This awareness is evident today in the interdisciplinary discourse in which diverse vantage points are considered and problems approached from multiple directions, in the collapse of subject and object in the field phenomena of atmospheric space, in the burgeoning awareness of interdependence with context, in the simultaneous borderless relativizing democratisation of internet communication. The constitutive empathetic interplay between self and other, whether that other is a member of the natural or constructed world, makes inhabiting, playing and healing the interactions to explore in this structure.

The mental-rational structure that Gebser critiqued is also the principle theme of Alberto Pérez-Gómez's well-known study *Architecture and the Crisis of Modern Science*, which argues that Western architectural thinking underwent a radical transformation around 1800, when the rational sciences took command of an architectural practice that had hitherto been grounded in the mythopoetic ethos of the classical tradition. Architecture in the industrial age was forced to choose between the newly sundered domains of art and science—and with the overwhelming ascendancy of the former's positivist approach, the poetic content of reality disappeared beneath a mire of formal explanations. This crisis culminated in the structuralist and post-structuralist linguistic theories of the 1960s and 1970s, which were inappropriately applied to architecture but nevertheless consumed the theoretical spotlight to the exclusion of other more valid approaches. That poetic dimension may have slipped off the knife-edge of the rational inquiry, but it never entirely disappeared. Alberto Pérez-Gómez's call to cultivate poetic language; Dalibor Vesely's call to reinstate analogy, metaphor and proportion; Juhani

Pallasmaa's call to remythologise; and Harry Francis Mallgrave's insistence to sophisticate the long-standing cultural role of architecture with a biological understanding—these are not nostalgic back-turnings, but acknowledgements of the need to restore lost dimensions of architectural consciousness that constitute the living ground of future work. In an integral approach, the obsession with quantification must shift to a concern for the quality of time. To magical consciousness the world is present in every part, macro/microcosm are homologous. To the mythic, time is cyclic and the world is a place of complementarity. To mental the world is not a place, but mathematised space, and to integral consciousness, the whole of the past and the possibilities of the future awaken in the fullness of the present moment.

Notes

1. Roger Ulrich, "A View Though a Window May Influence Recovery from Surgery," *Science* 224, no. 4647 (1984), 420–421.
2. Jean Gebser, *The Ever-Present Origin* (Athens: Ohio University Press, 1984), 41.
3. Ibid., 117.
4. Georg Feuerstein, *Structures of Consciousness* (San Diego: Integral Publishing, 1987), 54.
5. Gebser, *The Ever-Present Origin*, 43.
6. Ibid., 44.
7. Richard Wilhelm, *The I Ching or Book of Changes*, trans. Cary F. Baynes (New York: Routledge Kegan Paul, 1968), 57.
8. Chuang Tzu, *The Writings of Chuang Tzu*, trans. Brook Ziporyn (Indianapolis: Hackett, 2009), Book 6.
9. Daphne Maurer, Laura C. Gibson and Ferrinne Spector, "Synesthesia in Infants and Very Young Children," in *Oxford Handbook of Synesthesia*, eds. Julia Simner and Edward Hubbard (Oxford: Oxford, 2013), 46–62.
10. David Abram, *Becoming Animal* (New York: Penguin, 2012), 3.
11. Gebser, *The Ever-Present Origin*, 64.
12. Ibid., 60.
13. Edith Cobb, *The Ecology of the Imagination in Childhood* (New York: Spring, 1998).
14. Gebser, *The Ever-Present Origin*, 132.
15. Dalibor Vesely, *Architecture in the Age of Divided Representation* (Boston: MIT Press, 2004), 289.
16. Walter Ong, *Interfaces with the Word: Studies in Consciousness and Culture* (Ithaca: Cornell University Press, 1977), 299.
17. Gebser, *The Ever-Present Origin*, 68.
18. Leonard Shlain, *The Alphabet and the Goddess* (New York: Penguin, 1999), 3.
19. Ibid.
20. Gebser, *The Ever-Present Origin*, 19.
21. Claude Lévi-Strauss, *The Elementary Structures of Kinship* (Boston: McMillan, 1969), 15.
22. Gebser, *The Ever-Present Origin*, 18.
23. Ibid., xxvii.
24. Ibid., 25.
25. Ibid., 464.

26. Ibid., 9.

27. Sigfried Giedion was a student of Gebser, and openly acknowledged his debt to him. His books, *Mechanization Takes Command* (1948) follows Gebser's critique of the mental structure and his *Eternal Present: The Beginnings of Art and The Beginnings of Architecture* (1957) is a direct homage to Gebser's *Ever-Present Origin*. Eric Mark Kramer has also traced Gebser's influence on Marshall McLuhan and his colleague E. T. Hall at the University of Toronto. Lewis Mumford's influential critique of technology, which so closely parallels Giedion's, underlines Gebser's lingering influence.

28. Peter Blundell Jones, "Hans Scharoun and the Berlin Philharmonic: The Discovery of Aperspective Space," *Space and Society: International Journal of Architectural and Environmental Design* 45 (Jan–Mar 1989), 19.

The Primacy of Breathing   **7**

Inhaling, invisible molecules surround us, enter in—exhaling, our inner being courses outward to meet the world. Our life depends on this intimate exchange. What is more primal, more necessary, than this vital streaming? We are born breathing, or not at all. Breathing is synonymous with life; it is the primordial interaction par excellence. This air that is in my body was once in yours—and sooner or later, we will all breathe the same air. The most concrete expression of our being inside and outside at once, breathing, is the ultimate testimony of our utter dependence on something other than ourselves, that we dwell in a shared medium. This subtle melding of inner and outer worlds is so automatic that it goes unnoticed, unless it is interrupted by a loss of equilibrium, perhaps caused by illness within or pollution without. In the rhythm of breathing, divisions such as these—thinking of illness as only inside of us, or pollution as solely outside of us—are foiled. Breathing declassifies: the condition of my inner world, my wellness or illness, exhausts into the atmosphere, and that atmosphere, polluted or pure, inhabits my inner world—either washing me clean or sickening with its stain.

This quintessential interdependence is something we take for granted. Yet, breath is something we can only hold or possess at our own peril. Breath is movement and depends on openings. The primacy of breathing means that we are only alive to the extent that we are porous—to the extent that we are open. The word *pore* comes from the Latin and Greek meaning 'for passage' and 'journey,' sharing the same root with words *portal*, *door* and *gate*. Our life depends on the openness of this passage, yet this world we have built of blocks has exorcised the air. Too often our buildings are inert boxes on life support, that no longer breathe. The absence of breathing in our building practices is symptomatic of a larger forgetting—a loss first taken seriously by the philosopher Luce Irigaray—who noticed a persistent bias in Western thinking that favours the version of matter that is static and hard and more obviously possessed and completely overlooks matter that is subtle and flows. On the matter of air, Western philosophy has said nothing: "The vacuum that they create by using up the air for telling, without ever telling of air itself: [is a] chasm at the origin of their thought's appropriation."[1] Air escapes notice because it is nothing, no thing. Irigaray argued:

> No other element is in this way space prior to all localisation, and a substratum both immobile and mobile, permanent and flowing, where multiple temporal divisions remain forever possible. Doubtless, no other element is as originarily constitutive of the whole of the world.[2]

Air is the missing constituent of our obsolete physics; in our obsession with the particle, we have forgotten the wave. And our forgetting of the air has left us breathless.

Affirming the Breath

Paying attention to breathing restores this original vital inheritance. In creating buildings that breathe—in this most non-dualistic of interactions—we ourselves can breathe. Gebser named the structure closest to human beginnings 'archaic consciousness.' The word *archaic* comes from the Greek *archē*, meaning 'inception, origin.' And since "no other element is as originarily constitutive of the whole of the world"[3] as air is, perhaps the origin—the *archē*—of architecture is not made of a solid; perhaps it is built of breath. After all, "Is not air the whole of our habitation as mortals?"[4] Irigaray asks. In archaic consciousness, humans were fused to completion with their surroundings; the distinction between world and individual did not yet exist. To even begin to imagine this kind of bond, it is helpful to reflect on the rhythms of breathing. "Nothing is more important than breathing, breathing, breathing," declared the Zen master Shinichi Suzuki. Awareness of this original unity is the foundation of Eastern meditation practices bearing witness to the continuous cycle of union and reunion in breathing that we normally take for granted—concretely reminding us not to forget about the air. The Inuit word for 'breath' is the same as making poetry—imagine the halo that visibly surrounds one's breath when speaking in a cold climate. Their 12 names for the wind enable them to navigate an Arctic environment where there is often no horizon differentiating earth from sky. Increasing our awareness of free-flowing air by rendering it evident to multiple senses is a poetic affirmation of the breath. The artist Tomás Saraceno celebrates this vital dynamic in his *Poetic Cosmos of the Breath*. The otherworldly iridescence of this work was not achieved by mechanical means but by harvesting the invisible currents of air at dawn that warm to awaken the tissues of a simple silk parachute. His Aerocene flight tests are not propelled by fossil fuel but by harvesting forgotten currents of air. The artist Ned Kahn drapes the anonymous facades of parking garages with metal sculptures that shiver with a slightest breeze—flashing their mirrored surface like delicate leaves. Cloud Arbor, his collaboration with the landscape architect Andrea Cochran, creates a sphere of fog from a forest of stainless steel poles in a community park in Pittsburgh, immersing park visitors in its vaporous nebula. The rhythms of breathing animate that which is otherwise inanimate and bring otherwise invisible dimensions to conscious awareness.

Image 7.1 Poetic Cosmos of the Breath
Source: Photo Studio Tomás Saraceno.

Image 7.2 Cloud Arbor by Ned Kahn

Source: Photo Matt Niemi.

Image 7.3 Wind Arbor by Ned Kahn, Marina Sands, Singapore

Source: Photo Ned Kahn.

Empathy and Entrainment

The capacity for these artworks to engage us emotionally—to literally move us—is rooted in the movement of the works themselves. One reason for this is that we identify the movement in the work with the movement in our own bodies. At the turn of nineteenth century, the art historian Heinrich Wölfflin hypothesised this:

> Physical forms possess a character only because we ourselves possess a body. If we were purely visual beings, we would always be denied an aesthetic judgment of the physical world. But as human beings with a body that teaches us the nature of gravity, contraction, strength, and so on, we gather the experience that enables us to identify with the conditions of other forms.[5]

His precocious statement has since been developed in cognitive neuroscience, most notably by Vittorio Gallese, whose motor simulation hypothesis[6] argues that when we observe real or implied body movement—such as facial expression and gestures, footprints on the ground, the strokes of brush on a painting, or the etching made by a chisel on stone—we simulate those actions and emotions in our own mirror systems. This means that roughly the same neurons are activated in the observer as those that were engaged in making the original work. Other researchers have studied the ways in which artwork that exhibits actual movement or vestiges of movement provoke the same motor resonance in our own bodies compared to static content which causes us only to imagine movement.[7] Though varying in their technical details, the consensus among researchers is that we understand others by perceiving them as living bodies.[8] Another reason that these works move us is still more direct and can be explained by the tendency for entrainment. Entrainment is the universal tendency in living and nonliving systems to synchronise movements—the swing of pendulum clocks and the tendency of plants and animals to spontaneously respond to the cycles of light and dark caused by the earth's rotations are obvious examples. On the interpersonal level, infants entrain with the rhythms of their caregiver's heartbeat, blood circulation and breath. Two people in rocking chairs involuntarily synchronise their rocking frequencies,[9] while two people walking together tend to fall into the same pace, assume the same posture and mimic one another's gestures regardless of their familiarity.[10] On the social level, audiences at theatre or athletic performances not only tend to clap in unison[11] and assimilate the emotional tenor of the speaker or event, the mere co-presence of others sharing a common experience is enough for cardiac synchrony to occur spontaneously.[12] What this entails is that collective events are both physiologically and emotionally shared experiences simply by virtue of gathering together in the same space.[13] Entrainment is involuntary, preconscious, automatic and constraining, creating an *"implicit common ground"*[14] of conscious awareness. The basic rule of entrainment is that people synchronise with rhythms whether the originator of those rhythms is animate or not. Indeed, the very capacity to generate rhythm renders that stimulus animate—the billowing silken parachute, and the delicate shuffle of pieces of tin. To our baseline awareness, the stimulus seems alive. Synchronisation to shared rhythms is known to cause stability, reliability and predictability and therefore promotes cooperative action and feelings of familiarity and affiliation.[15] So, it is perhaps no surprise that rhythm is a well-known design principle in art and architecture throughout time.[16]

For Wölfflin, breathing was a paradigmatic example of rhythm. What is more, the rhythm of breathing had a decisive ordering effect on the body that the best architecture should strive to emulate: "The posture of the body affects the circulation of the blood and the rhythm of breathing. Our consideration of conditions of balance thus leads us *to what in architecture has been called serial regularity or 'eurythmy.'"*[17] The term *eurythmy* refers to harmonic balance in dance, music and architecture. The homology he suggests between body and building entails that the composition of the building should be arranged to ease the flow of blood and breath. He goes on to say:

> Of great interest is the relation of proportions to the rate of breathing. It cannot be doubted that very narrow proportions produce the impression of an almost breathless and hurried upward striving. Naturally, we immediately associate them with the idea of tightness, which makes it impossible for us to continue to breathe deeply with the necessary lateral expansion.[18]

The spatial composition of the building shapes the posture and breathing of the body in mutual entrainment. Proportion is not static imposition but an iteration of the rhythms of breathing. Using breathing as a measure of proportion truly tunes the design composition to the limits and possibilities of the human organism in a higher octave of harmony that sophisticates the Vitruvian model.

The Epistemology of the Skin[19]

Skin is primarily an organ of breathing. Our skin is our earliest and most fundamental medium of contact with our world—which is why we call touch the mother of the senses. We transmigrate from the aqueous womb to the outside world clothed in the same skin. This organ, which wraps us outside and in, exemplifies our most primordial interactions with the built world— breathing, resisting and touching—and it is also the most paradoxical. Our skin serves a dual, and seemingly conflicting, function, simultaneously protecting us from harm while remaining exquisitely sensitive to the slightest vibration. In the embryonic stage of fetal development, the nervous system develops from the ectoderm layer. Skin protects only to the extent that it is open; this organ is our nervous system turned inside out. The poet Paul Valéry captured this paradox when he wrote:

> That which is the most profound in the human being is the skin . . . the marrow, the brain, all these things we require in order to feel, suffer, think . . . to be profound . . . are inventions of the skin! . . . We burrow down in vain, doctor, we are . . . ectoderm.[20]

And in fact, our current focus on the brain as the centre and source of knowledge derives from a now exhausted epistemology. We tend to forget that the brain is the upper and expanded part of the central nervous system, whose primary function is to relate the organism to its environment—an environment that actively shapes thought and behaviour, one woven through with intelligence, of which our individual nervous system is but a part. The word *cortex*, used to designate the outer layer of neural tissue, is the Latin word for 'bark' or 'shell.' Our brain itself is skin, wrapped in skin—it is centre and periphery at once.

The difference between ourselves and other mammals resides not solely in the greater size of our brains, but also in the fact that our skin has shed its hardness and hairy cloak. Our lack of fur makes us depend upon our relations and our extensions ever more greatly; our intelligence and sensitivity owes to this very vulnerability. Our loss of fur was an adaptation that afforded intensified bonding between mother and baby. Skin-to-skin contact creates a thermal, emotional, communicative, sensorimotor envelope that extends the environment of the original womb. From this protected position, the baby's world gradually extends outward to the family, the community and the larger environment in an entourage of signals. Clues about external reality come forth in smiles, sounds, gentleness of contact, warmth of embrace, solidity of carriage, the rhythms of rocking, the availability of feeding, the quality of attention and the presence of others. Basic needs like feeding and protection are accompanied by tactile, visual, auditory and olfactory communication. The fulfilment of these vital needs in the absence of sensory and affective exchanges is known to cause irreparable physical and psychological damage and even death to the baby.[21] Evidence from the fields of interpersonal neurobiology and developmental psychology unequivocally concur that the biological and social consequences of this early matrix of care cannot be overstated.[22]

Our skin reveals our emotional condition with exacting accuracy. Sweaty palms, perspiration, blushing, goosebumps, hairs standing on end—researchers have studied the quickly fluctuating electrical properties of this somatosensory perception for over a century. Changes in electrodermal activity (EDA) and skin conductance have been used to study affective processes, attention, arousal, cognitive effort and even decision-making. In their study of the emotional basis of cognition, Hanna and Antonio Damasio have found that measuring electrodermal activity is a much more sensitive indicator of our thinking and eventual decisions than our rational minds.[23] Our brain is not only enskulled, it is enskinned. In our obsession with penetrating the core, we forgot about the shell—when in fact the two hold each other; they interdepend. "The shell itself is marked by what it shelters,"[24] wrote the psychoanalyst Nicolas Abraham. The epistemology of the skin demolishes the duality between form and substance, obviating the detachment of the container from the contained. As we now know, no such simple lines can be drawn in the living world where what appears to be a surface is merely the visible layer of much deeper terrain. Consider the polar bear's fur, which consists of three layers: the clear hollow hair, darker coloured skin and a wooly layer below. The clear hollow hair serves as a lens for sunlight to absorb on the darker surface below, which is retained inside the wooly blanket beneath. When the temperature warms in the summer, the structure of the hair allows the fur to change colour. Similarly, a chameleon not only changes the colour of its skin for camouflage and communication, but to exploit the thermal variations consequent to the daily cycles of light.

Practicing the principles of biomimicry, some architects are finally modelling building skins not only as barriers to the outside world, but as filters that breathe like natural skin. Thinking through the skin allows one to consider the building envelope as a complex membrane, a nervous tissue capable of information and energy exchange and even self-cleaning. The Council House 2 in Melbourne Australia designed by Mick Pearce mimics the ventilation strategy of a termite mound. Recycled timber louvres controlled by photovoltaics move according to daylight, and five shower towers cool the air through evaporation. Ilaria Mazzoleni and her students at SCI-Arc created a residence in Palm Springs modelled on the physiological characteristics and behaviours of lizard skin. Her living units for the Arctic mimic polar bears' behavioural and physiological adaptation strategies. Foliage facades integrate plants in the space between two glass panels that filter sun through leaves which vary in density according to light levels. Living walls of course serve similar multidimensional functions. Jenny Sabin and her colleagues at eSkin emphasise connectivity and context as primary determinants of form and functional layering; LabStudio develops intelligent skins in collaboration with biomedical researchers; others are exploring growing living tissues for use as building materials. These projects exemplify some of the inexhaustible possibilities that can result from thinking of surfaces of buildings as one considers the boundary of the skin—not as an inert delineation, but as the site of intense interactions.

Cultures of Breathing

The sense of layers that serve to maintain openness and flow while protecting and resisting is exemplified in desert climates that prior to industrialisation could not afford to forget the air. These vernacular arrangements were constellated around the constant movement of air in an elegant layering that was the fruit of compounding cultural, psychological, personal, social climatic and economic factors. The advent of fossil-fuelled mechanical systems forced a complete rupture with the past that abandoned the concepts and values that evolved over the course of millennia. The prototypical house design that was introverted and focused family life on the courtyard shifted to a plan that looked into the street. The architect Hassan Fathy laments:

> The cool, clean air, the serenity and reverence of the courtyard were shed, and the street was embraced with its heat, dust and noise. Also, the qa'a was supplanted by the ordinary salon, and all such delights as the fountain, the *salsabil*, and the *malqaf* were discarded in the name of progress and modernity.[25]

The vernacular technologies to which he refers each played cultural roles equally as important as the thermal function they served. And, as Ellen Dissanayake reminds us, the decorative arts in many cultures were rooted in acts of care, and developed to express and reinforce interpersonal and social connection. These thermal devices served both sociocultural and eco-biological roles that were gutted with the advent of mechanical air-conditioning—their loss commits a double devastation.

Like Icarus flying too close to the sun, architects were suddenly released from the tempering forces of local climates and traditions and hastily adopted modern technologies without considering their potential consequences on the complex web of culture. They failed to understand "that civilisation is measured by what one contributes to culture, not by what one takes from others . . . without assessing the value of his own heritage."[26] The havoc wreaked by mechanical air-conditioning extended well beyond disrupting the physiological, psychological, social and intimate life of the community. The refrigerants used in air-conditioning heavily contribute to global warming.[27] Where these technological advances were directed towards achieving mastery over the environment, vernacular cultures did not conduct themselves in this top-down, authoritarian manner. Their responses were not abstract, but local—they adapted to specific conditions in a dialect of strategies born from the intimate knowledge, moods and temperament of place. Their buildings were in-formed—that is, formed by these local, situational variables—and this gradual process of achieving equilibrium was a work in progress requiring continuous local attunements. We have scarcely fathomed the consequences of disrupting of this hard-won balance. As Fathy insists:

> However fast technology advances, however radically the economy changes, all change must be related to the rate of change of man himself. The abstractions of the technologist and the economist must be continually pulled down to Earth by the gravitational force of human nature.[28]

A Brief Study of Desert Thermal-Cultural Devices

Traditional architecture was tested and honed in the crucible of the desert climate. We tend to undervalue the extent to which the empirically achieved trial and error of tradition is based on scientifically sound principles. This process generated vernacular building strategies in which each element worked in balance with and served to reinforce the others, which means that altering one aspect of the building has cascading effects throughout the whole system. Changing even one small element can destroy the entire validity of the building as a satisfactory response to local climatic conditions. A closer study of the elements that evolved for living in extreme climates exemplifies the sophisticated intertwining of behavioural, social and biological adaptations. Like layers of veils that protect skin from aridity, dust and heat, dwellings were distributed according to a nested hierarchy of porosity. Their cellular pattern, unlike the gridiron arrangement with wide vistas that allow air to sweep through at a disturbingly high velocity, performs the same function as the courtyards; the narrow meandering streets with closed vistas retain the cool air deposited at night from being swept away by the first morning wind. The shared outer walls reduced the heat load by minimising the external surface while opening the inner one. The largest pore was the courtyard in the centre—dwellings turned their backs to the street to afford privacy and air circulation. Life was lived in the mutuality of building technology and cultural practices; one afforded the other in an organismic reciprocity.

The fountain that was placed in the centre cooled the passing air, distributing it through the complex, while its rhythmic murmur dampened and amalgamated other sounds. Describing his mother's childhood home in Yazd, Iran, Sina Sohrab writes:

> The courtyard's reflecting pool—a small body of water that operated beyond its practical nature—acted as the soul of the entire home. This label is not bestowed lightly, nor attributed to the pool's mere positioning; the notion that the reflecting pool contained the soul of the home is borne out of the many years of interaction that occurred around it. In a sense, these interactions elevated the physical space of the courtyard to an interpersonal experience by providing a calm center amid the surrounding humming energy, and ultimately a space conducive to connection.[29]

The courtyards were typically lined with a *takhtabush* loggia, a covered outdoor seating area at ground level opening completely onto the courtyard through a *mashrabiya* onto the back garden.[30] The porous perimeter of rooms allowed for a more intimate way of life—one that, Sohrab notes, "encouraged my mother's family to share experiences more consistently, and perhaps even more viscerally, for better or for worse; it was a kind of carousel of life always on display."[31] This centripetal

Image 7.4 *Mashrabiya*, Cairo, Egypt

Image 7.5 *Mashrabiya*, Cairo, Egypt
Source: photo Alamy.

concentration seemed to unite the family in overlapping moods and oscillations that were the visceral fabric of daily life.

The brise-soleil typically used in hot arid climates called the *mashrabiya* derives from Arabic—'to drink'—and originally referred to a place to have a drink. True to its name, it is a wood-screened cantilevered outcropping where jars of water were placed to cool the passing air through evaporative cooling. Like all vernacular technologies, it served a multitude of functions—controlling passage of light and airflow, reducing the temperature of air currents and increasing their humidity—and was also intricately configured to provide privacy. The lattice was designed with horizontal lines interrupted by protruding balusters producing a silhouette carrying the eye from one baluster to the next across the interstices. The louvers were adjustable so that the eye is not dazzled by the contrast between the brilliance outside and the darkness within. This design corrects the slashing effect caused by the flat slats while offering the outside view over the entire plane of the opening—superimposing a decorative pattern reminiscent of darkened lace.[32] From the inside, the *mashrabiya* appears as a lighted wall that affords the freedom of a view while simultaneously imparting a sense of privacy and security. It was a built amalgam of thermal, psychological, physiological, behavioural and aesthetic concerns finely tuned not only to climatic conditions but to human perceptual limits. The exterior wall surfaces, though simple in outward appearance, also served complex functions. The openings allowing air intake used elsewhere are typically windows but are not feasible in a desert climate because they let in excessive heat and dust. And, at street level, wind velocity is reduced, which makes an ordinary window inadequate for ventilation. The desert alternative is the claustrum—a multitude of small vents that function more efficiently than a few big ones to ensure privacy, security, airflow. They were originally used in high openings for Roman baths and are now used in modern architecture mostly for their visual effects and are stripped of their formerly sensitive thermo-cultural meanings. Domes and vaulted roofs were used to increase the speed of air flowing over their surfaces according to the Bernoulli effect. In concert with the domed ceilings was the distinctive wind catcher called the *malqaf* or *badgir*—a shaft rising high above the building with an opening towards the prevailing wind that traps the wind which is cooler and stronger and channels it down to the interior.[33]

Materials were chosen for their capacity to breathe, and the way they were used was crucial because cooling and humidifying functions are closely related. While the thick claustral walls were useful in resisting heat transfer, they caused problems because they radiated that heat back out, so they were used in combination with organic fibers. Plant-based materials have the

Image 7.6 Dome with *claustra*, Bazaar Yazd, Iran
Source: photo Sarah Robinson.

capacity to regulate their skin temperatures through transpiration—wood fibres retain this quality even after they are cut from the tree, as long as they are not coated with impervious paints. Organic fibres readily absorb, retain and release considerable amounts of water, making them able to cool the air that passes through them. It is important to remember that these technologies were not discrete formal elements, but functioned within a larger system. Configured to keep air moving, these nested strategies coupled building technologies with behavioural practices. Living patterns shifted according to the seasons, making one aware of their belonging in the larger rhythms of natural cycles. In these vernacular configurations, every detail is designed with the

Image 7.7 Four *badgir* structures placed over a water well in Yazd, Iran

Source: photo Sarah Robinson.

breath in mind, and they offer inexhaustible lessons for designing as if "air is the whole of our habitation as mortals." In buildings that predate the advent of air-conditioning, the actions of opening and closing shutters to keeping air moving synchronised body, consciousness and climate in a way that kept one in touch with the day, the passing of time in a larger entrainment with place. The suffocation of place—the fact that many live inside hermetically sealed rooms smelling of freon—has had devastating consequences for our environmental, physical and psychological health. "What is climate change if not a consequence of failing to respect or even to notice the elemental medium in which we are immersed?" David Abram asks. "Is not global warming, or global weirding, a simple consequence of taking the air for granted?"[34]

Resisting

An arch is two weaknesses which together make a strength.[35]

—Leonardo da Vinci

These bio-thermal-cultural strategies, collectively accrued over generations, exquisitely exemplify not only resistance, but flourishing in harsh conditions. They suggest a version of strength which is not impervious to change or disruption, but capable of enduring pain—to suffer, yet to remain standing. Such poetic responses emerge from the discipline of accepting that there is no escape from the embrace of and struggle with one's fundamental ground. The character of architecture, like the matter from which it is fashioned—is resistance. Yet, as these integrated techno-cultural practices testify, building thick walls to block the heat is only one way of thinking about resistance. We tend to associate resistance with that which is hard. The pyramids have resisted the ravages of time because of their sheer mass. But the walls of desert dwellings have lasted because of their strategic openings and their earthen materials which permit breathing. When we think through the skin, we remember that the protection afforded by our skin is a function not of its stubborn mass, but of its vulnerability—its sensitivity to pain. And perhaps this kind of sensitivity offers another way to think about resistance. "True resistance begins with people confronting pain," writes the poet bell hooks, "and wanting to do something to change it."[36] *Resist* shares the root with *exist*, 'to go on living'; if we have a strong immune system, we resist a cold; when we are ill, our health disintegrates. Perhaps resistance can be best achieved not through damming the pores, but through unclogging them. One of the most celebrated buildings in Western history is surely Rome's Pantheon. It has stood stubbornly for 2,000 years without steel reinforcement and continues to withstand the passage of time because it is open at its crown. Like the breathing hole of a great whale, the oculus allows in oxygen, light, rose petals and rain, while simultaneously girdling the 4,535-tonne compressive force of the entire dome. Meanwhile, the arches on its interior distribute the girth of its heavy walls. What they accomplish with opening and welcoming, heavy

Image 7.8 Pantheon, Rome

Source: Photo Devin Ford.

walls can only accomplish with sheer density and weight. Gravity—after all, is not a force, it is a curvature. The Pantheon curves to remain standing.

Resistance depends not only on the thickness of our walls, but on our finely tuned sensitivity and ability to connect. The way we resisted temperature shifts was first to gather around the fire and to build shelter. Think of the way mangroves dampen the onslaught of hurricanes through their innumerable connections—protecting coastlines with their profligate network of roots and resisting shock through their wealth of relationships. Adopting a similar strategy in the post-tsunami reconstruction master plan for the city of Constitución, Chile, the architect Alejandro Aravena planted a forest along the shoreline rather than a cost-prohibitive wall. Now both the residents and the local wildlife can enjoy the far-ranging benefits of a shoreline park. Richard Sennett has suggested that it is time to "rescue the clichés"[37] of sustainability and resilience, by more carefully considering how building approaches can be more adaptive. In adaptive strategies, borders function like cell membranes whose porosity and resistance function together in dynamic tension, while mitigation strategies emulate the model of a solid dam. Adaptive approaches are inherently open, while the mitigation approach tends to be closed. The difference is evident in two different strategies proposed for sea-level rise for the city of New York: the mitigation model is exemplified by the "Dryline" designed by Bjarke Ingels, which is essentially a large berm on top of which will be constructed gardens and parks. The problem is that this wall is fixed in height and can be inundated if waves are larger than mathematical models predict. An alternative strategy, rather than creating one hard-edged surface, proposes to create a series of wetland berms across from Manhattan that rise and fall as storms wax and wane, shifting in form, rather than remaining as a fixed construction. The first proposes a closed boundary, while the second proposes an open one.[38] Adaptive strategies of resistance feature openness, connection, elasticity—the capacity to bounce back after being stretched.

Perhaps the most accessible model for building resistance is through introducing plants and trees as much as possible into our living environments. And with over half of the world's population now living in cities,[39] dedicated green areas have never been more crucial. Already at the turn of the last century, Frederick Law Olmsted was concerned with the unhealthy living conditions of cramped tenements fouled with smoke from burning coal and intentionally designed New York's Central Park to serve as the "lungs of the city." Urban parks are not only social and recreational centres, they function as air filters, sponges, humidifiers, heat shields, wind blocks, carbon sinks, habitats, migration corridors, stress reducers, shock absorbers, sanity savers and playgrounds. Green walls, green roofs, vertical forests, pocket parks and gardens—designers are adopting evermore resourceful strategies to integrate plants in the urban landscape. The 2.5-acre green roof at the California Academy of Sciences in San Francisco, for example, replaces the footprint removed from the natural habitat with a 2.5-acre green roof that links a wildlife corridor along the Pacific coast. The landscape group RANA used 50 species of indigenous plants that host endangered insect populations in an intentional act of restoration. Understanding resistance in terms of interconnectedness means that we must recognise and tend the natural environments that sustain us as the very source of our sanity. Trees are gravitational loci for human well-being. Their shade softens heat: one mature tree produces the equivalent cooling effect of ten room-sized air conditioners and can lower surrounding surface temperatures by five degrees Celsius.[40] Their leaves rustle in the breeze to absorb noise, while releasing phytochemicals known to counteract stress. In tropical climates, trees grow large enough to serve as canopies for entire communities. Yet trees truly flourish and live to be very old when they grow together in ecosystems they co-create with other trees. To truly function as lungs of the city, urban trees must be urban forests, where their roots and canopies are free to entangle and support one another.

Images 7.9 and **7.10** Urban Carpet Installation Aarhus, Denmark by Polina Chebotareva in collaboration with Elias Melvin Christiansen

Source: Photos Rasmus Hjortshøj.

Beyond the obvious economic and ecological value of trees, what is more difficult to articulate is the calming power of their presence. Living among trees is to share in the company they keep with birds and insects. This kind of immersion in their physical being is akin to another aspect of resistance that Gernot Böhme suggests has to do with the need for mindful physical presence. In an increasingly virtual world, the starvation of physicality seeks its compensation. When tourists actually visit the places they dream about, they touch things to make sure they are real—to be real means that they resist their touch. "As virtual reality develops— what is real becomes harder and harder to decipher, to sense presence, there is no more accurate indicator than the sense of touch,"[41] Böhme insists. Working with friction through interrupting the habitual increases the awareness of touch. Polina Chebotareva accomplishes this with her Urban Carpet in Aarhaus, Denmark. The woven textile of charred wood releases its scent in the friction underfoot, and its location near the entrance of the train station causes people not only to slow their hectic pace, but to occasionally tap their feet and start dancing. The carpet makes sounds when walked upon and draws people's attention to the tree around which is installed in an unprecedented way. It also had the effect of increasing safety: its attraction compels people to stand on it while awaiting the green light.[42] Tadao Ando also insists that we can develop resistance through maintaining and developing our sense of touch. This is so important a task that it should be one of the primary objectives of architecture:

> Since there has been life on earth it is our feet which remind us we are alive. We know we exist when we feel it in the soles of our feet and all of us in infancy begin by learning how to walk. No matter how computerised the world may become we will probably keep on walking and that will probably be the last thing we feel. If we finally lose all perception of reality our psychological disintegration will follow and in the midst of environmental catastrophe, famine and natural calamities, being alive will mean nothing anymore. If the world is determined to destroy itself, the only thing architecture can do is make sure we don't lose our sense of touch.[43]

Touching

Keeping us in touch with the durable flow of matter is in itself a powerful act of resistance. As Diane Ackerman writes:

> We need to return to feeling the textures of life. Much of our experience in twentieth-century America is an effort to get away from those

textures to fade into a stark, simple, solemn, puritanical, all-business routine that doesn't have anything so unseemly as sensuous zest.[44]

The founders of the Bauhaus were already concerned about the atrophy of the senses that might result from the industrial processes they themselves championed. Sensitivity in all of its connotations is an undeniable skill to both artist and designer and sensory training was fundamental to their preliminary course. Bauhaus students explored different aspects of tactility through making devices enabling them to feel a scale of textures, as one hears a scale of music. These devices took myriad forms, from Otti Berger's woven tactile chart of varying thickness and patterns of thread, to a revolving drum of tactile values, tactile tables that tested pressure and vibration and registered pricking sensations.[45] Students then explored the varying textures while blindfolded and this practice was also extended to include the visually impaired who were asked to evaluate the success of their inventions. J. J. Gibson was also among the first to use hand sculptures to investigate the perception of shape and found that the visually impaired are reliably more accurate than those who are merely blindfolded.[46] László Moholy-Nagy understood touch as "a collective term for a number of different sensory faculties."[47] His primary device for exploring the foundational aptitude of touch were his hand sculptures. He asked students to create hand sculptures whose sole function was "to be agreeable for the hand to hold and to play with."[48] The hand sculptures figured prominently not only in his teaching, but in his later explorations of film and kinetic sculpture. According to him, the hand sculptures were "nearest to the timeless art of all ages mainly because they express the pure functions of the hands."[49] This 'pure function' of the hands has since been extensively studied; the kind of knowing that comes through touching imparts an authoritative knowledge unlike that given by the other senses, as in the case of tourists who are not certain of the reality of what they see until they touch it for themselves. Touch does not lie.

The hand sculptures bear an uncanny resemblance to the Inuit sculptures that Edmund Carpenter has studied. One of their distinctive characteristics is that their carvings do not stand up, but "rolled clumsily about" because they are not intended to be displayed or perceived from one perspective—but to be passed from hand to hand and played with. The sculptures were not objects per se but mediums of shared experience. Similarly, Moholy-Nagy's hand sculptures could not be viewed from any one side. Touch is local; immediate and relational does not admit dualities like subject and object. To touch is to be touched in return. Inuit art did not exist in a realm apart but was an

Image 7.11 Hand sculpture
Source: Photo Dorothy Pelzer.

integral expression of everyday life, and the process of its creation reflects this sense of embeddedness. As Carpenter described the process:

> They enter into an experience, not as an observer but as a participant. . . . He rarely sets out, at least consciously, to carve, say, a seal, but picks up the ivory, examines it to find its hidden form and, if that's not immediately apparent, carves aimlessly until he sees it. Then he brings it out: Seal, hidden, emerges. It was always there: he didn't create it; he released it; he helped it step forth. He has no real equivalents to our word create or make, which presuppose imposition of the self on matter. The

closest term means to *work on*, which also involves an act of will, but one which is restrained. The carver never attempts to force the ivory into uncharacteristic forms, but responds to the material as it tries to be itself, and thus the carving is continuously modified as the ivory has its say. It is their attitude not only towards ivory, but towards all things, especially people: parent towards child, husband towards wife. Where we think of art as possession, and possession to us means control, to do with as we like, art to them is a transitory act, a relationship.[50]

With touch, the resistance of the material says what it wants to be by pushing back. The hand sculptures were an occasion to learn the difference between working with and against the grain of wood. Wood will allow some forms more easily than others and through touch it makes its resistances and flows directly known. No other exercise, according to Moholy-Nagy, had "such a basic effect on a student's understanding of *form* as hand sculptures do."[51] Form known through touch opens the most basic understanding of the give-and-take that is the basic tension in all relationship. Cezanne's desire to "let us begin to paint as if we held things in our hands, not as if we were looking at them at all"[52] comes from this basic shared experience. We can close our eyes and our mouths and plug our ears, but touch is always on—even in our sleep; only our hair and our fingernails do not touch. Touching keeps us constantly exposed; to touch is to be vulnerable. To be tactful is to be tactile: how we touch communicates meaning far more than words. Touch is also highly sensitive to context, and soaked with emotional resonance. Social touch communicates different intentions and emotions: anger has been associated with hitting and squeezing; disgust with a pushing motion; sympathy and love with stroking. Dynamic slow touch is soothing, while quick and abrupt touch is upsetting.[53] Touch has pain and stress-alleviating effects mediated by the same neurobiological pathways involved in social bonding. Phylogenetically, touch is an 'earlier' sense, developing prior to vision—even bacteria possess a sense of touch. Touch is essential to communicating emotions and intimacy, and maintaining and reinforcing social bonds.[54] Touching accelerates brain development in infants[55] and likely accounts for our emotional involvement with inanimate objects.[56] And again confirming Böhme's earlier statement, haptic perception is crucial in determining a 'sense of presence,' a sense of being immersed in the surrounding environment in a way that vision cannot accomplish. Touch is always immediate and reciprocal, and as much as the surface of our body differentiates us from the objects that surround us, this differentiation is precisely what evokes a sense of empathy with the surface of those objects. If we could approach design work with this same humility and partnership—this sense of openness that allows the work to emerge as a collaboration between people, place, embodied skills and capacity to listen without prefixed ideas left over from other projects or unmet ego drives—we might recapture this authentic freshness.

Haptic Perception

Just as the pressure and emotional tenor of a person's touch unequivocally communicates their intentions, so do the materials we use insistently impress their meanings. And as we saw in the case of bio-thermal-cultural strategies, it is not enough to choose renewable materials. It all depends on how we use them—that is, how we touch them and allow them touch us. The sense of touch registers much more than just forces; through touch we perceive material properties such as roughness, give, coldness and friction and spatial properties such as curvature, orientation and quantity. Roughness is mediated by vibrations, and softness requires moving over the surface for the vibrations to be perceived. Coarseness can be perceived with or without movement. Textural differences are relative to what was last touched just like music or sounds—we adapt to different frequencies. Even materials that are the same temperature may feel colder as a function of their shape and texture. A rough surface has a smaller contact area with the fingers and higher contact resistance, so it will feel warmer.[57] Heat flows slower through long, thin object than a short, thick one. Research has shown that subjects could reliably discriminate between copper, bronze, stainless steel, epoxy, plastic and foam based on thermal cues alone.[58] This implies that we also draw on our personal history of perceptual correlations, and our experiences with material qualities may override the actual physically measurable properties of the materials themselves. Concrete may seem cold to us because of our prior emotionally negative experience of it in another context, and these experiences go on to condition future ones. Many of these studies in haptic perception come from computing and industrial design, fields acutely aware of the importance of haptic feedback to indicate resistances. In aviation, for example, a force feedback joystick enables the pilot to make more precise movements. Again, resistance gives a concrete sense of reality that communicates authoritatively. Texture invites life because absences create friction. Uniformity sickens because it makes us lose touch.

Image 7.12 Wall detail, Amateur Architecture Studio, Ningbo History Museum, China

Source: Photo Sarah Robinson.

The best architects have long-intuited these characteristics of haptic perception. Alvar Aalto sensitised matter in his meticulous attention to how materials touch the body—wrapping handrails and door handles with leather to allow contact between skin and skin. He similarly garlanded concrete columns, a perceptually 'cold' material, in rattan at body level, aware that in the presence of materials that were once living, our bodies can also loosen and relax. Juhani Pallasmaa has long-argued on behalf of haptic perception and its potential to compensate for the long-term design deficits consequent to our overreliance on retinal vision. The rich texture on the massive concrete walls of Wang Shu's Ningbo History Museum are pressed from the bamboo

Image 7.13 St. Ignatius Church, Seattle: Steven Holl, Architect
Source: Photo Steven Holl Architects.

formwork. He used traditional recycled materials in a way that expresses their handmade origins, and in the process gives history a sensuous body. In these humane treatments, concrete is not cold and clay tiles are not tired. Porosity and hapticity have been key to Steven Holl's practice. His chapel of St. Ignatius in Seattle is a rich amalgam of tactile experiences: the moist mirror of the reflecting pool, the glow of patina on the bronze handles on the carved-wood entrance doors, the striated plaster on the interior surfaces and the way it subtly interacts with the constantly morphing colored light. The especially moving Blessed Sacrament chapel's walls are dripped in beeswax and etched with golden prayers. The whole ensemble of touch contributes to making the

Image 7.14 Thermal Baths at Vals, Switzerland: Peter Zumthor, Architect
Source: Photo Trevor Patt.

place one of the most beloved in Seattle, which is a distinction usually earned only over the course of generations. The chapel is used by all and exemplifies how buildings can touch and restore us.

A modern masterpiece of touch is undoubtedly Peter Zumthor's Thermal Baths at Vals, Switzerland. Perhaps even more than sleeping, bathing is an interaction in which we are most vulnerable, without blanket or bed; to clean ourselves, we must remove every shred of protection to bear our skin. Before innovations in plumbing, bathing was a communal practice, and had not only hygienic but cultural and emotional meanings. Sharing this vulnerability together surely solidified communal ties. And in fact cultures that restrict bodily pleasure, particularly in childhood, have been correlated with higher degrees of violence at all stages of life.[59] As Bernard Rudofsky points out:

> We ought to remember that the thermae of old, with their daily regeneration, were as much a matter of course to their users as restaurants are to us. Only more so, they were considered indispensable. In the fourth century, the city of Rome alone counted 856 bathing establishments; six hundred years later, Córdoba boasted an even larger number.[60]

Bathing is a highly refined cultural practice with a rich history in Japan.[61] After his first Japanese bath, the novelist Niko Kazantzakis wrote:

> I feel unsurpassed in happiness . . . I have overcome impatience, nervousness, haste. I enjoy every single second of these simple moments I spend. Happiness, I think, is a simple everyday miracle, like water, and we are not aware of it.[62]

Indeed, water is soothing and filled with emotional resonance because of its capacity to hold us in a nurturing embrace. Water bends to support the weight of our bodies.

The geothermal activity channeled and celebrated in cultures of bathing is the guiding force of Zumthor's design. The bathers' experience parallels the elemental course of water coming to light from its deeper sources in the earth. One enters the baths through a subterranean tunnel followed by a narrow turning passage of stairs. The first indication of water is through the labyrinthine passage of the ear: beyond a shadowed corridor, one hears the trickle of faucets. Their resonant dripping, the liquid minerals emerging from their spouts, the history of their movements is recorded in rust. To the left, the changing rooms are draped with black leather; pushing the curtains aside reveals highly polished red mahogany harbouring cabinets. The act of undressing is thus honoured in this dramatic counterpoint to the ruggedness of the surrounding surfaces. This costume change prepares one for the first vista into the main pool; surfaces of massive granite rise into slits of light. To descend to the pools, one must follow a brass railing that feels soft and jewel-like against the hand; one's gait is slowed in platforms of gradual descent. Light filters in from a grass roof above and from massive openings that frame the mountain-rimmed valley. In orchestrating experience, this place is not as much building as it is a natural wonder, metamorphosed through the relentless pressures of geologic time. And within its enclosure, the fragility of human time is set apart. Vapour, steam, mist, sulfurous trickles, effervescing bubbles, rushing fountains, mirror surfaces, the icy reaches on the slopes beyond—water in all of its moods absorbs in its flow of elemental regeneration. The indoor and outdoor pools are separated only by the gesture of submersion. The baths touch in a way that only water can: complete and total immersion.

Notes

1. Luce Irigaray, *Forgetting of the Air in Martin Heidegger*, trans. Mary Beth Mader (London: Athlone Press, 1999), 7.

2. Ibid., 8.
3. Ibid., 7.
4. Ibid., 8.
5. Heinrich Wölfflin, "Prolegomena to a Psychology of Architecture (1886)," in *Empathy, Form and Space: Problems in German Aesthetics 1873–1893*, eds. Harry Francis Mallgrave and Eleftherios Ikonomo (Santa Monica: Getty Center, 1994), 151.
6. D. Freedberg and V. Gallese, "Motion, Emotion and Empathy in Esthetic Experience," *Trends in Cognitive Science* 11 (2007), 197–203; see also D. Freedberg, "Movement, Embodiment, Emotion" in *Cannibalismes disciplinaires. Quand l'histoire de l'art et l'anthropologie se rencontrent*, eds. T. Dufrene and A.-C. Taylor (Paris: INHA/Musée du quai Branly, 2012), 37–61.
7. C. Di Dio, M. Ardizzi, D. Massaro, G. Di Cesare, G. Gilli, A. Marchetti et al., "Human, Nature, Dynamism: The Effects of Content and Movement Perception on Brain Activations during the Aesthetic Judgment of Representational Paintings," *Frontiers in Neuroscience* 9 (2016), 705.
8. S. Gallagher, "Direct Perception in the Intersubjective Context," *Conscious Cognition* 17, no. 2 (2008), 535–543.
9. M. J. Richardson, K. L. Marsh, R. W. Isenhower, J.R. Goodman, and R. C. Schmidt, "Rocking Together: Dynamics of Intentional and Unintentional Interpersonal Coordination," *Human Movement Science* 26, no. 6 (2007), 867–891.
10. G. Knoblich, S. Butterfill, and N. Sebanz, "Psychological Research on Joint Action: Theory and Data," in *The Psychology of Learning and Motivation*, Vol. 54, ed. B. Ross (Burlington: Academic Press, 2011), 59–101.
11. Z. Néda, E. Ravasz, T. Vicsek, Y. Brechet, and A. L. Barabási, "Physics of the Rhythmic Applause," *Physiology Review* 61 (Jun 2000), 6987.
12. M. Ardizzi, M. Calbi, S. Tavaglione et al., "Audience Spontaneous Entrainment during the Collective Enjoyment of Live Performances: Physiological and Behavioral Measurements," *Scientific Reports* 10 (2020), 3813.
13. Ibid.
14. I. Brinck, "Empathy, Engagement, Entrainment: The Interaction Dynamics of Aesthetic Experience," *Cognitive Process* 19 (2018), 201–213.
15. Ibid.
16. H. M. Sayre, *A World of Art*, 8th ed. (New York: Pearson, 2015).
17. Wölfflin, "Prolegomena to a Psychology of Architecture (1886)," 173.
18. Ibid.
19. This section has been modified from my essay, "John Dewey, Didier Anzieu and Architectural Possibility," in *Architecture and Empathy* (Helsinki: Peripheral Projects, 2015).
20. Paul Valery, *Oeuvres Complètes* (Paris: Pléide, 1957), 215–216.
21. Harry Harlow's experiments with monkeys in 1958, 1959 and 1961 at the University of Wisconsin, Madison, had profound implications for attachment theory and subsequent research.
22. Daniel J. Stern, *The Developing Mind*, 2nd ed. (New York: The Guilford Press, 2012).
23. D. Tranel and H. Damasio, "Neuroanatomical Correlates of Electrodermal Skin Conductances Responses," *Psychophysiology* 31 (1994), 427–438.
24. Ibid., 81.
25. Hassan Fathy, *Natural Energy and Vernacular Architecture* (Chicago: University of Chicago Press, 1986), xxii.
26. Ibid.
27. Every refrigerator and air conditioner contains chemical refrigerants that absorb and release heat to enable chilling. Refrigerants, specifically CFCs and HCFCs, were once culprits in depleting the ozone layer. Thanks to the 1987 Montreal Protocol, they have

been phased out. HFCs, the primary replacement, spare the ozone layer, but have 1,000 to 9,000 times greater capacity to warm the atmosphere than carbon dioxide.

28. Fathy, *Natural Energy and Vernacular Architecture*, xxii.
29. Sina Sohrab, "Reza's House," *Maharan Stories*, at: www.maharam.com/stories/sohrab_rezas-house
30. Similar arrangement can be found in the tablinum arrangements at Pompeii also town squares see Fathy, *Natural Energy and Vernacular Architecture*, 64.
31. Sohrab, "Reza's House,"
32. Fathy, *Natural Energy and Vernacular Architecture*, 47.
33. Its earliest use dates back to 1300 BC and was used in the houses of Tal Al-Amarna and is represented on the walls of the tomb of Thebes in Egypt.
34. David Abram, "The Commonwealth of Breath," in *Atmospheres of Breathing* (New York: SUNY Press, 2019), 263.
35. *The Notebooks of Leonardo da Vinci*, trans. J. P. Richter (1888).
36. Bell Hooks, *Talking Back: Thinking Feminist, Thinking Black* (Boston: South End Press, 1989), 30.
37. Richard Sennett, *Building and Dwelling: Ethics for the City* (New York: Penguin, 2019), 274.
38. Ibid., 274–276.
39. J. Africa, A. Logan, R. Mitchell, K. Korpela, D. Allen, L. Tyrväinen, E. Nisbet, Q. Li, Y. Tsunetsugu, Y. Miyazaki, and J. Spengler; on behalf of the NEI Working Group, *The Natural Environments Initiative: Illustrative Review and Workshop Statement* (Boston, MA: Harvard School of Public Health, 2014).
40. See The U.S. Environmental Protection Agency website on Heat Islands. https://www.epa.gov/heatislands/using-trees-and-vegetation-reduce-heat-islands
41. Gernot Böhme, "Atmosphere as Mindful Physical Presence in Space," Sfeerbouwen/Building Atmosphere, *Oase* 91 (2013), 21–31.
42. Polina Chebotereva, "Urban Carpet," PhD Presentation at Aalborg University, Denmark 10/2/2019.
43. Tadao Ando, "Tadao Ando: Rokko Housing," in *Quaderni di Casabella* (Milan, Italy, 1986).
44. Diane Ackerman, *The Natural History of the Senses* (New York: Penguin, 1990), xviii.
45. Oliver A .I. Botar, *Sensing the Future: Moholy Nagy, Media and the Arts* (Zurich: Lars Müller, 2014), 26.
46. J. J. Gibson, "Observations on Active Touch," *Psychological Review* 69, no. 6 (1962), 477–491.
47. Ibid.
48. Moholy-Nagy, *Vision in Motion* (Chicago: Paul Thibaud, 1958), 73.
49. Ibid.
50. Edmund Carpenter, *Eskimo* (Toronto: University of Toronto Press, 1959).
51. Moholy-Nagy, *Vision in Motion*, 73.
52. Maurice Merleau-Ponty, "Cezanne's Doubt," in *Sense and Nonsense*, trans. Patricia Dreyfus (Evanston: Northwestern University Press, 1964).
53. M. J. Hertenstein, D. Keltner, B. App, B. A. Bulleit, and A. R. Jaskolka, "Touch Communicates Distinct Emotions," *Emotion* 6 (2006), 528.
54. J. T. Suvilehto, E. Glerean, R. I. M. Dunbar, R. Hari, and L. Nummenmaa, "Topography of Social Touching Depends on Emotional Bonds between Humans," *Proceedings National Academy of Science* (2015), 112.
55. A. Guzzetta, S. Baldini, A. Bancale, L. Baroncelli, F. Ciucci, P. Ghirri, et al., "Massage Accelerates Brain Development and the Maturation of Visual Function," *Journal of Neuroscience* 29 (2009), 6042–6051.
56. J. Hornik, "Tactile Stimulation and Consumer Response," *Journal Consumer Response* 19 (1992), 449–458.

57. Hsin-Ni Ho, "Material Recognition Based on Thermal Cues: Mechanisms and Applications," *Temperature* 5 (2018), 36–55.

58. Astrid M. L. Kappers and Wouter M. Bergmann Tiest, "Haptic Perception," *Cognitive Science* 4 (2013), 357–374.

59. James W. Prescott, "Body Pleasure and the Origins of Violence," *Bulletin of the Atomic Scientists* 31, no. 9 (1975), 10–20.

60. Bernard Rudofsky, *Behind the Picture Window* (New York: Oxford University Press, 1955), 118.

61. Hiroko Nakata, "Japan's Hot Springs part of Social, Geologic, Historic Fabric," *The Japan Times*, Jan 22, 2008, accessed Feb 20, 2013.

62. As quoted in Christopher Alexander et al., *A Pattern Language* (New York: Oxford, 1977), 683.

Homo Faber   8

Homo, Latin for 'human,' comes from the word for *earth*. Coupled with the word *faber*, meaning 'to make,' *homo faber* describes humanity in our impulse to shape the world. A drive so basic, Henri Bergson suggested that *homo faber* rather than *homo sapiens* would more fittingly name us.[1] We have so thoroughly coevolved with our tools, and our physiological and cognitive coextension in our environments is so complete, we must admit that *faber*, our ability to make, is a precondition for *sapiens*, the capacity for knowledge. Thinking and making have traditionally been relegated to two different domains—and like architecture and building, the former is privileged over the latter. Seldom do we consider the act of making as a method of knowing. For Tim Ingold, both the maker and the theorist are engaged in processes of knowledge—with the important difference that the craftsman thinks through making while the theorist imposes thought on matter. The top-down abstract knowing of the theorist versus the bottom-up embodied knowing of the craftsman has come to define our valuation of knowledge—and Bergson's was an early call to realign this age-old hierarchy. Yet, in preclassical Greece, knowledge *episteme* was knowledge as skill—knowing through making. And this embodied knowledge—or 'primordial techne,' to use Husserl's vivid term—is the very ground from which further diversifications of knowledge were built. "Kosmos was discovered through teknē," insists Indra Kagis McEwen, advancing the still more radical claim that "all Western thinking was first grounded in architecture."[2] Up until the eighteenth century, it has long been argued, architecture was built metaphysics. Ideas were made manifest in the body of architecture: form is born of an idea. She reverses this order, arguing that architecture shapes ideas: *ideas are born through the act of forming*. And, given what we are now learning about the building of knowledge through the acquisition of skill, her claim is all the more convincing.

We now know that our capacity for knowledge is an embodiment of skill developed and honed in the process of building a world. "Craft gives things life and it is no accident that *tiktein* is to give birth, *tektein* to build, and *technē*, a letting appear,"[3] writes Indra Kagis McEwen, who goes onto say: "It is through making that kosmos appears or does not. In fact, kosmos . . . seems to share the very identity of making."[4] This drive to create a cosmos originated, according to Gebser, in the magic structure of consciousness. The process of making is a magical act—and in fact magic and making share the same root. The word *magic* is a Greek borrowing of the Persian word for power, and this deeper sense comes forward in the family of words *machine*, *mechanism* and *might*. This structure marks the inchoate individuation through the act of making. Like the critical period in childhood that Esther Cobb described, in which a child discovers the capacities of their own bodies and realises their individuality for the first time, making exteriorises and extends internal capacities and conditions. All acts of making, from the early magical rituals of spell-casting to modern technologisation, are a process of projecting one's powers out into the world. The machine is an objectification of human capabilities.

> All basic physical and mechanical laws such as leverage, traction, bearing, adhesion, all constructions such as the labyrinth, the vault, etc, all such technical achievements or discoveries are pre-given in us. Every invention is primarily a rediscovery and an imitative construction of the organic and physiological.[5]

Through acts of making, early humans began to release themselves "from harmony or identity with the whole, with that a first process of consciousness began. . . . Therewith arose the gem of a need: that of no longer being *in* the world but of *having* the world."[6]

Gebser correlates the magic structure with the perceptual organ of the ear and the stress of emotion, in the historical period when masks and objects lacked a mouth. The preverbal emphasis on sound reveals the extent to which we are immersed in our surroundings. The sounds of nature were the primary signals of oncoming danger. In a striking parallel, Dewey called the ear the emotional sense for this very reason—emotion is not strictly an internal condition but a coextensive awareness gauging inner and outer situations, readying us for flight or fight. Where the eye is the organ of distance, the ear stimulates directly, exciting inner tissues by an outward commotion. Vision arouses interest, but sound makes us jump. Vision imparts a sense of certainty; sounds warn of impending danger and are always effects—we become aware of the effect before the cause and the effects are unsettling because they are so very uncertain. In this "theatre of endless conflicts,"[7] sound signals interruptions and moves us directly—this 'co-motion' gives rise to 'e-motion.' Sound is a "commotion in the organism itself,"[8] writes Dewey. The ear is receptive: we can close our eyes but we cannot close our ears. In our nondirectional immersion in sound we are utterly exposed. The German word for 'hear' means both to obey and to belong—and this primal vulnerability has long been manipulated to social, religious and political ends.[9]

The labyrinthine ear was evocative of the magical structure for its cavernous associations. The sun represents the brightness of day, whereas the labyrinth represents the cave-like darkness of dormant consciousness. The word *cave* is rooted in kēl—meaning shelter, hold, conceal, the earth, security, darkness. The rituals manifest in early cave art were the signature achievement of the magical period. Just as sound is always an effect, early humans *effected* their world through making sound. The rhythms of drumming set the tone of the period and gave birth to dance. Through the magical instrument of the drum, the rhythms of nature were transformed into time, marking a departure from purely natural rhythms. Auditory awareness becomes temporal and the cycles of nature become humanised. The constellation of interactions that effect this emergence are preserved in our earliest known art forms: the Paleolithic cave art in France and Spain. Cave paintings are found only in the deepest recesses of the caves, suggesting that the arduous passage of arrival was ritual of procession and preparation. In order to make the journey, one's posture had to conform to the internal topography of the cave. Similarly, the paintings were not so much painted on the surface as much as they were born of it. The body of the animal was moulded and afforded by the surface of the cave. Cave and creature belonged to a shared continuum. Perhaps for this reason, no art form has since been able to depict the living presence of animals with such minimal means. The fact that the paintings are located in the darkest part of the cave implies the necessity of artifice and tools in creating the ritual. The three-dimensional paintings were dimensioned further by the wavering flames of torches, the drumming resonance that magnified sound and image. While few would claim that this qualifies as architecture, this early atmospheric art does suggest the powerful ways that spatial and perceptual experience inform one another and can enrich our approach to design. The interactions evident in this prototypic structure worthy of further exploration are resonating, dancing and making.

Resonating

The capacity for resonance shared by both ear and the cave perhaps underlies Gernot Böhme's insistence that music is the paradigmatic atmospheric art.[10] Music is the dramatic reenactment of the instabilities, shocks and resolutions of nature, the humanising of sound and rhythm that has patterned human consciousness from the very beginning. "It is we ourselves who are tortured by the strings,"[11] Schopenhauer proclaimed. The primitive power of sound to both signal danger and to confer a sense of belonging has made music both the highest and lowest of the arts. Because hearing has more reverberations and resonances than any other sense, music is a uniquely powerful means to organise raw material into an intensified and concentrated medium of experience. Dewey writes:

> It is the peculiarity of music and indeed its glory that it can take the quality of sense that is most immediately and practical of all the sense organs (since it incites most strongly to impulsive action) and by use of formal relationships transform the material into the art that is most remote from practical preoccupations.[12]

No known human culture lacks music, and all humans are capable of creating and responding to music. Neurological studies indicate that music is a biological competence rather than a generalised social function. Music is a highly multifunctional adaptation, serving a diversity of functional roles in all cultures, suggesting just how deep-seated is its evolutionary importance.[13]

Music: A Technology of Bonding

Perhaps music evolved in tandem with our emotional lives—one enriched, regulated, formed and informed the other in an interweaving in which cause and effect cannot be teased apart. Music moves us in certain ways because it not only represents our emotion but is itself an exteriorisation of our emotional lives. Similar to color, with which we also resonate, certain colors make us blue just as music does. "All arts, we must remember, are phases of the social mind," wrote the sociologist Franklin Henry Giddings in 1914.

> We are in the habit of thinking of them in terms of art products that we forget that the arts themselves are groups of ideas and acquisitions of skill that exist in the minds, muscles and nerves of living men.[14]

Music involves not only the auditory system but the somatosensory and motor systems as well. There is no doubt that music induces and modulates different emotional states. The ancient Greeks correlated three main classes of music with distinct emotional states.[15] And we now know that these states are accompanied by the release of neurohormones correlated with certain emotions, just as they surmised. Walter Freeman called music a technology of emotion, and argued that music evolved to regulate emotional states—suggesting that the tendernesses, ecstasies and agonies of music coevolved with our emotional lives. Music together with dance coevolved biologically and culturally to serve as a technology of deep bonding that could not be achieved by words alone. Freeman argues:

> The role of music as an instrument of communication beyond words strikes to the heart of the ways in which we humans come to trust each other. Trust is the basis of all human endeavours and a case is made that it is created through the practice of music.[16]

Brain chemistry interacted with evolving culture, leading to the development of chemical and behavioural technology that altered states of consciousness. The trance states induced by music and dance were particularly important in forming social cooperation based on trust. The bonds formed in this way were not only the result of neurochemistry, but also of the social action of singing, playing music and dancing together, which led to new forms of behaviour. "It is reasonable to suppose that musical skills played a major role early in the evolution of human intellect, because they made possible the formation of human societies as a prerequisite for the transmission of acquired knowledge across generations."[17]

According to Ellen Dissanayake, the strong emotions elicited by the temporal arts of music and dance create emotional dispositions that through the medium of ritual ceremonies instil and reinforce shared cultural values, promoting feelings of confidence and unity. The temporal arts are integral to ceremonies precisely because of their role in promoting affiliative behaviour and conferring a shared social identity and sense of belonging. As she puts it: "In ceremonies, bodies swayed to music result in minds relieved of existential anxieties, firmed by convictions, and bonded with their fellows in common cause."[18] The capacity of the temporal arts extends beyond social bonding to restore psychic balance as well. Oliver Sacks noticed that two things restored balance to his patients more than drug treatments: experiences in nature and music. In a testimony to music's capacity to tune our emotions, he writes:

> Music, uniquely among the arts, is both completely abstract and profoundly emotional. It has no power to represent anything particular or

external, but it has a unique power to express inner states or feelings. Music can pierce the heart directly; it needs no mediation. One does not have to know anything about Dido and Aeneas to be moved by her lament for him; anyone who has ever lost someone knows what Dido is expressing. And there is, finally, a deep and mysterious paradox here, for while such music makes one experience pain and grief more intensely, it brings solace and consolation at the same time.[19]

Buildings as Musical Instruments

This restorative and affiliative capacity suggests a far deeper significance of the familiar analogy between music and architecture than has hitherto been acknowledged. Goethe's frozen music image descended from Pythagoras's observation that the geometry of shapes is solidified music. Shifting the metaphor of frozen music to understanding architecture as an instrument that actively *makes* music was suggested by Dalibor Vesely almost two decades ago. Analogous to the communicative role of architecture, like a musical instrument, architecture, "can send reverberations through a culture and help embody them."[20] It is not only that our bodies are, by their very nature, resonant bodies; our buildings are resonant bodies—instruments that constantly reverse the roles between the player and the played. We not only tune our instruments but are *tuned by them*.

Like entrainment, resonance is invisible, involuntary and preconscious. But where entrainment is an interaction between two independent vibrating entities that synch to a shared frequency and if parted will go back to their former respective frequencies, resonance, as its etymology suggests, is to 're-sound,' to sound again. If a tuning fork producing sound waves inside a resonant chamber is removed, the oscillations inside the chamber will also cease. All matter vibrates, so the resonance chamber, by definition, vibrates to its particular frequency— the wood used for the cavity of the violin or cello changes the oscillations that take place inside of it. The synergy between materials has to do with their harmonic likeness, so the choice and organisation of materials is critical to shaping the interaction between body and building. The forming power of sound is easily visualised on a resonating plate. Ernst Chladni, who was a physicist and musician, found that when he drew his violin bow across the edge of a metal plate with sand particles on it, the particles arrayed themselves into distinct patterns.[21] Chladni figures are graphic signatures of different vibrational frequencies. The sand particles align to areas of the plate that are the calmest, that have the least amount of agitation: *form follows vibration*.

Image 8.1 Chladni Patterns, generated on a resonating plate, make it possible to visualise sound. From *Entdeckungen über die Theorie des Klanges* (Discoveries in the Theory of Sound), a late eighteenth-century work by German physicist and musician Ernst Chladni.

It is telling that a far more accurate indicator of space is not our sense of vision but our sense of hearing. Not only has music coevolved with our emotional lives, its history developed in tandem with the built environment. "Music is pure context," Iain McGilchrist reminds us, "even if the context is silence."[22] Because it depends on reflective surfaces in order to resound, resonance can only occur in an enclosed environment, and the characteristics of that environment join in making the sound. This fact is the basis of Wallace Sabine's theory of music. Long before Jay Appleton's prospect and refuge theory, Sabine, who originated modern acoustics, discerned two basic models of music: one arising from the enclosed cave and the other from the open savannah. The most basic musical forms developed according to the spaces in which they took place: outdoor music is necessarily rhythmic, while more resonant indoor spaces afford music that tends to be harmonic and melodic.[23] Building on this insight, Hope Bagenal was able to show that until recently, musical forms were determined as much by the spaces in which the music was performed as by the genius of their composers. The difference between the slow-moving Gregorian chants of the Gothic cathedrals with their long reverberation times, and the music Bach composed for the wooden interiors of the Thomaskirche in Leipzig, which allowed sharp articulation and the quicker harmonic shifts characteristic of Baroque music, were consequences of architectural design.[24] The polychoral music that gave rise to Baroque music of sixteenth- and seventeenth-century Venetian composers was determined not only by the acoustics of Saint Mark's Basilica, but by the particular spatial configuration of the choir galleries within the building.[25]

The highly refined aural sensitivity of ancient builders enabled them to select building sites they could acoustically enhance. Gebser also pointed out that "the acoustic-labyrinthine magic emphasis is the basis for all theatre."[26] In the Asclepius theatre at Epidarus theatre in Greece, one can hear a pin drop from each one of its 14,000 seats. R. Murray Schafer has long argued that the history of architecture cannot be properly understood until it is interpreted according to the ear, rather than the eye.[27] Schafer himself came to this insight after an extended visit to Iran, where he experienced the visual and acoustic perfection of Shah Abbas Mosque in Isfahan. Known for its perfect seven-second reverberation time, a whisper in the very centre of the dome can be heard by a crowd of 15,000 people with no mechanical intervention. Other structures in the complex exhibit the same acumen. The music room in the Ali Qapu Palace, whose high-volume ceilings are perforated with *muqarnas*, which are cutouts shaped like musical instruments, bring the reverberation time to a level appropriate for conversation and intimate music that the room is intended to serve. The cutouts have since been studied in their function as precocious anechoic devices. At the entrance to the palace where guests are received, guards are positioned at opposite corners. The ceiling and walls are configured so that their whispers are audible only to each other. The acoustics allow the guards to communicate in a most subtle form of surveillance.

Improvements in mechanical acoustics have since allowed music to dissociate itself from spaces altogether. In the pursuit of perfect sound, the resonance that situated performer/listener in place was sacrificed to the ideal acoustics of the neutral white box—the equivalent of a museum in which art objects are displayed interchangeably regardless of situation. In this severance, music became yet another formal object, conceived in the manner of Ingold's theorist—that is, rather than emerging from the play of situated variables, it was conceived in the head to be performed in neutral environments. Despite this strong bias, some exceptional performers have intentionally sought out

Image 8.2 Muquarna patterns, Ali Qapu Palace, Isfahan, Iran
Source: Photo Sarah Robinson.

spaces whose distinctive acoustic properties enhance, and even challenge, their musical works. Pauline Oliveros practices 'deep listening' in an empty underground cistern in Port Townsend, Washington that has a reverberation time of 45 seconds. John Butcher toured Scotland, investigating acoustic personalities of various vernacular structures: an ice house, the interior of an oil tank, a mausoleum—each space an integral partner in performing the piece. Luigi Nono performed his composition *Prometeo* in a specially designed arc by Renzo Piano which cultivated, in his words, "a listening that is able to shrug off the idolatrous fetes of the image"[28] in a kind of plural-directional listening in his native city of Venice. The sonic and geographical poetics of particular places make us aware of our own acoustic inheritance that, as the composer George Crumb insists, moulds the ear during our formative years of development. "Living in a city, the seashore, the desert would be different from living in an Appalachian river valley," where he grew up. He "always thought the echoing sense of my music is distilled really from the sense of hearing I developed there."[29] The composer Oliver Beer insists: "Every space has got its own frequencies . . . and can be made to resound and sing. Every space has got its own unique harmonic fingerprint." Scott Arford and Randy Yau of Infrasound show that not only is building an instrument, but one that contains its own score: "Simply listening closely to a space will reveal its score. The music is in there, but it requires some coaxing to bring it forward."[30] What if we apply the same attentive patience to listening to the geography, the sounds and stories, the plants, the animals and the historical situation of our buildings—and with the same sensitivity, nudge those voices forward? Deep listening and respectfully patient coaxing are methods of situated poetics that reveal the music latent in place.

Sound as a Building Material

This understanding is operative in the work of the architect / sound artist / composer Bernard Leitner, who has been using sound to explore the bodily experience of space since the 1970s. According to his work, space not only surrounds us but penetrates through the body. His *Ton-Liege* Sound Chair is a somatic sculpture which transmits sound allowing one to hear from the soles of the feet up though the full length of the body, out through the head and back again through the lower region of the legs— touching all of the organs. This artistic experiment informed a medical investigation demonstrating that this sonic touch works as a sort of lullaby enhancing relaxation, leading to positive surgical outcomes and increased healing.[31] In another shift away from the emphasis on vision, the presence

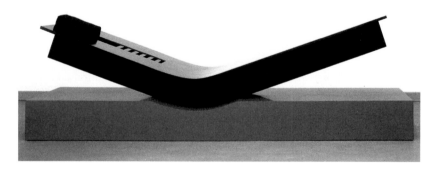

Image 8.3 Bernhard Leitner, Sound Chair III (Ton-Liege III) 1991
Source: Photo Bernard Leitner.

Image 8.4 Bernhard Leitner, Le Cylindre Sonore, Parc del la Villette, Paris 1987

Source: Photo Bernard Leitner.

of his Sound Cylinder in the Parc de la Villette, Paris can be detected only with one's sense of listening. Its nested cylinders, lined with flowing water, are hidden in a lush grove of bamboo and can only be reached by a descent of stairs. The archaic concrete curves create an inner sanctum in which the movement of water becomes a sort of 'sound tissue' coextensive with the human body. Leitner's extraordinary explorations of space articulate the model of the plastic, resonant body and demonstrate that one is never strictly outside of space, but truly *in*. In his hands, sound becomes a building material of an active kind, collapsing distinctions between outside and in—it very literally moves us.

The engineer/architect/composer Iannis Xenakis also critically explored the capacity of sound to transcend traditional boundaries. His composition Terretektorh intermingled performers and audience in an analogy with an electronic synthesiser, "an accelerator of sonorous particles, a disintegrator of sonorous masses."[32] Tearing down the psychological and auditory curtain that typically separates the passive listener from the active performer, he made the audience an active and necessary ingredient in the work. Xenakis also broke down interdisciplinary categories—his site-specific works interwove architecture, light and sound to pioneer the field of multimedia installation art. His Polytope of Cluny transformed the Roman baths in the heart of Paris into a multisensory spectacle that played electroacoustic music and threaded hundreds of flashbulbs through underground chambers to project

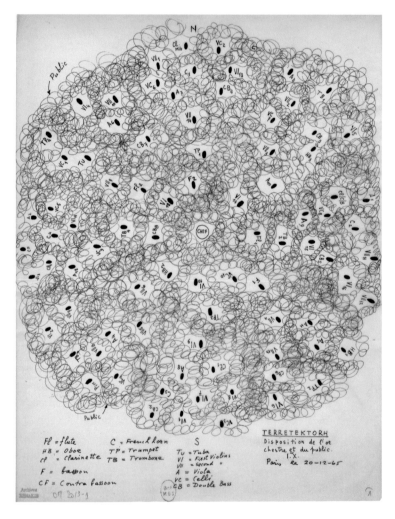

Image 8.5 Iannis Xenakis, Terretektorh, 1965. Study drawing for an orchestral performance in which 88 musicians were distributed throughout the audience, this image evokes the sense of energetic envelopes that neuroscientists describe as peripersonal and extrapersonal space.

light onto a network of adjustable mirrors that washed the interior vaults with vivid patterns of colour. The whole installation was controlled via computer in an unprecedented feat of coordination and programming. The dynamic fusion of sound, light and ancient history revealed new textures of the urban experience to the hundreds of thousands of people who made the pilgrimage to Cluny to participate in the work. There could hardly be a more compelling example of architecture fulfilling its primary communicative and socially integrating role.

In his collaboration with Le Corbusier on La Tourette, Xenakis's musical sensitivity and acumen undeniably helped to make it the masterpiece that it is. His undulating fenestration system is based on the stochastic series to evoke musical rhythm. And this evocation of rhythm appeals beyond the visual sense to engage deeper dimensions of perceptual experience. The chapel which he

Image 8.6 Le Corbusier and Iannis Xenakis, Le Couvente Sainte-Marie de la Tourette, d'Éveux, France 1959. Xenakis developed the undulating fenestration system based on the stochastic series of the *modulor*.

Source: Photo Sarah Robinson.

Image 8.7 Xenakis's contribution is particularly evident in the analysis of light levels and acoustic qualities in the chapel.

Source: Photo Sarah Robinson.

was left to design concretely tunes one's body to its particular signature. One enters the chapel through the sole orifice in an otherwise impenetrable wall. Yet one does not even reach this threshold until circulated through promenades lacking a clear destination, which feels more akin to passing through the labyrinthine ear than following the commanding march of the eye. Opening the heavy brass door thrills with the sensation of violating a bank vault, yet the light touch needed to pivot the hinges cannot but be an invitation. Light enters through slanted coloured sills, and only on the periphery, the eye evolved to detect subtle movement from the sides—its soft wash accentuates blemishes, wrinkles, the poverty in its making, the patience of its resistance. Lowered light weakens the eye, activating the ear as the primary organ of sensing space.

Image 8.8 The Canons of Light in the side chapel were among Xenakis's distinctive innovations.

Source: Photo Sarah Robinson.

For Le Corbusier, the truest way to experience architecture was at night. Darkness awakens resonant bodies. The chapel breaks the vows of silence taken by the monks, amplifying their vespers in the same reverberation time as a cathedral. Its signature: its voice, scale, gravity and light are medieval but its arrangement is not. The chapel—like ear, mouth, violin—is open at the centre and needs touch and breath to make music.[33]

Dancing

Sound is patterned in music and expressed through the body in dance. "Dance is tone made visible: the medium of conjuration and of 'being heard' by the deeper reality of the world,"[34] insisted Gebser. Music changes the vibrational patterns in our body fabric, literally tuning us to its strings and accompanied no less by dancing as its outward counterpart. Different types of music each have their distinctive emotional signature. And we now know that certain postures and gestures also leave their chemical fingerprints as well. The philosopher Suzanne Langer was the first to study dance as an emotional body language, calling it "the art of the Stone Age, the art of primitive life par excellence."[35] Dance is not only an art of movement in space, but a relation of forces. "The forces that [dancers] exercise, that seem to be as physical as those which orient the compass needle toward its pole, really do not exist physically at all. They are dance forces, virtual power."[36] She suggested that these dance forces are the proto-symbolic capacity at the heart of ritual, ceremony, language and art. And while music and dance are cross-cultural constants, the names that refer to them are not. Some cultures use a single word to refer to music—making, singing, dancing and ritual: participatory activities which all contribute to and reinforce group bonding and self-identification. The anthropologist Jerome Lewis argues that music structures dance and ritual activities and together they serve as foundational cultural schemas to organise shared values.[37] Playing music and dancing together reenacts and reinforces those social and cultural ties. In a similar vein, Jean Molino understands music, chanting, dance and language in their common primeval origins, growing out of the muscular and neural control of rhythmic bodily movements. As we saw with empathy research, perceiving emotions and emotional body language in others engages the same regions of our own brain as those we perceive being experienced.[38] Because dance is an emotional body language par excellence, it has been used as a stimulus for such studies. Several of these found that the gestures of dance intended to convey sadness, love, peace, heroism and shyness were consistently correlated by people with and without dance experience, irrespective of cultural origin, with the emotional states intended by the gestures.[39]

Perhaps in light of these studies it is time to reevaluate Goethe's frozen music metaphor. If music and dance were early technologies of affective and social affiliation, whose modulation of rhythm and tempo shaped emotional and cultural temperaments and behaviours and were reenacted ceremonially to reinforce those patterns in the plastic nerves and tissues of generations, how do these rhythms echo in architecture? In his study of rhythm, Steen Eiler Rasmussen pointed to the Spanish Steps as a paradigmatic case of petrified rhythm. The steps were constructed in a cultural consciousness modulated by the Baroque waltz, and consequently in the Spanish Steps, "we can see a petrification of a dancing rhythm of a period of gallantry; it gives us an inkling of something that was, something our generation will never know."[40] Unlike other stairs connecting two places, the bends and turns of the Spanish

Steps seem to mimic the bodily habits of those for whom they were intended: for people, who knew little about walking, but much more about ceremonial dance.[41] Yet, that which was once frozen need not necessarily remain so. The stairs are Baroque artefacts that have an active life today, subtly tuning our neurochemistry with every step. The mutual shaping of body and place is captured in the Greek word *choros*—the root of choreography referred not only to dance, but also to the dancing place, and the group that dances, as in the chorus of Greek tragedy, but it can also refer to any group with a shared purpose. *Chora* and *topos* were two words used to refer to space. *Topos*, like its modern usage in topography suggests, was space that can be mapped. *Chora*, closer to the meaning that Suzanne Langer articulated, is the space of forces that invisibly magnetise the compass needle towards its pole. Chora is a generative place that depends on participation, a territory that appears through continual remaking and reweaving.[42]

The sense in which all places, not just iconic ones like the Spanish Steps, are not only crystallisations of movement but generators of movement, comes through in the geographer David Seamon's notion of place-ballet. The way we inhabit our everyday spaces reveals the extent to which our bodies extend into and integrate with the features of our surroundings. Consider Merleau-Ponty's description of his apartment in Paris:

> My flat is, for me, not a set of closely associated images. It remains a familiar domain round about me only as I still have 'in my legs' the main distances and directions involved, and as long as from my body intentional threads run out towards it.[43]

This threading that Merleau-Ponty describes is a common occurrence—we can navigate our living spaces in the dark because we have already integrated the location of our furnishings into our repertoire of movement. Introducing a new piece of furniture requires an update to those habitual patterns. Seamon refers to this zone of familiarity as our 'body-routine'—a set of integrated gestures, behaviours and actions that sustain a particular task or aim, such as doing the dishes, making a repair, cooking a meal or going to sleep. The reciprocity between one's body-routine and the environment that supports its integrated movements becomes a place-ballet—a fusion of interpersonal and communal exchange and affective attachment. Places like a lively neighbourhood café or pub, a well-used office lounge, a tree-filled public park and a crowded urban plaza are place-ballets that are meaningful because they support our personal body-routines in an interpersonal setting.[44]

Kinesthetic Awareness

While musicians and composers were busy dismantling the box of the static concert hall and finding the music in common sounds, the dancer and choreographer Anna Halprin was breaking free from the same pretensions in dance. Fed up with the cult of personality that typified modern dance and its extraction from the context of life, she was inspired by John Cage to take dance to the forest and to the streets. Her lifelong partner was the landscape architect Lawrence Halprin, and from the deck he designed for her suspended in a redwood forest north of San Francisco, she developed an approach to dance that cultivated its capacity to heal personal, social and racial divisions. Perhaps the most convincing testimony to her legacy are her many students who left the theatre to use public spaces for performances and social action. Like composers for whom spatial qualities are shaping partners in music, so for these choreographers did places shape the dance—effectively restoring the original meaning of *choros* in which place and dance are interdependent. Anna Halprin cultivated a technique of kinesthetic awareness that she and Lawrence Halprin developed into their RSVP cycles. They led workshops and events involving

Image 8.9 Keller Fountain, Portland Open Space: Lawrence Halprin, Landscape Architect

Image 8.10 Keller Fountain
Source: photo Sarah Robinson.

architects and landscape architects designed to refine kinesthetic awareness and to supplement the shortcomings of representing movement graphically—by experiencing movement first in the body, before translating it to the page. An outstanding outcome of this method is his Open Space Sequence in Portland, Oregon—a series of parks and walkways in the heart of the city imagined as a participatory place of movement and play. These parks with fountains sculpted from the local topography, waterways threading through the places of daily life and work whose platforms and stairways invite a diversity of movements, are a contemporary expression of the special capacity for dance to weave place. The architecture of this work could hardly be called frozen—it bubbles and baptises with all the exuberance of water.

Emile Jacques Dalcroze is another figure who understood dance and music in their potential to organise and stabilise emotional and social life. His experimental movement and music workshops at the garden city of Hellerau, Germany were designed to harmonise emotional and nervous systems.[45] The key to this attunement was to tap into the body's natural rhythms through a method he called "eurhythmics." Young musicians could not play their instruments until they performed rhythmic exercises. Once the natural rhythms of the body were understood and experienced, students could then learn to play music with more ease and transfer this rhythmic knowing to other forms of art. The school was visited by thousands of members of the public and the full lineup of the European cultural avant-garde—among them, Le Corbusier, whose brother taught music there. The promising and much-lauded experiment was abruptly ended with WWI, and as Harry Francis Mallgrave observed: "We can only speculate what a major impact it might have had on the cultural world at large . . . Its influence was nevertheless significant, if not predominant, in the postwar conception of the Bauhaus."[46] Indeed, the attention given to developing sensory and perceptual awareness on the basic course can clearly be traced to the experiment at Hellerau. And the efficacy of the training that Le Corbusier experienced there perhaps contributed to his sensitivity towards kinaesthesia that clearly underlies his architectural promenade. His careful orchestration of ramps and stairs at La Tourette very precisely choreograph one's sense of expectation and carefully calibrate one's centre of gravity with a deep respect for bodily experience.

Mechanisms of Mutuality

Perhaps one of the most celebrated choreographies of arrival is the approach to Frank Lloyd Wright's Taliesin West. He was also keenly sensitive to music, played piano himself and habitually surrounded himself with musicians. No picnic at Taliesin was unaccompanied by a cello or violin. He seemed to intuitively employ what Ellen Dissayake calls "mechanisms of mutuality"—techniques used by artists in all media that mimic the processes of ritualisation that have been shown to promote bonding and mutuality. These techniques are formalization, repetition, exaggeration, elaboration, manipulation and delay. These processes of ritualisation transform ordinary behaviours into something distinctive that have the potential, when organised temporally, to elicit emotional responses. To consider the choreography of Taliesin West with these techniques in mind, rather than studying a floor plan to analyse orienting landmarks, alignments and terminals, let us listen to Philip Johnson's narrative of arrival. Suspend for a moment whatever you may think of his own architecture; his account remains without parallel. It was written in Wright's lifetime and deserves to be quoted in full:

> (Wright) has developed one thing which I defy any of us to equal: the arrange-ments of the secrets of space. I call it the hieratic aspects of architecture. The processional aspects. I would like to tell you about it briefly. You drive up from Phoenix, about 20 miles out, up a dusty desert road, wondering why you came because it's terribly hot, and you go up a slight rise. Finally you turn into a particularly dusty, nasty and ill-kept road. But there is a little sign that says 'Frank Lloyd Wright.'
> You come to an agglomeration of tents and stones where the car stops. There is a low wall and you realise after you have been there and come back again,

that he has been putting out the spot where the car stops further and further from his place. I'd like to recommend that to you and me. The car, of course, is one of the deaths of architecture. It's out of scale, it makes noise, it doesn't please the eye. And you cannot from a sitting position, even look at architecture. It has to be by the actual muscles of your feet.

He now makes you walk about 150 feet, until you get closer to this meaningless group of buildings. You've seen the plans many times and I am sure you did not understand them anymore than I did before I'd been there. As you approach, he starts you off on a slight slope, with the mountains to your left, and so up the first steps you go, away from the buildings instead of towards them. And now he takes your eyes and makes you follow. You go down the steps this way but the buildings are over there.

Then the steps turn at right angles and you go between two low walls, very much narrower this time. You have the sensation that you are always changing your point of view of the buildings. You turn, pass his office, you climb four more steps and pass a great stone that he has put there with Indian hieroglyphics on it, which he found on his place. There is no door in sight. You just begin to wonder.

The path takes you down a long walk, about 200 feet perhaps, with this tent room on your right, the mountains to your left. You begin to wonder what is happening when, at your left, you pass the tent room, the building above goes overhead. But the view—two enormous piers—and you look again (a trick) through a dark room, a 6-foot room, over the terrace of Taliesin West: an enormous prow that sticks out over the mountains.

Now you've been climbing all this time and you never knew it because you never looked back; but for the first time, you realise you have been climbing and for 90 miles you look across the desert through that darkened hole. And again, of course, the steps start rippling. You go down three steps more and you are pulled out into this prow of the desert. He calls it his 'ship of the desert.' That's where Frank Lloyd Wright is usually standing to greet you with his purple hair, his cape, and you say, 'Now I've arrived at this magic place.'

But you've just begun your trip. He then leads you thorough a gold-leaf concrete tunnel that turns three times and you are pushed out into the single most exciting room that we have in this country. It is indescribable except to say that the light, since it comes from the tent above, has filtered and mellowed. You are just beginning to absorb this room when he opens a few of the tent flaps and this is when it really hits you. You look out—but not onto the desert. You look out this time on a little private secret garden that he has built beyond this room, where water is playing unlike any water in the desert. The plants are 20 feet high in this garden, and there is a lawn such as you have only seen in New England.

You say, 'Now I see what I have come to Taliesin for'; you have not. He makes one more turn, two more turns. This time the door is 18 inches wide and you have to go sidewise. It is entirely an inside room, no desert or garden. One wall is of plants. To be sure, you cannot see them: that is, you can't see through them, but that gives you the jungle light that comes into the room. There is a shaft of light that comes from 12 or 14 feet above (this is a very high room now). The room is 21 by 14 feet, all stone. One entire length of it is fireplace, on the other long wall is a table and two chairs—and that is where you have come to be. You sit down with Frank Lloyd Wright and he says, 'Welcome to Taliesin West.'

My friends. That is the essence of architecture.[47]

This narrative can easily be read in terms of formalization, repetition, exaggeration, elaboration and most importantly . . . delay. The dusty road required for entry is common: it subverts your expectation because of its unruly condition, which leads you to believe you are going to a construction site, not to a completed complex of buildings. Johnson failed to mention that the scale of the buildings beyond follows the horizontality of the land, so they are completely obscured by saguaro and mesquite trees as you drive up the hill, leading you to think you are approaching the buildings, but they constantly escape your grasp, adding even more to the tension that sets the imagination spinning. We are predictive creatures; our minds ceaselessly calculate our possibilities for action.[48] Frank Lloyd Wright manipulated habitual predictions to extraordinary aesthetic effect. Johnson hardly noticed scaling the steps because the risers are low and the treads are generous, which necessarily slows the gait. With such proportions, one flows rather than steps. You simply cannot rush when you move on stairs proportioned in this way. How many turns does he make before he arrives? In what direction do you turn in a labyrinth, and where might it lead? What about the crunching of gravel underfoot or the effervescing fountains of water? Or the scented tunnel of bouganvillea whose day-glow pink clashes madly with the desert tan? Another trick Wright used was constant transition between light and shadow—which in the desert has seriously thermal consequences that you feel very viscerally. Looking out over the prow, through a breezeway, means that the view is framed as much by the wall as by the breeze that is continually passing through. The refreshment you feel at this point is thus magnified: an expansive view for the eyes and refreshed air for the skin, all the more so because the passing air is moistened by the pools of water. Rough stone walls made from desert rocks—made with imperfect formwork and too much sand in the concrete because it was built by amateurs in the best sense of the word—contrast with very fine gold leaf! The raw desert harbours a lush lawn. Harsh sun filters through canvas sails and is saturated with the chlorophyll of jungle light. Formal categories of expectations are completely blown apart. Here, the journey is more important than the destination. And by the time you reach it, you are emotionally exhausted and exhilarated all at once.

Making

Making "is a question of surrendering to the wood, then following it where it leads . . . instead of imposing a form upon a matter," insisted Gilles Deleuze and Felix Guattari. The resonant oak balconies at Thomaskirche played their role in shaping musical history—one could say that Bach's symphonies surrendered to the wood. Anna and Lawrence Halprin transformed urban settings through listening to the body of dance and following where it led. These approaches exemplify a way of making that does not impose form, but bodies it forth. The sounds of music and the movements of dance pattern the matter they touch in ways specific to their frequencies, pressures and flows. And the matter so shaped is not the passive recipient of their design manipulations, but *informs* the processes of its shaping. To the craftsperson, the rings in wood are not nouns but verbs—rings trace the growth of tree and act differently if worked with or against. According to how one follows the line of its growth, wood *rings* in cooperation or opposition, and in this process matter informs its destiny. The story of making is rooted in this subtle kind of coupling. *Making* comes from the word for *magic* and *matter* from the word for *mother* and *matrix* and is also related to the Greek word *hylē*, a word which comes from *forest* or *woodland*. In preclassical Greece, *hylē* belonged to a divine and deathless *physis*, and was not treated as dead timber but was "cut with all the circumspection devoted to the cutting up of a sacrificial victim, to be remade in order that it might reappear in another guise,"[49] as Indra Kagis McEwen reminds us. It was not until Aristotle that *hylē* was set up in opposition to an intelligent formative principle in the matter/form differentiation of the hylomorphic model. The origins of architecture predated this division and cannot be truly understood in its terms. The magic at the heart of making— that living wood was cut, only to appear in a different guise—both awakened and exercised humanity's inner powers. Making allowed cosmos to appear. The carefully cut wood was made to reappear as a boat, or when burned, transformed magically into a flame. In this early understanding, order was not imposed on chaos—chaos merely preceded cosmos but was not yet set up in opposition to it.

The way that *hylē* was used to make a boat illustrates the underlying unity of this approach. The anthropologist Lionel Casson has shown that the wooden hulls of ancient Greek boats were not made with a skeleton frame to which planks were attached, but were painstakingly crafted of planks interlocked with mortise and tenon joints. The skin was simultaneously the structure. The Greco-Roman shipwrights "carried out the joinery with such care that it resembles cabinetwork more than carpentry . . . The work involved was laborious, but the reward was a hull of remarkable strength with great savings in weight and bulk,"[50] Casson writes. The technique of ancient boatbuilding is clearly analogous to the technique of weaving. Mortising tenon and joint is to weave with wood—the planks are laid at right angles to the pegs, binding them together like the warp threads are bound with the weft threads on a loom, which must also interpenetrate at right angles to make cloth. *Textile* comes from 'to weave,' which shares a root with *tecton*, the craft of carpentry

Image 8.11 Greek Weaving Urn, Metropolitan Museum of Art

and boatbuilding. Building a boat, or weaving cloth, was to make something like skin, in which structure and material are fused. The technique of forming is itself the form.

Both the mast of a ship and the upright loom were referred to using the word *histos*, which generically referred to anything set upright. *Histos* also means the web woven on the loom as well as the cloth used for the sails of ships.[51] The skill involved in making their boats watertight, and the skill involved in the tight weave that lofted their sails, enabled Athenians to colonise hundreds of islands. The success of their endeavour very concretely depended on the solidity of the joints. And in fact the Greek word *harmonia*, which applies both to governance and music, originally refers to a perfectly crafted joint. The emergence of the Greek polis is therefore clearly rooted in and made possible by the craft tradition. And it is no accident that the craft specific to Athena was weaving—the goddess of the city was the goddess of weaving. When boats were sent to establish the far-flung sanctuaries that were integral to the emergence of the Greek polis, they carried in them two things—fire from their mother cities and a loom. Hestia, which means 'hearth'—like a ship mast and an upright loom—is also rooted in the word *histia*, and in this case refers especially to 'setting up' a home. The loom and the hearth share a constitutive role not only in the establishment of the early Greek households, but in the setting up of the cities. Kagis McEwen has shown how the temples which were essential to each new site were modelled according to the post and beam structure of upright looms, and also served the cultural function of the loom; polis was very concretely woven and "weaving the city was a perennial undertaking."[52] The temple at once embodied the interdependent arising of craft and community and replaced the caves and sacred groves of earlier divine appearances to become a place apart—a crafted place where divinity was revealed. The world appeared, for the first time, through something people made. Through building the temple, cosmos was discovered through making.

She is not alone in identifying the origins of architecture in weaving. "With upright forked props and twigs put between, they wove their walls,"[53] declared Vitruvius, clearly honouring the Greek tradition he so admired, for Vitruvius's community was born of gathering around fire and weaving walls. Gottfried Semper also argued that the earliest buildings were woven structures.[54] Spelling out the implications of understanding building as weaving, Tim Ingold argues that just as baskets are woven, so buildings are grown; their form emerges from the process of growth rather than from the mandates of a preconceived design on formless raw material. Materials are not understood in terms of their component parts, but in terms of what they *do*.

Making is not a matter of imposition but of intervening in the fields of force and flows of material. What this understanding entails is that rather than interpreting the creative process 'backward' from a finished object to an idea in the mind of an agent, one must rather 'read it forward' in "an ongoing generative movement that is at once itinerant, improvisatory and rhythmic."[55] For Ingold, making is not a question of objects and images, "but about the coupling of awareness, and of movements and gestures, with the forces and flows of materials that bring any work to fruition."[56] In his comparison of the practices of carpentry and drawing, he traces the transition from the textile to the architectonic, in which the former was debased as craft while the latter was elevated to technology. The skill that built the original polis of Western civilisation may have been scorned and forgotten, but the more we learn about our own bodies and minds, the more are recognising the primacy of the role of this skilled intelligence in human becoming.

> If we could rid ourselves of all pride, if, to define our species, we kept strictly to what the historic and prehistoric periods show us to be a constant characteristic of man and of intelligence, we should say not *homo sapiens*, but *homo faber*. In short, *intelligence, considered in what seems to be its original feature, is the faculty of manufacturing artificial objects, especially tools to make tools, and of indefinitely varying the manufacture.*[57]

This is from Bergson—and to emphasise his point, he put the italics there himself.

Notes

1. Henri Bergson, *Creative Evolution*, trans. Arthur Mitchell (New York: Dover, 1998), 139.
2. See also Douglas MacLeod, "The Architecture Hypothesis," in *Intertwining*, issue 2 (Milan: Mimesis, 2019), 25–43.
3. Indra Kagis McEwen, *Socrates' Ancestor* (Cambridge, MA: MIT Press, 1993), 43.
4. Ibid.
5. Jean Gebser, *The Ever-Present Origin* (Athens: Ohio University Press, 1984), 132.
6. Ibid.
7. John Dewey, *Art as Experience* (New York: Perigee, 1934), 236.
8. Ibid.
9. Church bells, public clocks, calls to prayer, police sirens, political rallies all exploit the capacity of sound to organise emotional states and behaviour.
10. Gernot Böhme writes, "Music is the Fundamental Atmospheric Art Form," in *The Aesthetics of Atmospheres*, ed. Jean-Paul Thibaud (London: Routledge, 2017), 170.
11. As quoted in Dewey, *Art as Experience*, 248.
12. Ibid., 239.

13. N. Wallin, B. Merkur, and S. Brown, eds., *The Origins of Music* (Cambridge, MA: MIT Press, 2001), 11.

14. Franklin Henry Giddings, *The Principles of Sociology* (New York: McMillan, 1914), 241.

15. The ancient Greeks correlated Phrygian music with battle, Lydian music was somber and religious, while Ionian music is convivial and social. It is interesting, too, that the name Pythagoras, who was the first to measure tone, comes from pythian, a mantic-magical element.

16. Walter J. Freeman, "A Neurobiological Role of Music in Social Bonding," in *The Origins of Music*, eds. N. Wallin, B. Merkur, and S. Brown (Cambridge, MA: MIT Press, 2001), 411–424.

17. Ibid., 423.

18. Ellen Dissanayake, "Bodies Swayed to Music: The Temporal Arts as Integral to Ceremonial Ritual," in *Communicative Musicality*, eds. Stephen Malloch and Colwyn Trevarthen (Oxford: Oxford University Press, 2009), 542.

19. Oliver Sacks, *Musicophilia: Tales of Music and the Brain* (New York: Knopf, 2007), 15.

20. Dalibor Vesely, *Architecture in the Age of Divided Representation* (Cambridge, MA: MIT Press, 2004), 8.

21. Ernst Chladni, *Entdeckungen über die Theorie des Klanges* (Discoveries in the Theory of Sound) (1787).

22. Iain McGilchrist, *The Master and His Emissary* (New Haven: Yale University Press, 2010), 72.

23. Wallace Clement Sabine, *Collected Papers on Acoustics* (New York: Dover, 1964), 114.

24. Steen Eiler Rasmussen, *Experiencing Architecture* (Cambridge, MA: MIT Press, 1962), 231.

25. Deborah Howard, *Sound Space in Renaissance Venice: Architecture, Music, Acoustics* (New Haven: Yale University Press, 2009), 26–42.

26. Gebser, *The Ever-Present Origin*, 81.

27. R. Murray Schafer, *Our Sonic Environment and the Soundscape: The Tuning of the World* (Rochester, VT: Destiny Books, 1997).

28. Luigi Nono, *Écrits*, ed. Laurent Feneyrou (Paris: Christian Bourgeois, 1993), 500.

29. Edward Strickland, *American Composers: Dialogues on Contemporary Music* (Bloomington: University of Indiana Press, 1991), 163.

30. Scott Arford and Randy Yau, "Filling the Void: The Infrasound Experience," in *Site of Sound: Of Architecture and the Ear*, Vol. 2, eds. Brandon La Belle and Claudia Martinho (Berlin: Errant Bodies Press, 2011), 202.

31. Bernard Leitner, *Sound as a Building Material*, publication for the exhibition 'Tonraum-skulptur' (Berlin: Hamburger Bahnhof, 2008), 14.

32. Iannis Xenakis, *Formalized Music: Thought and Mathematics in Composition* (Hillsdale, NY: Pendragon, 1992), 237.

33. Some parts of this section have been modified from my essay, "Resonant Bodies in Immersive Space," in *Architectural Design: Neuroarchitecture*, ed. Ian Ritchie (London: Wiley, 2020).

34. Gebser, *The Ever-Present Origin*, 145.

35. Suzanne Langer, *Feeling in Form* (New York: Routledge and Kegan Paul, 1953), 204.

36. Suzanne Langer, *Philosophy in a New Key* (Cambridge, MA: Harvard University Press, 1953), 175–176.

37. See Michael Arbib, ed., *Language, Music and the Brain* (Cambridge, MA: MIT Press, 2013), 45–65.

38. J. A. Underwood and Craig Ayrey, "Jean Molino," *Music Analysis* 9, no. 2 (Jul 1990), 105–111.

39. Julia F. Christenson, Anna Lambrechts, and Manos Tsakiris, "The Warburg Dance Movement Library: A Validation Study," *Perception* 48, no. 1 (2019), 26–57.

40. Rasmussen, *Experiencing Architecture*, 136.

41. Ibid.

42. McEwen, *Socrates' Ancestor*, 82.

43. Merleau-Ponty, *Phenomenology of Perception* (London: Routledge, 1962), 130.

44. David Seamon, "Merleau-Ponty, Lived Body and Place," in *Situatedness and Place: Multidisciplinary Perspectives on Spatio-Temporal Contingency in Human Life*, eds. Thomas Hünefeldt and Annika Schlitte (New York: Springer, 2018).

45. Harry Francis Mallgrave, *Architecture and Embodiment* (Abingdon: Routledge, 2013), 4.

46. Ibid., 7.

47. Philip Johnson, "100 Years, Frank Lloyd Wright and Us," *Pacific Architect and Builder*, March 1957. Reprinted in *Johnson: Writings* (New York: Oxford University Press, 1979), 193–198.

48. Zakaria Djebbara, Lars Brorson Fich, Laura Petrini, and Klaus Gramann, "Sensorimotor Brain Dynamics Reflect Architectural Affordances," *Proceedings National Academy of Sciences* 116, no. 29 (2019), 14769–14778.

49. McEwen, *Socrates' Ancestor*, 51.

50. Ibid., 50.

51. Ibid., 71.

52. Ibid., 111.

53. Vitruvius, *Ten Books of Architecture*, ed. and trans. Frank Granger (Cambridge, MA: Loeb Classical Library, 1979), 2.1.3.

54. Gottfried Semper, *The Four Elements of Architecture*, trans. Harry Francis Mallgrave and Wolfgang Herr (Cambridge: Cambridge University Press, 1989).

55. Tim Ingold, "The Textility of Making," *Cambridge Journal of Economics* 34, no. 1 (2010), 92.

56. Ibid.

57. Henri Bergson, *Creative Evolution*, 139.

Collective Dreaming   9

An abrupt sound ushers fear through our body, a hearty laugh expands us with delight, a gentle voice softens our mood. Each sound thoroughly permeates with its chemical-emotional counterpart. The stress on emotion that marked magical consciousness shifted to an emphasis on the imagination in the mythical period and the aura that enveloped the entire body became concentrated in the mouth. Casting a spell became the power to spin a tale. Language belongs to everyone and was invented by no one—it is a communal agreement born of the trust built of the resonances of sound and the shared gestures of the body. And the inchoate language of magical sound in the mythical period became utterance. Gaining a voice, individuals gradually distinguished themselves from the group. The word *person*, from the Latin *persona*, originally referred to the megaphone-mouthed mask worn by actors in the open-air theatres of ancient Greece and Rome, the mask through *per* which the sound *sonus* came. Mouth and myth are inseparable—the Greek word *mythos* originally meant 'speech,' 'word,' 'report.' The mouth is the threshold between inner and outer worlds, and through myth collective dreams are formed into words. "Through speech a person dramatically identifies himself with potential acts and deeds; he plays many roles, not in successive stages of life but in a contemporaneously enacted drama. Thus mind emerges,"[1] wrote Dewey.

Every emergence of consciousness externalises something that has been pressing towards awareness, and until words find their expression in poetic form they remain latent processes. The inner world of the psyche issues forth in the shape of myth. Myth is not static—in mythic consciousness there is nowhere a dead thing—wind, rain, trees and stones not only make sounds, they have voices. Every detail is saturated with significance. Time is not linear; it is liquid dream time that does not unfold sequentially but is marked by intensities of condensed events and morphing colours. Myth is powered by polarity and characterised by animism, imagery, mirroring and complementarity. The language of myth lies hidden in primal words whose meanings are ambivalent. *Ambi* means 'both' and *valence* comes from the word for 'strength'—meanings moved in at least two directions. Primal words are not either/or propositions, but simultaneous tensions that give fullness to one another in their coincidence. The acoustic similarity between the German words *stimme* ('voice') and *stumme* ('silence'), for example, points to a time in earlier cultures when the speaker was as important as the listener. Again, polarities are not oppositions; they are mirrored interdependencies.[2] The word *stimmung*, as Alberto Pérez-Gómez has shown, has an astonishing breadth and depth of significance irreducible to any single word such as mood or atmosphere. Its meaning speaks to the unity once experienced between humans and their surroundings. To capture its more encompassing sense, he chooses to translate it as *"an attunement of embodied consciousness."*[3] The ultimate task of architecture, he argues, is to attune person and place, to effectively restore the dynamic unity that lies latent in the word *stimmung*. To refine our ability to design places that engage the imagination, we must first venture to understand how imagination shaped and was shaped by myth and is intimately tied to the capacity for remembering and reinforced in the act of storytelling that paradigmatically embodies both.

Imagining

"Architecture is always inhabited by spirits,"[4] writes Juhani Pallasmaa. Already this statement sets the imagination in motion—the suggestion that the settings we design house not only bodies but spirits. There is just enough tension here to nudge us into pondering other possibilities. It might be obvious to say that *some* architecture—temples, mosques and churches—house spirits, but in this case, the categorical *always* loses its deterministic ring. The verb *inhabit* suggests something ordinary, and coupled with *spirit*, something extraordinary—there is some reality, but not too much. Imagination plays in this realm between the concrete and the abstract; it is neither and it is both. Imagination is open-ended or not at all. And though the imagination is inexhaustible, it is not unlimited. Limit is rooted in *limen*, the word for 'threshold'; imagination respects certain thresholds, is nurtured or diminished according to certain rules. Gaston Bachelard, who left his chair in the philosophy of science at the

Sorbonne to study the imagination, insisted that imagination has not only an anatomy but a physiology. The imagination has a certain structure as well as a characteristic way of interacting. Like the body, imagination is a noun that describes a collection of verbs—a bounded collection of organs whose inter-actions are its life. If the imagination is a body—it is a body in suspension—a subtle body that operates in an intermediate zone of possibility, in the pause between what has already happened and what might possibly be. This zone of possibility awaits an invitation to enter in. And the invitation must respect the nature of the pause. It must not complete or resolve the suspension, but must offer—indeed, encourage—a departure from the known.

"To imagine is to absent oneself, it is a leap forward to a new life,"[5] declared Bachelard. This absence is what Keats called a "negative capability"— imagination depends on holding an emptiness, allowing one to identify with something outside the self. "A poet has no identity—he is continually in for— and filling in some other body."[6] This negative capability opens new dimen-sions of inner space. Bards like Homer are blind because they do not need vision to see the inner world. Rilke called this capacity in-seeing. The imagi-nation does not go to a place that is already full. It cannot be summoned but can be seduced. Rilke begins his poems with 'as if'—asking the reader to suspend rational judgment and embark on a journey. "Every poet must give us his invitation to journey. Through this invitation, our inner being gets a gentle push which throws us off balance and sets in motion a healthy, really dynamic reverie,"[7] wrote Bachelard. His *Poetics of Space* explores how things like nests, chests and houses, in their ordinariness, become departure points for the imagination's journey. The nest that is formed with the curve of the bird's breast is a birthplace of possibility: the chest harbours secrets. Houses with attics and basements are more amenable to dreaming because they offer hiding places—nooks and corners that are open but also conceal. The stability of support allows the tension of flight. The movement of imagining is often compared with flight—suspension is a kind of tension—both come from the word for 'stretch.' As the poet May Sarton puts it: "When I imagine wings that come and go, what I see is a house and a wide open window."[8] The wing is a fragile thing—the innocence of reverie can easily be broken and can only flourish with limits. Imagination alights from a basis of trust—trust that is born in the resistance of the real.

Like Darwin's insistence that the mind cannot be understood by "attacking the citadel itself,"[9] Bachelard realised that something as subtle as the imagina-tion cannot be approached directly. So, rather than asking what imagination is, he focused on what the imagination *does*—he studied the imagination's *characteristic way of interacting*. His study of poetry did not end with the poem; the poem was a trace left in imagination's wake. And, in studying imagination's movements, he concluded, "the physiology of the imagination obeys the law of the four elements."[10] As the heart is to the circulatory system, the psyche is to the imagination, and its function is not to form images, but quite the contrary; the imagination *deforms* what we perceive. It is, above all, the faculty that frees us from immediate images and changes them."[11] It is important to remember that for Bachelard the word *image* did not refer to a picture, nor did it apply to one sensory faculty. The power of an image can be measured by the compass of its aura, the reach of its web of associations and the number of sensory faculties it engages. The elements widen to hold multiple possibilities simultaneously. His books devoted to fire, water, air and earth are inexhaustible sources of inspiration for designers, since these are the basic elements of our craft. The elements are not those itemised on the periodic table; they are the elements of the alchemists that undergo transfor-mation. "Once imagination has set into motion an attentive sensibility in us, we realise that qualities are not so much states . . . as they are processes of

Image 9.1 Temple of Segesta, Sicily

Source: Photo Sarah Robinson.

becoming."[12] In designing the Thermal Baths at Vals, Peter Zumthor meditated on mountain, stone, water—and the outcome of that process is a place that acts like a poem to embody the mystery of all three. The mutating personality of water, the patience of stone, the mountains' deep history—are each restored to their own particular movement.

Complementarity

The formal typologies of the ancient world, the cave and column, have deeper roots than the superimposition of the anatomy of the womb and the phallus onto architecture. Gebser wrote:

> In antiquity, it is principally their psychic reality and polarity which are evident, for both Hades and Hell are vault-like and cavern-like; they reflect the nocturnal aspect, maternal mystery, shelter and the parturient principle. The columnar aspect, in turn, corresponds to the sky and to Olympus: in architecture it expresses the very essence of open, in-between space. It is the diurnal aspect, paternal illumination, exposure, the seminal principle.[13]

The cave and column were mythic structures that mediated between earth and sky; they were not dualities but polarities that held the human world in balance. *Their form was their meaning.* The imagination that emerged within mythical structure is characterised by a field of tension expressed in the two-dimensional polarity between the depths of the earth and the counterpole of the heavens. The architecture of the period is marked by the stretching upright columns of Greek temples that marked their emergence from the cave. Plato was a pivotal figure whose life spanned the transition from the mythical to the mental period and it is significant that he introduced the allegory of the cave. In his rendering, the dark resonant cave was no longer a place of protection, refuge and birth but a dungeon of dim shadows that impeded the clear thinking symbolised in his ideal forms.

The nascent interdependence of the mythic polarity between prospect and refuge is present in the German words *höhle*, which means 'cavern,' and *helle*, which means 'brightness.' The roots of the words *hell*, *hole* and *brightness* derive from the word 'clam,' 'hollow,' 'husk'.[14] Imagination operates as a field of tension in which the dynamics of dark and light, cave and pillar, prospect and refuge, presence and absence, part and whole are not contradictions but animating complementarities.[15] In the mythic period, architecture embodied the human imagination in nature and was not separate from it. "The action of buildings and landscape was fully reciprocal in meaning as in form," wrote Vincent Scully, "and this is the essential fact, form and meaning were the same."[16] The deep sense of action and effect of landscape in the Homeric myths portray the human and natural worlds in a complementary relationship. Yet, the word *landscape* did not yet exist as we know it—landscape literally means 'land that is cut off from the rest,' and this severance in the mythic world did not yet happen. The nonhuman context is not an aesthetic backdrop of action; the hard line between the human and the nonhuman did not yet exist. One cannot even use the word *landscape* to interpret the relationship between earth and temple—in mythic consciousness, they are woven of the same thread. Human feelings were expressions of more profound commotions, which is evident in Greek verbs whose meanings have both physical and psychical dimensions: The verb *melt* refers to the state of ice and human tears at the same time. Things do not resemble other things; they share the very same processes.[17] In the animistic mind of myth, there is no dead thing. Spirits were physically embodied in the earth and temples were outcroppings of that spirit—the Greeks built sanctuaries at particularly potent places and were situated and related to one another in such a way that enhanced, developed and complemented the meaning that was felt in the land. The temple was an instrument of conjuration, and in order to fully act it had to be an embodiment, not merely a "construction, or an abstractly perfect shape, or a pictorial element."[18] The patterns of the temples were not static templates, but were adjusted according to site characteristics and the persona of the gods and goddesses they were intended to serve. Greek temples were oriented in relation to the shape of the earth and the patterns of the sky—uniting above and below. The act of placing an oblong structure in a cyclical world—effectively squaring a circle—is another polarising act in the magic of making, exciting the current between positive and negative poles.

Suspension

This presence/absence dialectic seems to be at the heart of the Greek temple design and rituals. The presence of the goddess was a necessary precondition for the unfolding of the ritual act. On the one hand, temples were built to house spirits, but those spirits did not seem to reside in them full-time. The tension of their appearance and disappearance was kept aloft by human actions. And perhaps this distinction speaks to the emergence of the imagination as a place in-between. The temple was the medium for the appearance of the goddess, like the shiny surface is the medium of your reflection in a mirror. The temples effectively embodied the imagination as a place of appearance. "The active Imagination is the preeminent *mirror*," writes Henri Corbin, "the epiphanic place of the Images of the archetypal world."[19] The Greek *epiphaneia* means 'surface, a place of appearance'—a place where the subtle bodies of image are suspended and made visible. The word *imagination*, after all, comes from the word *magic*, and acts of the imagination are indeed subtle acts of magic.

Architecture can enact this kind of suspension, and there could hardly be a better model than Luis Barragán's chapel and convent of the Capuchinas in Mexico City. Its anonymous facade belies the treasures hidden inside, and already the imagination is activated in this tension. One enters into a spare courtyard open to the sky where a wall-height crucifix appears in a recess. The cross itself is also recessed in such a way to collect dust—the earth, particle by particle, filling in the edges of its absence. Directly across lies a polished black granite basin, filled to the brim—allowing one to see only its shimmering surface, but not its hidden depth. And on that surface, or rather its *epiphaneia*, floats the reflection of a bright yellow screen woven of concrete. As one climbs the stairs behind, the screen casts its glow on the adjacent white walls.

Image 9.2 Luis Barragán's Chapel of the Capuchinas in Mexico City

Once inside, another screen appears, this time woven of wood through which the altar of the chapel is visible from its side. Beyond it, on the left, a giant pink cross is poised in front of a wall of a deep orange plaster. Both are made visible by light which enters from an unseen source. The light illuminates the wall behind the cross, but touches the cross only on its side, leaving its face in shadow. All this drama is happening at the chapel's periphery. When the altar is faced directly, one sees not the cross, but only its shadow, which looms larger than the cross itself, and keeps mutating. We therefore see the cross—the symbol of contradiction, only in its absence. The shadow brings the subtle body of the cross to light. It is not stable, but shifts according to the

Image 9.3 Ernest Mundt sculpture for San Miguel School, San Francisco, 1959, seen from top to bottom at morning, noon and afternoon.

Source: Photo Ira Latour.

cycle of day and disappears at night. This law of mirroring, the suspension of presence and absence, is at the heart of the ceremonies that took place in Greek temples in which the rituals of making coaxed the goddess to presence. More subtle levels of mind cannot be approached directly and in his mastery of this rule, Barragán accomplished Chekhov's request: "Don't tell me the moon is shining, show me the glint of light on broken glass."

As we saw with the approach to Taliesin West, it is not enough to cast a veil—it all depends on how it is shed. The chapel suspends the rational because it unfolds in layers: the disclosure of one veil leads only to another. One cannot confront mystery head-on, but only from the periphery, with tenderness and patience. Giving presence to the more subtle but equally real dimensions of shadow suspends rational thinking precisely because it undermines Plato's famous allegory. He derided shadows for their uncertainty. They soften the edges of his perfect forms; their ephemerality defies clarification. His allegory marked the transition from polarity to duality and the presence of shadow depends on the mutuality of light and solidity. It is an expression of complementarity and interdependence that underlie the white light of reason. Shadows offer perhaps the most enticing invitation of all to the imagination because they bring subtle bodies to light. The artist Ernest Mundt's proposal for a shadow sculpture for the San Miguel School in San Francisco, for example, can only be appreciated in four dimensions—when regarded face forward, it appears in thin outline; its thickness and depth only appear as light casts their shadows. Like the imagination, shadows are never still and cannot be touched directly, but can be felt and experienced in their softening coolness, in their ever-shifting glance. In paying as much attention to the play of shadows as to the solids that cast them, we engage these subtle dialectics.

Gottfried Semper recognised that the imagination is activated when reality is suspended:

> I think that the dressing and the mask are as old as human civilisation and that the joy in both is identical to the joy in those things that lead men to be sculptors, painters, architects, poets, musicians, dramatists—in short, artists. Every artistic creation, every artistic pleasure, presumes a certain carnival spirit, or to express it in a modern way, the haze of carnival candles is the true atmosphere of art. Destruction of reality, of the material, is necessary if form is to emerge as a meaningful symbol, as an autonomous human creation.[20]

The mask was a vestige of magic, and signified a phenomena outside the bounds of space and time. It did not destroy reality so much as suspend it.

And to understand the technique of suspension, the mask is instructive. To mask is to leave certain things unsaid, to screen certain realties from consciousness temporarily. Donning a mask liberates reality from its gravitational grip just long enough for the spontaneous to enter. This loosening of fixity is the essential ground for imagination's mercurial play. One must refrain, at all costs, from succumbing to the obvious. An airport shaped like a bird is like a hyperrealistic children's toy suggesting only one way to play. A wing torn from its generative body is no longer the organ of flight but a finite form—its closure is double—its aura repelled.

Metaphor: Patterning Fields

The 'as if' invitation to imagine plays out most fully in the open-ended capacity of metaphor. Metaphor operates in the shared field of tensions that is imagination's unique terrain. The function of metaphor, as Alberto Pérez-Gómez points out is "to discover by approaching two distant realities, a new reality that jolts us like a voltaic arc."[21] Indeed, electricity is powered by the poles of positive and negative, the animating dynamic of myth. Aristotle defined *metaphor* as "the *transport* to one thing of a name that designates another."[22] This crossing of identities opens a fluid transitional domain that loosens meanings from their rational categories, yet at the same time is grounded in a long history of shared bodily experiences. As Mark Johnson and George Lakoff have shown, metaphors are patterned biologically in relationships between physical, emotional and cultural experiences. The 'warmth is affection' metaphor, they argue, arises from the childhood experience of being held affectionately and the pleasing thermal envelope that coincides with that experience. The physiological profile of the metaphor shows "neuronal activation occurring simultaneously in two separate parts of the brain: those devoted to emotions and those devoted to temperature. As the saying goes in neuroscience, 'Neurons that fire together wire together.' Appropriate neural connections physically constitute the Affection is Warmth metaphor,"[23] they write.

In their rootedness in the body, metaphor shares common ground with Jung's notion of archetypes. Gebser called archetypes "organs of the soul" and Jung himself referred to them using Bergson's phrase *les éternels incréés*, uncreated eternals, and was convinced they were also physiologically grounded. Like metaphor, archetypes are open-ended psychic tendencies towards patterns.

> What an archetypal content primarily expresses is first of all expressed as a simile or metaphor. It speaks of the sun and identifies it with the

lion, the king, the hoard of gold guarded by a dragon, and of the power of man's life and health, it expresses neither the one nor the other, but rather an unknown third which to a greater or lesser degree is expressed by all of the metaphors—although, to the perceptual organ of the intellect, it remains unknown and inexpressible. For this reason the scientific intellect repeatedly falls prey to the temptation of trying to explain it.[24]

Jung emphasised the biological-neurological anchorage of allegory and imagery and the way both behave as a force field, an organising medium, as epistemic filters.[25] Similar patterning structures have been suggested by Rudolph Arnheim, who referred to these tendencies as *sensory symbols*, and Joseph Rykwert, who spoke of a *structured complex of symbols*. Dalibor Vesely suggested *primal configurations*, Alvar Aalto suggested the *psyche of form* and Juhani Pallasmaa has suggested the notion of *primary images*. These structures all share several important similarities: they are open-ended, elusive and immune to the strictures of space and time. They are not static configurations but operate, if latently, in the present, and as such, they are not representations but experiential complexes rooted in a long history of embodied experience.

In helping us to understand what Aalto meant by *psyche of form*, Juhani Pallasmaa draws our attention to the inspiration Aalto found in Fra Angelica's Annunciation. In this painting Aalto witnessed the essential act of entering a room. This event may have been suggested by the tectonic formal elements of door and vestibule in the painting, but could not be reduced to or explained by them. The painting concretises the experiential complex of crossing a threshold, setting in motion all the nuance of anticipation bound up in the emotional residues of the embodied event. Aalto was able to transfer these metaphoric layers into built form. Speaking about his experience at Aalto's Villa Mairea, Colin St. John Wilson writes:

> We are here considering a phenomenon which has a direct impact on the nervous system of the beholder and I believe that this operates through a body language that we have all learnt long before words, in the earliest days of infancy. It is a kind of sixth sense.[26]

In his essay "The Geometry of Feeling," Pallasmaa insists that within the pragmatic program of architecture, the more subtle and significant role of the architect is to appeal to this sixth sense, this deep language of the body. The primary emotions he outlines are not emotional states correlated with tectonic elements—they are verbs—the unfolding experiential actions of approaching, entering, crossing the threshold, gathering, encountering light,

Image 9.4 Door Threshold, Palermo Sicily

Source: Photo Sarah Robinson.

looking out of the window, connecting with landscape.[27] Each of these actions does not end once it is completed, but when honored and respected sets the imagination and memory in motion.

Rudolph Arnheim called metaphors *sensory symbols*, the most powerful of which were rooted in shared human experiences.

> Symbols could not rely on the expressive qualities of sensory experience if that experience were not endowed with metaphoric overtones in daily practice. Sunlight streaming through windows when the shades are raised in the morning is not perceived as a mere change in brightness level. Only because it is received as a gift of life, exposing the world to us and us to the world, can illumination serve us as a broadly valid symbol. The most powerful symbols derive from the most elementary perceptual sensations because they refer to the basic human experiences on which all others depend.[28]

The symbolism in the arts would not move us so nor be so prevalent were it not rooted in the most universal of human experiences—the warm envelope of touch, the bright sky of deliverance, the adventure of ascent, the healing mystery of the forest. And this loops back to our earlier discussion of dance, and the way dance space is a magnetic field orienting the needle on a compass. These experiences are grounded in the musicality of movement. The body language of entry, passage, ascent and descent are actions—not finished forms that repel the imagination precisely because they are static and completed. According to Bachelard, two conditions alter the sense of temporality in the realm of the imagination: resonance and reverberation. Resonance, for him, was the dynamic condition through which the world discloses its

Image 9.5 Shadow patterns and light from above: Sarah Robinson, architect
Source: Photo Sarah Robinson.

imaginary openings and oscillates at a larger amplitude at some frequencies than at others. In resonance, the rhythm of the world and the rhythms of one's body become attuned, a condition which sounds very similar to the one Dalcroze tried to achieve through his eurhythmics. Reverberation is technically a further step, a reconfiguration of our rhythmical settings through the intrusion of alien vibration. "In reverberation . . . we find the real measure of the being of a poetic image. In this reverberation, the poetic image will have a sonority of being. The poet speaks on the threshold of being."[29]

To these I would suggest another category of metaphor: the primal metaphor that operates similarly to primal words in language. Primal words simultaneously have two antithetical connotations: Latin *altus* meant 'high' as well as 'low'; *sacer* meant 'sacred' as well as 'cursed.' Primal words testify to an undifferentiated psychically stressed unity whose bivalent nature was familiar to the early Greeks. This is the language of word images formed from sounds in an animate world— prior to antonyms and conceptual opposites. As we saw earlier, with *hell* and *hole*, they share the same root and are acoustically similar, but have polar connotations that stretch their field of associations, their aura radiating from a deeper source. Like the elements of matter in their transformative capacity, primal metaphors stretch back into time into the kinaesthetic memory of muscle, and their formative capacity has shaped human cognition. They are complexes that weave together the mysteries of the elements, sending reverberations through our body—to shape our perception, our values and our cultural practices.

The cave, as we have seen, is obviously a primal metaphor that continues to reverberate throughout the history of architecture. Another, still undeveloped in its full potential, is the primal metaphor of the forest—the original, deathless *hylē*. The most quoted passage in Western literary history, the first canto of Dante's *Inferno*—"In the middle of our life's path, I found myself in a dark forest, where the straight way was lost"—speaks of the forest as a threatening and bewildering place. And interestingly, the word *bewildering* comes from the word *wilderness*. Yet, we know that few places are more nourishing to body and spirit than a bath in the forest. This polarity is what makes the primal metaphor of the forest so activating. The architects Charles Moore and Donlyn Lyndon have stressed the ordering effect that orchards—humanised forests—have on the temperament. Charles Moore recollects:

> The building in all the world that has the most magical orchardness, is for me, the Great Mosque at Córdoba. Forty years later I remember still the moment when I arrived at its door, which was open and admitted enough light into the shadowy interior for me to discern the first rows of columns marching into the darkness beyond. It was my first glimpse of Islam, of an order of rhythm, not hierarchy.[30]

The neuroscientist Tom Albright relates this sense of order to the way our vision has been shaped by selective pressures over the course of human evolution. Certain regularly recurring features and conjunctions of features are more preferable than others because vision exhibits highly specific and tunable, organizational properties representing key characteristics of the environment.[31] In particular, he refers to Hubel and Weisel's work on orientation selectivity, relating our preference to vertical lines to the architectural prevalence and popularity of columnar arcades and cable stay bridges. Certain visual patterns yield a sense of order because they tap into neuronal substrates that adapted to recurring features in the environment. Perhaps we prefer these colonnades because our sensory perception adapted for life in the forest canopy. Discerning the fine branches that connect the vertical rise of tree trunks with the horizontal plane of the forest floor was the perceptual triumph of the primate. The ecologist Paul Shepard attributed the emotionally calming effect of trees and forest settings to the arboreal origins of early humans. He speculated that our aesthetic preferences for symmetry and balance, our tendency to abstract vertical and horizontal lines, and even our attraction to the tension provoked by the obtuse outline of an occasional leaning tree, are shadows that linger in our Paleozoic memory. "Restfulness to the eyes and temperament, unspoken mythological and psychic attachments, remain part of the forest's contribution to the human personality."[32]

Yet beyond the arrangement of columns evoking tree trunks, the forest metaphor suggests an experience of space lacking a strong gestalt. In the forest, no one feature stands out more than the others and aside from its heroic verticality, the forest is all texture—which is likely why some find it disorienting. In the forest, there is no one centre—every centre opens out to another centre—and simply being in a forest makes you a centre—among centres. An architectural work that operates in just this way is Juha Leiviskä's Myyrmäki Church just outside Helsinki in Finland. Finnish architecture has perhaps the richest relationship to the forest, and this tradition comes through this work in the subtlest of ways. One approaches the church through a forest of birch trees past a crisply edged bell tower, through the invitation of a wood canopy into a modest room lined with thin slats of wood, evocative of the papery bark on the trees just outside. The wood floor cushions footsteps like a bed of fallen leaves. This lowered space heightens the anticipation of entry into a drama of the most ethereal light—the Japanese have the word *komorebi*, an amalgam of the characters for *tree* and *shine*, to describe the kind of light that shines through the forest—and it is perfectly suited to describe this sanctuary. The light filtering in from on high gives the impression of being in a very tall space, yet in section the space is perfectly square. Its asymmetrical balance of

Images 9.6 and **9.7** Myyrmäki Church, Myyrmäki Finland: Juha Leiviskä, architect

Source: Photo Arno de la Chapelle.

light and form and horizontal and vertical elements evokes Paul Shepard's observation about the tendency of arboreal perception to abstract vertical and horizontal lines. Even the details of the unevenly hung brass fixtures that sparkle in the light suggest a passing flock of birds. The layering of white reenacts the presence of the birch forest in an interweaving of human and natural realms. Even the shadows are shades of white on white. Layers upon overlapping layers is the enveloping pattern of the forest. And the opposite, the uneasy sense of exposure we feel in open spaces, is another indication of our forest past, suggests Paul Shepard:

> There is yet an enduring nostalgia that is reinforced by the relentless glare and feeling of vulnerability in the open. An affinity for shade, for the nebulous glimmering of the pillared interior, for the tracery of branches against homogeneous backgrounds.[33]

The complex layering of light, suspended cloth, the dynamic interplay of shadow and plane evokes the forest that lies deeply hidden in human consciousness. In this tranquil, soothing and enveloping place, one would never guess that its back wall affronts a major railway line. This grand illusion is the power of architecture to uniquely do.

Remembering

The places that exist in your mind are in many ways as real as the places themselves—all places have this power. They deposit their residue whether we will them to or not. "Every site is haunted by countless ghosts . . . that lurk there in silence to be evoked or not,"[34] writes Michel de Certeau. We can get a hint of the interweaving of the mental and physical when we recognise that memory is a capacity that is spatial and practiced. Before the Greek alphabet appeared, knowledge was enacted in craft and passed on in story. And, the temporal distance separating the Greek alphabet from today—less than 3,000 years—is a mere fraction of the time that humans have been on earth. Crafted buildings, objects and stories were the means through which the human mind emerged. This is why Indra Kagis McEwen can claim that architecture was a precondition for Western thought. Building architecture built the mind. We now recognise that the notion of memory as something exiled to the skull of an individual is a relatively recent idea—and it is, just that, an idea. The capacity of memory developed together with the development of craft and building.

Memories are not passive traces of past experiences stored like coins in our 'memory bank.' Memory and imagination travel the same circuits. The words 're-member' and 're-collect' mean to put back together what has been scattered—memory is active, constructive and must be exercised. The Roman orator Cicero adopted the *ars memoria*, the art of memory, from the Greeks. He built a mental scaffolding to help him remember his speeches by situating memory images in specific locations of the theatre in which he was to deliver the speech. He performed his speech by mentally travelling through the room and reeling in those memory images in the correct order. This memory palace came from a cultural legacy in which mind was already externalised. In his study of Roman town formations, Joseph Rykwert showed how the town was "a mnemonic symbol or at any rate, a structured complex of symbols" and functioned "as a machine for thinking with, as an instrument for understanding the world and the human predicament in it."[35] The physical layout of towns was a means to reconcile human experience through monument and ritual action. Citizens participated in and were protected by the regenerative and reconciling pattern of the town itself. This sense of order that was patterned by and embodied in the town schema has since been lost, and Rykwert suggested that it can now be found "in the constitution and structure of the human person."[36] Both of these examples from antiquity are still operative in us today. Our cities are sedimentations of mental and physical habits, as Alva Noë has argued.[37] Physical spaces correlate with mental places, and vice versa. All of our behaviour relies on the intertwined capacities of memory and the innate sense of space that we share with other animals. The neuroscientist John O' Keefe was the first to recognise that many forms of explicit memory— that is, memory about objects and people—rely on spatial coordinates. We remember a face in the context of a place; the two fuse together in our minds. And, the art of associating memories with specific spaces has a biological basis. Unlike our other senses, we do not have a particular organ dedicated to sensing space. Instead, our brain weaves together information from multiple sensory modalities, in myriad areas in many different ways to record spatial experiences. O'Keefe has since been awarded a Nobel prize for his discovery in 1971 that the hippocampus area of the brain specialises in multisensory perception of the environment. When an animal enters an enclosure, certain neurons ignite action potentials only when that animal moves to a particular location. This pattern of activation is so distinctly related to a particular area of space that O'Keefe named these neurons "place-cells." Because our environments shape corresponding patterns of neuronal activity, every act of memory can also be considered as a recapitulation of a specific place.

Awareness of place has profound evolutionary advantages: locating a safe place to nest, finding a refuge from predators, navigating a migration corridor, all depend on knowing the intimate curvature of the surrounding world. Inscribed into the genes of every animal, this highly evolved sensibility sculpts our anatomy. Birds who store their food at numerous different sites, for example, have a larger hippocampus than other birds. This enlarged hippocampus is also evident in another population whose livelihood depends on the precise cartography inscribed both inside and outside their bodies: London taxicab drivers. Unlike cabbies in other parts of the world, cab drivers in London must study the names, layout and most efficient route between the city's streets. After two years of this rigorous orientation, magnetic resonance imaging revealed that their hippocampus was significantly larger than their civilian peers and that it continued to swell over time. And even more, brain imaging showed that their hippocampus lit up even during imagined travel.[38]

This research suggests that our nervous system is very concretely configured by our environment—memory and imagination reinforce patterns of neuronal activity that go on to shape experience. The close ties between imagination and memory suggest that what captivates imagination also triggers memory. If imagination relies on openness, memory too, relies on gaps. Memory palaces function only if they shelter openings; Cicero could not place his memory images in niches if such openings were already full. The memory scholar Frances Yates has noted the idiosyncratic character of the palaces built in the ancient art of memory. "It reflects ancient architecture but in an unclassical spirit, concentrating its choice on irregular places and avoiding symmetrical orders."[39] Memories were recollected with greater facility in settings that were not completely uniform, possessing knots of roughness and even unsavoury imagery. In his study of memory, Donlyn Lyndon also noticed that "good places are structured so that they attract and hold memories; they are sticky—or perhaps you would rather say magnetic."[40] A place deserves its name because of its capacity to hold memories. And like memory itself, place is not a passive container that holds memories as an album holds photos. It operates like a force field magnetising memories in intimate collaboration with your active imagination, and to do so it must have openings, hinges. Buildings that try too hard to control experience ultimately fail to become true places. "Seeking to make each place a singular, memorable work of art often makes the insistence of its vocabulary resistant to the attachment of memories—to the full engagement of the people who use and live with the building,"[41] Lyndon insists. This insight resonates with Bachelard's claim that a stable and completely realised image clips the wings of the imagination.[42] Memorable places are not already filled but allow and even create space— I have referred elsewhere to the research showing that Europeans who walk on cobblestone sidewalks retain their sense of balance longer than their American peers who walk on smooth concrete sidewalks.[43] But I would go further to suggest that negotiating unevenness exercises one's sense of balance because one's attention must fill in the gaps that lie between the stones. With every step, one completes the work. This is true participation: the body does not participate in its fullness without also engaging the mind. Texture invites life and uniformity deadens.

Michel de Certeau has emphasised the close bond between memory and place, and his practice of space could be correlated with what we now know about the externalisation of memory.

> Places are fragmentary and inward turning histories, pasts that others are not allowed to read, accumulated times that can be unfolded but like stories held in reverse, remaining in an enigmatic state, symbolisations encysted in the pain and pleasure of the body. 'I feel good here': the well-being under-expressed in the language it appears like a fleeting glimmer is a spatial practice.[44]

Though his work tends to emphasise the linguistic dimensions of spatial practices, even he acknowledges the limits of language to express the subterranean role of place on the imagination. Memory and imagination are so closely bound that those who suffer from amnesia not only lose their capacity to remember, they lose their capacity to imagine their future as well. De Certeau seemed to be aware of this interdependence and was concerned that the privatisation of stories eroded the capacity of both memory and imagination:

> The dispersion of stories points to the dispersion of the memorable as well. In fact memory is a sort of anti-museum: it is not localisable. Fragments of it come out in legends. Objects and words also have hollow places in which a past sleeps, as in everyday acts of walking, eating, going to bed, in which ancient revolutions slumber . . . It is striking here that the places where people live are like the presences of diverse absences. What can be seen designates what is no longer there: you see, here used to be . . . but it can no longer be seen . . . it is the very

Image 9.8 & 9.9 Palermo, Sicily
Source: Photo Sarah Robinson.

definition of a place in fact, that it is composed by these series of displacements and effects among the fragmented strata that form it and that it plays on these moving layers.[45]

His insistence that memories are encysted in the pleasures and pains of the body underlines the importance of presenting both dimensions of the human experience. When wounds are not hidden, the scar becomes stronger than the surrounding tissue. Pain acknowledged, is pain that is shared. The hollow places in which the past sleeps are pores that must remain open in order to breathe. When cleansed of their suffering, and dried of their tears, the strata in which memories and dreams dwell is exiled as well.

Storytelling

The familiar metaphor that depicts consciousness as the visible tip of a vast submerged iceberg of the subconscious could equally be applied to written and oral language. Eric Havelock insisted:

> The natural human being is not a writer or a reader, but a speaker and a listener. This must be as true of us today . . . as it was 7,000 years ago. Literacy at any stage of its development is in terms of evolutionary time a mere upstart, and to this day it is in our spoken communication with each other that we reveal and operate our biological inheritance.[46]

The written word is the visible tip of the better part of language. Fixing words on a page took the pressure off the environment to play its mnemonic role. The buildings, ceremonies, rituals, rehearsals of epics, rhymes and proverbs that all served to build up and reinforce memory gradually lost their status. "One must imagine the transformations of epic forms occurring in rhythms comparable to those of the change that has come over the earth's surface in the course of thousands of centuries,"[47] writes Walter Benjamin. And this momentous transition had consequences that are more far-reaching for architecture than has yet been fully recognised. In Victor Hugo's *Notre Dame de Paris*, a scholar looks out from manuscript-stuffed shelves of his study at the silhouette of the cathedral and declares, 'Ceci tuera cela'—the book will destroy the building. Hugo was warning against far more than an eclipse of architecture's communicative role. His parable might be applied to the sacrifice of the ancient art of memory once externalised in buildings. The arrival of the printing press would effect a throughgoing shift in perception that changed how we see, think, remember, behave, cooperate and govern. "More than any other single invention," Walter Ong writes, "writing has transformed human consciousness."[48] What was once collectively available and externalised became private domain, the imagination of myth that was once shared, atomised in a book—which is not to discount the breakthrough that the book was, but to point out that the atrophy of the communal imagination that began with trapping words in print has only been exacerbated. The internet effectively split the atom of the book, releasing a tremendous amount of energy, at once democratising the text while distancing it even further from its living *context*. Unleashing the word from the body and situation has not yet been compensated for with an attendant richness and articulation of the material tissue that buildings once embodied and expressed.

The human mind was born in the cradle of architecture. The form of buildings was their meaning—and neither buildings, nor their meanings, could be *read*. Architecture did not cease to communicate; it lost its audience of listeners. The skill with which buildings were constructed was a kind of knowledge that could only be practiced. It is knowledge that can be transferred from body to body through craft, ritual and inhabiting, and through the tongue and tale of story. Storytelling is fundamentally different from reading. "Familiar though its name may be to us," writes Walter Benjamin, "the storyteller in his living immediacy is by no means a present force . . . less and less do we encounter people who know how to tell a tale properly."[49] In its proximity to myth, storytelling passes experience from mouth to mouth, and its telling relies on the mutuality between speaker and listener. Storytelling is context-dependent and improvisatory like jazz—it is open-ended but works within a certain stylistic form. It is a performance art that engages memory rhapsodically—*rap* and *rhapsody* come from the Greek *rhaptein*, meaning 'to stitch.' Homer stitched his epics from prefabricated mnemonic parts that came alive in the telling. Storytelling weaves counsel into the fabric of daily life through gradual buildup, rhythm and suspense—it neither fixes, nor dictates. Benjamin writes:

> Half the art of storytelling is to keep a story free from explanation as one reproduces it . . . the most marvellous things, are related with the greatest accuracy, but the psychological connection is not forced on the reader. It is left up to him to interpret things the way he understands them, and thus the narrative achieves an amplitude that information lacks.[50]

It is this foregoing of explanation that strengthens the story's claim to a place in the listener's memory. This process of assimilation takes place in depth only when the listener is in a state of relaxation, a condition which even in Benjamin's time was becoming increasingly rare.

Buildings once served the role of the storyteller—not only in the epics recorded on their surfaces, or through storing memories inside their crevices. They were and remain the embodiment of skill. As we have seen, the Greek *epiphaneia* means 'surface,' a place of appearance—and its close relative *hyphainein*, the word for weaving, or plying the loom—means 'to bring to light.' Weaving tales, brings things to light, reveals in a way that coaxes, threads, works through connecting and relating. Weaving has long been correlated with not only architectural origins, but the art of storytelling. And the slow, repetitive craft of weaving is the context in which storytelling developed its intellectual role. "A great storyteller will always be rooted in the people, primarily in a milieu of craftsmen," Benjamin reminds us. "The old coordination of the eye, soul and hand are brought in connection. Interacting with one another, they determine a practice, it is the world of the artisan where the art of storytelling is most at home."[51] Storytelling does not aim to abbreviate like news or information, but rather as Benjamin puts it, "sinks the thing into the life of the storyteller, in order to bring it out of him again. Thus traces of the storyteller cling to the story the way the handprint of the potter cling to the clay vessel."[52] Words emerged from and were knitted within the tissue of voice and experience. *Histio*, again the Greek word for loom, is used in medicine to indicate tissue—the structural element in the human body is also the tissue of story. Restoring the visceral presence of the body in architecture is key to reclaiming its constitutive role in shaping and sustaining culture. Architecture did not lose its capacity to communicate—consciousness transitioned to faster, reductive, visual modes of communication, but the "old coordination of eye, soul and hand" still lives, and retains its authority, as the inimitable veracity of touch testifies. Architecture belongs to the modes of communication that are slow and wordless, that occur on another time scale, more similar to that of craft, which can be tedious, repetitive, rhythmic and reliant on the textures of habit to make their impression. Unlike the role of information that does not survive past the instant of its newness, this slower mode does not

Image 9.10 Alhambra

Source: photo Sarah Robinson.

readily expend itself. Its hard-won accretion is precisely what concentrates its strength, releasing it gradually over a longer period of time. Charles Moore remembered the moment he stepped into the Great Mosque at Córdoba in vivid colour 40 years later. The silent voices of the buildings at Taliesin continue to resonate in my body memories today. What other fabricated mode of communication puts us more closely in contact with the enduring resistance of the real?

Narrative and Self

The parallel partnership of weaving and story suggest the way that a person, a couple, a family and a community come to understand themselves. The verb 'to narrate' is rooted in the word for coming to know—and the presence of narrative in all cultures and historic periods suggests the critical role that narrative plays in ordering human experience. Memories are inherently unstable—since they are not stored in a vault in the mind, they must constantly be repeated, rehearsed and retold. The narrative thread that is story is critical to developing a sense of identity—the stories we tell ourselves and each other define and stabilise who we are. Our self is woven of threads of experience that are ordered into coherence through narrative. Those who have suffered neurological damage have lost their ability to construct a narrative have lost their sense of self.[53] Again, unlike news and information that are communicated speedily and presented in bits, story seeks a body—a story is a story because it is cohesive and complete in itself, but whose process of unfolding entails remaining in suspense. The coherence of one's story becomes the coherence of one's self.

This binding of concrete experience through the threads of story underlines the importance of narrative in making memorable places. If every memory is the recapitulation of a certain place, those places are critical characters in the stories of our lives, the lives of our families and communities. History is ultimately a collection of stories whose repetition and inculcation into the imagination of the future is decided and arbitrated by those in command. Wiping out the presence of the past destroys not only our memories but our capacity to imagine our future. Invigorating historical buildings with new uses is crucial to the self-understanding of those who dwell in its midst. In the Castelvecchio Museum in Verona, Italy, for example, Carlo Scarpa wove a modern museum into the fabric of a medieval palace that had been severely damaged during WWII. The palace itself was built on top of Roman ruins. The easiest and cheapest strategy in this case would have been to tear down and start over, perhaps leaving a residuum of ruins as a static reminder. But instead, Scarpa approached the past not as a corpse or a fetishised fragment—but honoured the narrative of its continuous habitation. Every detail of the museum plays on the tension between fragile memories and stabilising story by juxtaposing the old and new together. More than a storehouse for the display of artefacts, the museum is a place that holds together the heart of the city. Places without traces of their history cannot properly be called a place—it is the very definition of a place, as Michel de Certeau reminds us, that it plays on the moving layers, among the "fragmented strata that form it." Historic fragments are made whole when woven into the body of story, when integrated into our daily present.

Empathy and Story

The mirroring and suspension of the imagination, its preservation in memory and reinforcement and exploration in story, are all aptitudes that come together in empathy. Empathy is the imaginative capacity to put ourselves in place of the other—the human capacity of stitching par excellence. And the mutuality inherent in storytelling remains a powerful way to access the kind of visceral communication that speaks more softly, slowly and therefore requires more effort to access.[54] "For an architect, the capacity to imagine situations of life is more important than the gift of fantasising space,"[55] wrote Aulis Blomstedt. The architect Klaske Havic has developed a method of using narrative techniques to exercise the critical capacity to imagine the situations of life.[56] Developing the negative capacity that Keats spoke of—looking through the eyes of another—places the writer in a position of empathy. "Stories are vehicles for empathy, able to make readers acquainted with the perspective of the 'other.' Indeed, this focus on empathy is part of plea for a more humanist understanding of architecture and urbanism,"[57] Havic writes. Everyone has an autobiography of places inscribed into their body of memory whether they are aware of it or not. Reflecting on the places that have emotionally moved you and identifying the patterns of meaning in those movements are the necessary basis for developing the ability to design meaningful places. Recapitulating your own stories makes you more skilled in listening to and locating the stories of others. Every site has its ghosts and spirits whose storyline precedes us. It is the task of the designer to reshape the plot. A receptive, listening consciousness is more suited to discerning these hidden presences. And like the musicians able to coax a tune from the acoustics of a situation, so can architects conjure stories from place. Just as we have seen with the art of storytelling, that the mode of consciousness employed in its creation is transferred to the listener applies equally to the work of architecture. We know that through the process of empathy, we experience the handprint on the clay vessel within the tissues of our own bodies. Bodies have a way of communicating with each other through these visceral traces. Tapping into this level of consciousness also serves to reinforce it. Our work has the capacity to open or close certain avenues, grooves and possibilities of sensory awareness to access memories of pleasure and pain, and to determine how and which stories get to be told.

Notes

1. John Dewey, *Experience and Nature* (New York: Dover, 1958), 170.
2. Jean Gebser, *The Ever-Present Origin* (Athens: Ohio University Press, 1984), 128.
3. Alberto Pérez-Gómez, *Attunement* (Cambridge, MA: MIT Press, 2016), 34.
4. Juhani Pallasmaa, *Encounters 1*, 2nd ed., ed. Peter McKeith (Helsinki: Rakennnustieto, 2012), 96.
5. Gaston Bachelard, *On Poetic Imagination and Reverie*, trans. Colette Gaudin (New York: Spring, 1987), 21.
6. John Keats, *Letters* 1:193.
7. Gaston Bachelard, *The Poetics of Space* (Boston: Beacon, 1994), 3.
8. May Sarton, "Of Havens," in *A Private Mythology* (New York: Norton, 1996), 66.
9. Charles Darwin, *Charles Darwin's Notebooks, 1836–44*, eds. Paul H. Barrett, Peter J. Gautrey, Sandra Herbert, David Kohn, and Sydney Smith (Ithaca: Cornell University Press, 1987), 564.
10. Gaston Bachelard, *Air and Dreams*, trans. Edith R. Farrell and Frederick Farrell (Dallas: Dallas Institute of Humanities and Culture, 1988), 7.
11. Ibid.
12. Gaston Bachelard, *Earth and Reveries of Repose*, trans. Mary McAllister Jones (Dallas: Dallas Institute, 2011), 89.
13. Gebser, *Ever-Present Origin*, 66.
14. Ibid., 126.
15. In their book, *The Complementary Nature*, J. A. Kelso and David A. Engstrom provide an empirically based investigation of complementary pairs in terms of coordination dynamics, a theory of the way human beings and human brains are coordinated. Their thorough survey of complementary pairs is a helpful study in this context.
16. Vincent Scully, *The Earth, The Temple and The Gods: Greek Sacred Architecture* (New Haven: Yale University Press, 1962), 6.
17. Paolo Vivante, *The Homeric Imagination: a Study of Homer's Poetic Perception of Reality* (Bloomington: Indiana University Press), 1970.
18. Scully, *The Earth, The Temple and The Gods*, 6.
19. Henri Corbin, "Mundus Imaginalis, the Imaginary and the Imaginal," *Spring* 19 (1972), 1–19.
20. Gottfried Semper, *The Four Elements of Architecture*, trans. Harry Francis Mallgrave and Wolfgang Herr (Cambridge: Cambridge University Press, 1989), 102–103.
21. Pérez-Gómez, *Attunement*, 102.

22. Aristotle, *Poetics* (1457), 6–9: 275.

23. George Lakoff and Mark Johnson, *Metaphors We Live By* (Chicago: University of Chicago Press, 2003; orig. 1980), 243.

24. Carl Jung, as quoted in Gebser, *Ever-Present Origin*, 400.

25. See Sarah Robinson, *Nesting: Body, Dwelling, Mind* (Richmond, CA: William Stout, 2011).

26. Colin St. John Wilson, "What is it Like 30 Years Later? An Assessment of Alvar Aalto's Work," *RSA Journal* 143, no. 5463 (Oct 1995), 52–62.

27. Pallasmaa, *Encounters 1*, 94.

28. Rudolph Arnheim, *The Dynamics of Architectural Form* (Berkeley: University of California Press, 1977), 209.

29. Bachelard, *Poetics of Space*, XVI.

30. Charles Moore and Donlyn Johnson, *Chambers for a Memory Palace* (Cambridge, MA: MIT Press, 1999), 30.

31. Tom Albright, "Neuroscience for Architecture," in *Mind in Architecture*, eds. Sarah Robinson and Juhani Pallasmaa (Cambridge, MA: MIT Press, 2015), 97–217.

32. Paul Shepard, *Encounters with Nature* (Washington, DC: Island Press, 1999), 53.

33. Ibid., 54.

34. Michel de Certeau, "Practices of Space," in *On Signs*, ed. Marshall Blonsky (Baltimore: Johns Hopkins, 1985), 124.

35. Joseph Rykwert, *The Idea of a Town: The Anthropology of Urban Form in Rome, Italy and the Ancient World* (Cambridge, MA: MIT Press, 1988), 162.

36. Ibid., 202.

37. Alva Noë, *Out of Heads: Why You are Not Your Brain, and Other Lessons from the Biology of Consciousness* (New York: Hill and Wang, 2009), 122.

38. Eric R. Kandel, *In Search of Memory: The Emergence of a New Science of Mind* (New York: W.W. Norton, 2007), 306.

39. Frances Yates, *The Art of Memory* (Chicago: University of Chicago Press, 1966), 16.

40. Donlyn Johnson, "The Place of Memory," in *Spatial Recall: Memory in Architecture and Landscape*, ed. Marc Treib (New York: Routledge, 2009), 65.

41. Ibid.

42. Bachelard, *On Poetic Imagination and Reverie*, 2.

43. See Robinson, *Nesting*, 49.

44. Michel de Certeau, *The Practice of Everyday Life*, trans. Steven Rendall (Berkeley: University of California Press, 1984), 108.

45. Ibid.

46. Eric Havelock, Interviewed by David Cayley for a CBC Radio series on "Orality and Literacy," in *Listen: The Newsletter of the Listening Centre* (Winter 1989/90, Toronto, Ontario).

47. Walter Benjamin, *Illuminations* (New York: Schocken Books, 1968), 88.

48. Walter Ong, *Orality and Literacy* (London and New York: Routledge, 2002), 77.

49. Benjamin, *Illuminations*, 89.

50. Ibid.

51. Ibid., 101.

52. Ibid., 92.

53. Kay Young and Jeffrey L. Saver, "The Neurology of Narrative," *SubStance*, 30, no. 1/2 (2001), 78.

54. Hannah and Antonio Damasio have found that empathy and compassion rely on biological processes that are inherently slow. See Guy Claxton, *Intelligence in the Flesh* (New Haven: Yale University Press, 2015), 280.

55. As quoted in Juhani Pallasmaa, *The Thinking Hand: Existential and Embodied Wisdom in Architecture* (Chichester: Wiley, 2009), 114.

56. See Klaske Havic, *Urban Literacy: Reading and Writing Architecture* (Rotterdam: nai010 Publishers, 2014).

57. Klaske Havic, "Terristories: Literary Tools for Capturing Atmospheres in Architectural Pedagogy," *Ambiances International Journal of Sensory Environment, Architecture and Urban Space*, Direction Générale des Patrimoines (2019).

This Lesser, Rebellious Field 10

The Spanish philosopher José Ortega y Gasset describes the decisive action that has come to define Western culture like this:

> The Graeco-Roman decides to separate himself from the fields, from 'nature,' from the geo-botanic cosmos. How is this possible? How can man withdraw himself from the fields? Where will he go, since the earth is one huge, unbounded field? Quite simple: he will mark off a portion of the field by means of walls . . . the public square. It is not like the house, an 'interior' shut in from above, as are the caves which exist in the fields. The square, thanks to the walls which enclose it, is a portion of the countryside which turns its back on the rest, eliminates the rest and is set up in opposition to it. This lesser, rebellious field, which secedes from the limitless one, and keeps all to itself, is a space *sui generis*.[1]

Walling off and narrowing one's focus inward created this space *sui generis* of Western culture, and the pivotal moment of this severance from the natural world was documented in Petrarch's celebrated letter. The chronicle of his hike up Mount Ventoux in Southern France may seem unremarkable today, but it is widely regarded to be the earliest account of someone climbing a mountain purely for pleasure.[2] And one can only write about an experience from the other side of it—the act itself implies a certain separation. Compelled by his overwhelming desire to see from its summit, the God's eye that opened before him upon his arrival filled him simultaneously with a sense of awe and foreboding of his newly emergent power. The letter is more a confession of transgression than an account of the scenery, but that definitive stepping into power marked the conscious moment that nature became Other. The "huge, unbounded field" became landscape—land literally cut off, *scraped*, from the rest. The spirited world of myth became dualised—polarities lost their energetic dynamism and became pitted against one another in opposition. Earth was no longer Mother, but the decisive Other, to be romanticised, dominated or dissected. Like Petrarch's view, human experience too was no longer within the world, but viewed from a vantage point outside of it.

The trajectory of this detached perception initially signalled in Plato's allegory was reinforced as humans were physically able to achieve new heights. Indeed, the spatial term 'achieving new heights' has come to be synonymous with progress and the ultimate goal of intellectual achievement. Plato's figurative ivory tower was eventually built of the actual stuff. Towers materialised what was once only imagined. "Architecture is always dream and function, expression of a utopia and instrument of convenience,"[3] writes Roland Barthes. In his essay on the Eiffel Tower, he points out that the vision from the tower was first intimated by Victor Hugo's description of the view from the steeple of Notre Dame 50 years before. Hugo was the tower's probe, conceiving in advance what the technology of the tower eventually afforded. Like Petrarch, Hugo understood the transformed vision of the newly available bird's-eye view. "The Tower is the only blind point of the total optical system of which it is the center and Paris the circumference."[4] This centre, for the first time, shows us a world not only to be merely perceived, but to be *read*. This vision elevated above the hurried sensations of the street permitted one to see things in their structure—it was the advent of a new category of perception that Barthes called "concrete abstraction."[5] For Barthes, the Eiffel Tower was a technology of perception allowing Paris to be read. Michel de Certeau also chronicles a view from on high, but his perch was the summit of New York's Twin Towers—and his critique begins from what that particular vantage point leaves out. To scale the towers is to feel the exhilaration of an all-seeing eye, yet from this position, forms can be seen in their structure, but not in their flesh.

> The city-panorama is a 'theoretical' (i.e. visual) simulacrum in short, a picture, of which the preconditions of feasibility are *forgetfulness and a misunderstanding of processes*. The seeing god created by this fiction . . . knows only corpses, must remove himself from daily behaviour and make himself a stranger to it.[6]

The detached perception afforded by Plato's ivory tower, Petrarch's summit, Victor Hugo's Notre Dame, Roland Barthes's Eiffel Tower and Michel de

Certeau's Twin Towers—in every case—reinforced the limits and constraints of that way of seeing, one that locates and determines the observer as well as the observed. Like Petrarch, whose perception unwittingly separated land-scape from land, the 'seeing god' separates the whole from the part which his view can encompass, and forgets the zones that lie adjacent, beyond or even behind. These technical processes created an omni-visual power in an eclipse of context from which we have yet to recover.

Abstracting

More than a century of the critique of vision has shown us that the faculty of seeing is not so clear. We simply cannot see form in its detached perfection—what we see is always mediated by something else. "No visible form is vis-ible enough,"[7] wrote Paul Valéry. Vision is unstable and interdependent and like imagination and memory is ecological, embodied and constructive. The ubiquitous expression 'seeing through the lens' of something when we want to understand another thing in its terms betrays the habit of thinking that interprets the world through an ever-narrowing aperture. J. J. Gibson already contrasted two basic visual practices: the visual world and the visual field. In the former, sight is ecologically intertwined with the other senses to gener-ate depth shapes, whereas in the latter, seeing is detached by fixating the eyes to produce the projected forms represented by means of perspective. Yet, the very idea that we can fix our vision to stabilise what we see in order to examine it analytically contradicts the physiology of vision. Vision is always crossed with the other senses and seeing itself is a matter of constant motion: the eye does its work by rapidly jumping from one briefly fixated point to another through what are known as saccadic movements. Seeing is inherently ecological, and the experience of seeing color is an exemplary case. The color blue that we see when we look at the sky, for example, is not a property exist-ing independently, but a dynamic interaction between the wavelengths in the electromagnetic spectrum reflected by objects, ambient lighting conditions, the colour cones in our retinas that absorb the corresponding wavelengths and the complex neural circuitry connected to those cones. The meanings and correspondences of colors to emotional states and cultural symbols further layer the situational character of seeing. This complex interplay lies behind Merleau-Ponty's observation that "color is where the brain and the universe meet."[8] As the process of color vision so characteristically demon-strates, seeing does not take place solely in the brain; it is an embodied, skill-based, exploratory activity.

What we see changes from moment to moment—we never see the same thing twice. Paul Valéry wrote:

> The objects about me are as *active* as the flame of a lamp. The armchair decays in its place, the table asserts itself so fast that it is motionless, the curtains flow endlessly away. The result is an endless complexity. To regain control of ourselves in the midst of the moving bodies, the circulation of their contours, the jumble of knots, the paths, the falls, the whirlpools, the confusion of velocities, we must have recourse to our grand capacity for forgetting.[9]

This capacity for forgetting is what abstraction evolved to accomplish. The sensory abundance of the world is so replete that we cannot possibly absorb it all. We must necessarily economise the resources of our attention. According to the neurobiologist Semir Zeki, vision obeys two 'supreme' laws: the law of constancy—"registering the constant and essential characteristics of objects" and the law of abstraction—"the process in which the particular is subordinated to the general, so that what is represented is applicable to many particulars."[10] Vision is an editing process honed over millennia tuned to what is meaningful in "the whirlpools, the confusion of velocities" that we take in at any given moment. This is why what we see is always a question of situated attention. This strategy, Zeki warns, is potentially costly—abstractions are not ends in themselves, but perceptual shortcuts that help us to navigate the complexities of life. An abstraction, after all, simply means leaving out part of the truth, as Whitehead so matter-of-factly reminds us. What we choose to cut out and what we choose to leave in has implications for what we see. Yet seeing is hardly a matter of choice. What we see is a matter of physiology, local ecologies, and deeply ingrained cultural values and habits. And, the technology that channels how we see in turn reinforces a certain way of seeing. We are always seeing through something else, but that something has only recently been confined to the circumference of a lens.

From Panoptics to Peripheral Vision

Vision has a dual structure—two pathways that attend to different kinds of visual cues. What is referred to as the 'where' pathway deals with the perception of motion, depth, spatial features, position, figure and ground segregation and has lower acuity—it is lightning quick, sensitive to contrast, but cannot see colors. The 'what' pathway specialises in recognising faces,[11] objects and colors.[12]

Without one kind of vision we miss high-definition details and without the other we lose salient meanings—we rely on the fluent integration of both kinds of vision. But we cannot attend to both kinds of vision at once. We cannot text while driving because the two activities call for two very different kinds of attention—one focused on the task, while the other involves more relaxed scanning, ever on the watch for impending perils. This is analogous to what the poet Jane Hirschfield observed about the exclusivity of certain sounds: "It is difficult to feel intimacy while shouting, to rage in a low whisper, to skip and weep at the same time."[13] The physiological differences in the function of the visual cells in the central cone cells and the peripheral rod cells yield two different kinds of perceptual awareness that serve discordant purposes. Some have compared the double structure of vision to the double structure of consciousness, correlating peripheral vision with preconscious and focal vision with conscious processes.[14] Peripheral vision excels in twilight conditions and registers movement without our conscious awareness, and because it is nearly impossible to shift our attention from the focus to the periphery, when we do, the forms appear vague, shapeless, unstable and highly suggestive to the imagination—and for this reason is important to creative endeavours. Anton Ehrenzweig called peripheral vision the "playground of our unconscious imagination"[15] for its flickering, elasticity, evasiveness and openness to imaginative infill.

The neurobiologist Margaret Livingstone suggests that peripheral vision more finely gauges emotion and nonverbal cues and is therefore important to determining whether someone is trustworthy. The high-resolution details that focused vision has evolved to detect are the surface features of the more pervasive, spontaneous body language in which motives are so often cloaked. Nervous twitches, hesitations, jaw tensing—all these micro-movements can be perceived with stunning accuracy by peripheral vision. An inordinately large number of the more than 600 muscles in our bodies happen to be located in the face. The high concentration here allows the subtlety of movements that finely articulate communication. Livingstone has shown how Mona Lisa's enigmatic smile, which seems to change when you shift position yet disappears when focused upon, was accomplished by using painting techniques that blur the facial muscles around her mouth. Leonardo da Vinci was able to capture the nuance of these movements about to happen by masterfully engaging peripheral vision.[16] Paul Cezanne was also preoccupied with capturing the act of seeing, and developed techniques that engaged perception in the process of movement. Rilke described Cezanne's artistic practice as continually "beginning at new center,"[17] perhaps because the shift towards the periphery enlarges the perceptual field to include the full range visual experience. The world of peripheral vision does not possess a fixed and orthodox centre; it is one in which each centre opens to another centre.

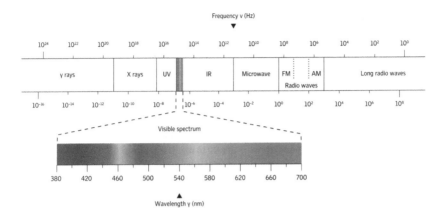

Image 10.1 Electromagnetic spectrum, a fraction of which is visible to the human eye

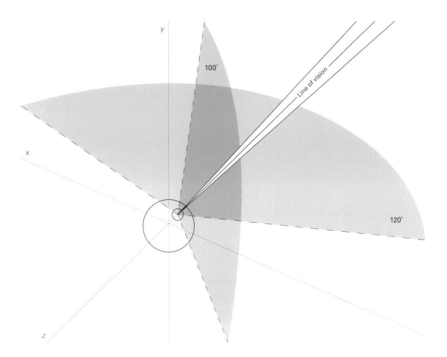

Image 10.2 Peripheral field of vision

The bandwidth of the visible on the electromagnetic spectrum is thin, and within that visibility the range of focused vision is narrower still. Yet, this is the knife-edge that has aligned human consciousness since the Renaissance. Juhani Pallasmaa critiques not only the overwhelming emphasis on vision to the exclusion of the other senses, but urges a reconsideration of sight itself. The bias towards centralised vision that took hold with the discovery of Renaissance perspective created architectural and urban settings that make us feel like outsiders because they impoverish our field of peripheral vision. "Peripheral vision integrates us with space, while focused vision pushes us out of the space, making us mere spectators,"[18] he insists. Research has since confirmed that architectural experience necessarily engages the entire visual field.[19] Focusing on the centre to the exclusion of life at the fringe fails to heed Semir Zeki's earlier warning that abstraction is potentially costly. Abstraction is an achievement gained in millennia of sifting, selecting and refinement. At its finest, abstract art distills the processes of perception to become itself an organ of perception. "In our abstract art there is a dramatic short circuit between its high sophistication and love of geometry on the one hand," writes Anton Ehrenzweig, "and an almost oceanic lack of differentiation obtaining in its matrix in the unconscious mind."[20] The complete critique of vision does not deny the achievements of focused vision, or discredit the vague certainties of the periphery—nor exclude the heat of street from the chill atop the tower. What is important is an approach, insists Jean Starobinski

> that knows how to demand, in their turn, distance and intimacy, knowing in advance that the truth lies not in the one or the other attempt, but in the movement that passes indefatigably from one to the other. One must refuse neither the vertigo of distance nor that of proximity; one must desire that double excess where the look is always near to losing all its powers.[21]

Learning From the Japanese Garden

Like the correlation between central and peripheral vision with two different varieties of consciousness, Alan Watts explained the differences between Western ways of thinking and Zen Buddhism by making the same parallel.[22] The reductive abstracting rationality so valued in the West does not share the same esteem in the Eastern way of thinking. Preference for fluidity, process and the value of intuitive knowledge subsumes the urge for fixed and singular points of view. The difference between the two approaches and styles of vision is evident in the comparative approaches to landscape design—the Renaissance axis is utterly alien to the Japanese garden that has no commanding central route, where space is deepened and comes alive through its veiling, obfuscation and layering that intentionally engage peripheral vision. Garden designers were routinely 'Renaissance men' who were painters, calligraphers, poets—and the close affinity between poetry and garden design developed a very precise vocabulary to articulate design methods that modulated emotion, imagination and mood. The Japanese word *fuzei*, for example, is written with the characters for *breeze* and *feeling*. *Fuzei* has a similar meaning to the German *stimmung*, with no exact counterpart in the English language— it means both 'feeling tone' and 'atmosphere' and refers simultaneously to the person experiencing the garden and the qualities of the garden that elicit that feeling. *Fuzei* suggests a poetic, qualitative approach to the way materials evoke a mood. The finely tuned awareness of the power of materials to evoke atmosphere frees the designer from simply reproducing features of the natural landscape in order to recreate the moods associated with them. The Zen tradition is rooted in Shinto animism, in which *kami* spirits were thought to reside in certain rocks, trees and aspects of flowing water. Japanese garden designers developed the skill to evoke the moods and feelings once thought to

Image 10.3 Ryoanji Temple Garden, Kyoto, Japan

Source: Photo Teo Romera.

reside in those special features through carefully tuning perceptual awareness through the use and arrangement of materials. The wealth and subtlety of the vocabulary used to describe and the skill to modulate mental states with design techniques testifies to the larger purpose of these gardens. Gardens were not intended for detached viewing, but for integrally engaging a shared consciousness.

The two main types of Japanese gardens, the stroll garden and the scroll garden, both involve and provoke movement. One unfurls through walking and the other through engaging the full range of vision—both were intuitively aware of the range and scale of human perception. The anthropologist Edward T. Hall who worked extensively in Japan called it a high-context culture and noticed how Japanese designers are more attentive to the influences of the direct environment, the scale of surfaces and texture relative to kinaesthetic awareness. This sensitivity is particularly evident in the garden where they stretch

> visual space by exaggerating kinaesthetic involvement . . . to watch his step as he picks his way along irregularly step stones . . . At each rock he must pause and look down to see *where to step next. Even the neck muscles are deliberately brought into play.*[23]

Oral cultures are also high-context cultures, meaning they rely on cues and practices embedded in the fabric of the environment for cultural order and meaning. Bodily actions belong to the fabric of context—the body is not abstracted out as a figure against a ground. The stroll garden was more recently developed in the context of the tea ceremony and worked like a promenade to prepare one's consciousness for the ritual of drinking tea. The scroll garden, like its Baroque counterpart, was intended to be viewed from a favoured position that would reveal 'a thousand trees' all at once. A key difference between the Baroque and scroll garden, which eludes to the different consciousnesses they intended to evoke, is that although the view was intended to be seen from a fixed point, *the view that was framed was not fixed.* The word for this kind of garden, *shakkei*, means 'to capture alive.' Lacking the compulsion to fix what they see, a splendid distant view is not enough, but must be *captured alive* and made a living part of the garden. The view thus perceived is animistic, not taxidermic. What is seen must remain alive like myth is alive—and in fact the word *capture* is used the way it is commonly used to say 'capture the imagination.' Imagination too, can only be captured *alive.* This is accomplished through the device of the middle ground, seeing through the trunks of trees is often the most common net used for capture.

Peripheral vision is carried along by the texture-laden motion of trees. One could compare this technique to the way da Vinci was able to portray Mona Lisa in the act of smiling. He captured her smile alive through obscuring the mouth edges and expressing the muscles of motion in the *sfumatura* that contextualises smiling; he portrayed her smile as an action, not as an image. As Ehrenzweig observed, "blurred plasticity is more important for the efficiency of vision than making precise shapes and patterns."[24]

Where the Baroque imagination compensated for Renaissance fixity with voluptuous fountains and lascivious figurines, their Japanese contemporaries found dynamism in restraint—engaging the imagination with what they left out. The most celebrated *shakkei* garden, Ryōnaji, is a meditation garden in Kyoto whose spare outcroppings of stone amongst a gravel sea has been a paragon for Western abstract minimalism. Japanese gardens abstract in a way that does not represent nature, but distills its action—involving you in the process. What appears to be negative space is not empty, but latently awaits fulfilment. It is, like the space *sui generis* that Ortega y Gasset described, a place that is walled in, yet the walls do not act to divide as much as they do to refine and concentrate. The walls of Ryōnaji delineate what Rilke called a "world-immanent space"[25] an intensification of a broader landscape. Much fuss has been made by art historians over the symbolism of the groupings of stone with little attention given to the space that the presence of the stones creates around them. When researchers studied the arrangement of the so-called empty space, they found that it is configured like the branching patterns of a tree.[26] The landscape architect and Japanese garden designer David Slawson has shown how the slightly elevated vantage point afforded by the wooden verandas of traditional architecture were exploited to accentuate a sense of movement between the ground and vertical and diagonal planes, which Rudolf Arnheim called the directed tension of a visual pattern.[27] What is more, the depth-to-width ratio of the vantage point on the veranda employs the same technique used in wide-screen cinematic projection by removing the frame of reference at the edges of the screen. They intuitively arrived at the exact viewing field that engages the full range of human vision, anticipating what is now routinely used in cinema by five centuries. Photographs convey nothing of Ryōnaji, because it engages the full range of animate vision. It refuses representation because it was designed to be experienced with living eyes.

The key difference between the abstraction of Ryōnaji and most of the idiom of minimalism as it is practiced today is that the former involves while the latter deprives. The perspective employed at Ryōnaji does not narrow but widens to include the natural history of human perception, relying on movement, shadow and suggestion in an intentional engagement of peripheral vision. The removal of the extraneous allows one to sense the subtle. The scene is carefully calibrated tension and texture, eliding the boundary between observer and observed—*observe* means 'to stand against,' and at Ryōnaji, one does not observe, but is integrally included in the scene. In this shared medium of consciousness, figure is not severed from ground. The means of abstraction retains some of the tissues of its becoming. "Abstraction becomes truly empty whenever it is dissociated from its unconscious matrix," wrote Anton Ehrenzweig. "It will then turn into a vacuous generalization. Empty generalisations can be handled with such facility because they have cut themselves loose from their anchorage in the deep."[28] Often the idiom of minimalism abstracts for the sake of abstraction, forgetting the nature of the achievement that abstraction actually is. Abstraction is the consequence of the series of sacrifices that preceded it. The sifting process that leads to the abstraction must necessarily leave variables out, but too often those variables lost to the process are critical to the vitality of the process itself. This results in surfaces shorn of handprints and polished of rust, chairs that cannot be sat upon, or in landscape design a monoculture of plants that are supposed to represent gravel and not the other way around. Barren minimalism excises form from the vital residues that gave it shape. The achievements of Cezanne and Rothko were distillations of the process of perception. They are liberations from form in the way that Japanese gardeners were freed from representation the minute they developed the skill to use their concrete materials to release the spirits once thought to reside in specific rocks and trees directly into human perceptual experience. Their paintings retained the tissue of its story of becoming within their frame. Ehrenzweig was optimistic about the potential for abstraction to open new depths of human experience. The key was to distill the full range of perceptual expression. "The close cooperation between precisely focused reasoning and almost totally undifferentiated intuition has, to my mind, made our time so abundantly creative, both in art and in science," he wrote. "A truly potent abstract concept has the same full emptiness."[29]

Framing

The point of abstraction in the case of Ryōnaji is to contain the multitudes in the one. The frame from which it is viewed is neither Petrarch's panorama nor a reductive reading of the text. It is a frame suited to the perceptual limits and potentials of human vision. When we think of architecture in terms of framing one's life, too often we refer to the finished tectonics of the frame—columns, doors and windows, rather than the desires, needs and actions from which those openings were born. The threshold of the door was an obsession to the ancient Greeks and its reverence was inherited by the Romans, and a vestige of this importance is still evident in Italy today. One cannot enter a space without saying *permesso*—a question asked at the threshold, asking permission to enter into another space. This courtesy that could be dismissed as an anachronistic formality vividly testifies to an earlier consciousness in which passages from the inside to the outside were of the utmost significance. Thresholds were time's spatial counterpart and were venerated because they were built reminders of the events that they once marked. Crossing the threshold was a reenactment, a remembering of those uncertainties in life that were made tolerable and manageable when appropriately framed by ritual acts that the material configuration of building was designed to support. But the rites of passage that thresholds embodied have all but disappeared from private and

Image 10.4 Brion Cemetery, Carlo Scarpa: entrance from public cemetery

Source: Photo Sarah Robinson.

Image 10.5 Brion Cemetery, Carlo Scarpa: syncopated stair, leaning tombs beyond

Source: Photo Sarah Robinson.

Image 10.6 Brion Cemetery, Carlo Scarpa: public chapel

Source: photo Sarah Robinson.

communal life, along their built counter forms. Walter Benjamin lamented the loss of the framing rituals, *rites de passage*—the designation in folklore for the ceremonies that mark birth and death, adolescence and marriage. "In modern life, these transitions are becoming ever more unrecognisable and impossible to experience. We have grown very poor in threshold experiences. Falling asleep is perhaps the only such experience that remains to us."[30]

Few experiences are more in need of rituals to honor them than the death of a loved one, and few architectural responses could be more poignant than Carlo Scarpa's Brion Cemetery in the Veneto region of Italy. The cemetery is an extension of a small town's graveyard built by the wife of a prominent industrialist in honour of her husband. Scarpa made his first trip to Japan while he was working on the project and the influence of his fascination with Japan is palpable. This memorial is a decentralised collection of places set in a contemplative garden—composed of tombs, chapel, meditation pavilion, pool and lawns for use by the public, and like a classical Japanese garden, the space between each distinct element is as important as the elements themselves. Each building element offers a counter form to support and even facilitate necessary cathartic actions—remembering, mourning, praying and imagining a possible future. The cemetery can be approached from multiple entryways—the principle entry frames two interlocking mosaic-framed circles. Scarpa referred to this approach as a *propylum*, the Greek term meaning 'that which is before the gates' and is customarily a grand platform of entry stairs. In Scarpa's hands, the sense of monumentality appropriate to the gravity of the place is achieved at a human scale. Three oversized, asymmetrically placed risers lead to a shaded threshold. The steps are more akin to geological formations at the entrance of a cave than a formal set of stairs. Once inside the entry, the accompanying drop in temperature and light initiates the first of many subtle shifts in consciousness enacted by this place. This is the threshold that Walter Benjamin carefully distinguished from a boundary. Where a boundary is a line that separates, the German word for threshold is *schwelle*[31] and the origin of the English verb *to swell*. The etymology of the word remains hidden in the ceremonial meaning of a threshold, which initiates a transformation, the rising of a powerful wave. Turning to the right, a darkened passage resonates with one's every footstep. Solid gradually gives way to liquid as the passage dissipates to square platforms—allowing one to briefly walk across a pool of water. Turning again to the left, the lotus-strewn pool opens towards a view of the spire of the San Vito d'Altivole church beyond the lawn. Below, and in front of the spire, is a shallowly arched bridge, sheltering two tombs beneath it. This nadir of the complex, accessed through descending four arched risers and shielded from direct light or rain, holds the tombs of husband and wife, placed so that they slightly lean into one another. Between and before them lies a basin of water, the culmination of a series of fountains and streams that quietly thread through the lawn. Water has long been an emblem of the passage of time, reflecting the ever shifting sky in its round frame, the basin poeticises this ephemerality.

The movement through the elements at Brion Cemetery is orchestrated with a delicacy of attention given to materials and views worthy of the ancient Japanese garden masters. As one steps down, one is accompanied by the gravitational flow of water. The stairs alternate between the smoothness of concrete and the calculated roughness of mosaic. One set of steps has irregular risers, forcing you to pay careful attention to an act that is typically taken for granted.[32] The disruption of our habitual use brings awareness to the living present. The jog in the stairs reminds one that time flows, but can also be interrupted. And from this rupture, the view of the nodding tombs is seen from the periphery. One's vision of death is thus aligned, not framed, by arrested movement. Another entrance leads through a concrete gate, leading to a chapel that does not rise from the earth, but from water. To enter the chapel, one must walk on water. The irregular steps are reminiscent of those in Japanese temple gardens, forcing one to engage the neck and abdomen to cross them. The heavy door through which one enters pivots lightly upon its hinges in a gesture of welcome. Once inside, the massive concrete walls are illuminated with full-length vertically stepped windows, opening on all sides to water. A bronze altar sits in an area rotated diagonally, lit through small square openings lined with alabaster and from a deep-set skylight above. The use of heavy walls penetrated with alabaster, adorned in mosaic and touches of gold, are reminiscent of the Galla Placidia in Ravenna not so far away, yet they are used with restraint, in a manner that looks towards the future. Elsewhere in the chapel, walls are patterned like Shoji screens and light has the effect of shining through a veil of paper. Downspouts are intentionally different lengths, terminating in pools or basins of stone, so that rainfall makes a subtle symphony. "Transcendence is immanent in life,"[33] wrote Georg Simmel. In this 'world immanent place,' the meaning of transcendence is envelopment. This place does not hide the instability of life, but affirms and gently emphasises it. The tombs enter their afterlife by honouring the passage of this life.

Thinking

The compassionate attention to detail, the respect for gravity of the low-lying walls and the shallow arched bridge—the only heroic vertical in the whole of Brion Cemetery is the spire of the church that lies beyond its walls. Even the walls that surround the compound lean inward, in a gesture of embrace. Brion Cemetery is the fruit of an entire lifetime spent discovering and honing his creative process, building trust with craftspeople, refining experience and the never-ending struggle to translate that lived depth into lived form. Some have lamented that Carlo Scarpa never had the opportunity to work on larger international projects, as if meaning were exclusive to scale, assuming—as is so common to do—that life exists more fully in what is commonly thought large. Such a sentiment completely misunderstands the nature of Scarpa's achievement. Where the large and the international are generally replicable and transferable, Carlo Scarpa worked in the very opposite direction. His work is rooted deeply in place, and the layers of exotic influences within it are rendered autochthonous in the crucible of his personal experience. His details are resolutions of local conditions that were arrived at and crafted from the embodied knowledge welling up in that place. The process of its creation comes through for those who experience it—one simply cannot race through a Scarpa work because the density of conscious effort that went into its realisation has the effect of thickening the atmosphere that is its fruition. The handprints on the clay vessel are left intact.

Like his built works, Scarpa's drawings were notoriously layered—he was the consummate craftsperson who thought through making. The drawings began with measured studies, the basis of his thinking process, that were then spun with sections, sketches, alternatives, inventive refinements, small views tucked in crevices. He overlaid drawing upon drawing until the accretion grew so dense that he sometimes resorted to painting over it with white tempera to begin anew, the rhythms of his vision slowly growing with each layer. The drawings thickened to absorb the sundry dimensions of his thinking—and were strewn with delicately lined comments, human figures, vining plants, wine stains, cigarette ashes and late nights, reminiscent of Pablo Neruda's "consummate poetry soiled by the pigeon's claw, ice marked, tooth marked, bitten delicately with our sweat drops and usage perhaps."[34] Scarpa's student and former associate Marco Frascari was convinced that the materials Scarpa used in his drawings—the sensual discrimination between the red of a red waxy pencil, the red of India ink or the red of an earthen brick—modulated his thinking process in a synaesthetic fusion of colour and meaning. "Architectural drawings then became metaphors, not in the literal meaning, but factually they are a *metaphorein*, a carry over, a moving sensory information from one modality to another modality, from one emotion to another emotion."[35] This joining of one sense with the perception of another sense, he goes on to say, "is the essence of architectural thinking."[36] In the impure poetry of sweat, and the oil of his fingerprints, the two dimensions of his drawings seemed to open to others in return for his patient effort, played without respite, they yielded their solacing surfaces, "shaped by the pride of the tool."[37]

Trained as an artist, with no formal education as an architect, Scarpa's drawings were art forms in and of themselves. And as we have seen, true art rarely stops at form but keeps on becoming. Drawing was not an imposition of an idea. Rather, ideas came from the act of drawing—he actively thought with his hands. Thinking is not something that goes on solely in our heads; we underestimate the extent to which thinking is very literally fleshed out through gesture. When children are asked to sit on their hands while they are speaking, for example, they are unable to articulate their fullness of their understanding. When deprived of gesture, the unfurling of their understanding is hampered.[38] And this gestural way of thinking did not stop when the drawings were completed. His drawings were not finalised when construction began—his open-ended embodied process of discovery continued on the jobsite. His lifelong relationships with blacksmiths, woodworkers, plasterers, glass blowers, masters of concretework were integral to the work. The process of designing and building was a confluence of this skilled embodied intelligence. Their skills were not only instrumental in executing the work, they were essential to the genesis of the work itself. Scarpa practiced in the long line of masters that included Brunelleschi and Michelangelo[39] who oversaw every detail of the construction process, from conception to implementation. Time spent on the construction site always opens new design alternatives that could never be planned or foreseen in advance. And like the old masters before him, he never made final decisions before the construction process began. Opportunities were seized and problems resolved in partnership with those who built the work, on the ground, while the work was in motion.

Improvisation

Thinking through making can be compared to the process of improvisational jazz, in which every performance is unlike any other, yet the variation and newness take place according to a certain set of rules implicit in the structure of the practice. We have seen how habit binds us to certain methods—and instilling those habits into our unconscious repertoire frees our energy for other pursuits. The grooves worn by habit are lined with the skills needed to move forward. For chess players, memorising the structure of openings and endgames allows the improvisation of the middle game. Scholars must master the research of their field, so they know what terrain remains untilled, and are able to recognise original work when it arrives. Artists and architects are no less constrained by what has preceded them. "Radical novelty is almost impossible," writes Alva Noë, "if we were to stumble upon it, it would take unusual strength and power to see anything of value in it."[40] The challenge faced in making something novel is that to be comprehensible, it must already exist. The truly new could not be recognised, because we have no grounds of making sense of it. What distinguishes an improvised jazz performance is that it manages to do something surprisingly new within a highly structured and conventional scheme. *Improvise* comes from two words—*unforeseen* and *provide*. The process itself provides unforeseen openings, as often happens on the musical stage, the drawing board or the construction site—but the key to this dawning possibility is openness. Our freedom is tempered by the limits of the craft. The embodied skills and practices of architecture are the woof and weave through which improvisation enters, yet the creative process, as we have discussed in the case of Carlo Scarpa, is enriched the longer it remains open. The beginning of the creative process is a wide-rimmed funnel, open to all input, in which simultaneously competing demands mix and meld. The field of the possible narrows through the mind and body of concentration until the intensified work ripens at the other end. The longer the wide rim stays open, the more opportunity the softer, gentler and deeper influences have to make their claims. Anton Ehrenzweig argued that an open scanning process, synonymous with the perception of peripheral vision, was crucial to the creative process.

> Ambiguity prevents a preconceived idea from setting hard too early. Keeping the final realisation of an idea wide open allows the artist whole range of his sensibilities and his whole personality while he struggles with a flexible and unformed vision.[41]

When we are at the funnel's helm, we are not on the lookout for results, but flexibly vigilant for the provision of the unforeseen. Gertrude Stein describes the process in terms of writing:

> You will write, if you will write without thinking of the result in terms of a result, but think of the writing in terms of discovery, which is to say that creation must take place between the pen and the paper . . . It will come to you if it is there and if you will let it come, and if you have anything you will get a sudden creative recognition.[42]

Yet it is far easier for a writer to speak of her craft, because the means of thinking, whether through pencil or pen or laptop, directly indicate the outcome of that thinking. Architects are in a curious position because our means of thinking and the fruit of that thinking take place in entirely different mediums, and at utterly different scales.

Nature of the Medium

Scarpa's drawings were isomorphic with his buildings because of the nature of the medium he used for their expression, and the improvisatory style that pervaded his entire process of making. The medium of drawing, its historical accessibility, its conventions and tools of inscription allowed a way of thinking that was tentative and forgiving; "its solacing surfaces" were amenable to erasures, yet retained a vague impression of what went before. One thinks differently in different mediums because of the nature of their histories, densities and resistances. One must surrender oneself to the medium, as the craftsperson must surrender herself to the veining of the wood. Certain mediums are more allowing of the flexibility of the creative process than others. Two factors that predominate this interaction are the relative closeness of the medium to the body, and possibility to see a direct result of our actions. When playing the violin, for example, its sound immediately tells us whether the movement that made it was worth repeating or not. The same can be said for the tennis racquet, golf club, skateboard, paintbrush or pen. In these cases, the "thorniest suavities shaped by the pride of the tool" make themselves immediately known. When we write with our laptop, pressure on the keys produces words that we can immediately see or hear. And those same words may eventually reach the mind of the reader through a similar means. When we draw on a computer, the lines that appear on the screen make no sense unless they are understood in terms of their context and the complexities of how they are constructed. The long chain of their becoming form ultimately results in a material surface or thing experienced by someone else's body. Yet, even with hand drawings, this virtuality is still present. The difference is that the hand is involved in a way that directly touches the line, leaving at least a trace of materiality. For artists, on the other hand, their medium immediately informs them of what they can and cannot do according to the character of its resistances. Yet, the architect must imagine these resistances either extrapolating from our own memories of places, or from the rich ore of experiences accrued in our bodies. The pushback that matter asserts is often not encountered until much later—gliding through the space of a computer screen, we do not become aware of what is lost in the abstraction until it is often too late, and so the architect does not reach her prime until much later in life. Each project is a learning experience for the next one and since the forces of gravity play so heavily in our craft, the profession demands an extraordinarily long time to ripen.

Scarpa's erasure marks, etchings, iterations left on the page are evocative of a walk through an old Italian city, half-buried arches left framed in new coats of plaster, the tracings and gestures all have their say, each embodies the history of the process. This accrual and spontaneity are what is lost in the computer—the difference in the media suits them for two different purposes. Drawing is a fluid means to discover and the computer is a precise means of documenting that discovery. They both speak a language: the first is akin to the language of poetry, the second to the language of specification. You cannot start a poem or a drawing knowing where it is going to end, but you execute a computer drawing precisely so that you can specify that end. The powerful possibilities of digital tools to convey our design intentions are unquestionable, but their limitations need to be critically considered and compensated for by other modes of representation. Some have used narrative and storytelling, comic strips, film, dance, performance art and ceremony, while others emphasise watercolour and sculpture. Methods of direct contact between body and building, intensity and effect, action and matter are fundamental to fully fleshing out the process of design, which always transfers to the mind and bodies of those who experience the work.

The Bottom-Up/Top-Down Dialectic

Another difficulty in the process of design is that we create the paths, grooves, surfaces and flows of people's lives from the vantage point of above. Looking down at our drawings as if they were maps is exactly the viewpoint from which we started this discussion—one that bestows the incomparable power of *intellection*, giving us the world to *read* and not only to perceive. Yet, the places we create from that vantage point can only ever be 'read' from a viewpoint that doesn't exist to the inhabitant, in a perceptual mode that is simply inadequate to the whole-body manner in which the work will actually be experienced. The preconditions of feasibility of such a starting point are *forgetfulness and a misunderstanding of processes.* Inscrutable from this vertiginous position are the arabesques of gesture, the paths worn by habit, the textures of speech, the not-so-hidden iceberg of language of which the written word is its tip. The panoptic eye created gridiron blocks that are not named but numbered and Hausmann's boulevards designed for the march and not for the stroll. We now know that there is no view from nowhere for even the most 'detached' observer. This vantage point biases not only a certain way of seeing, but a whole array of behaviours, thinking, cultural habits, economic values and policy decisions.

Rudolph Arnheim distinguished two different organisational approaches: one that begins from the top looking down and one that begins from below. In top-down approach, the overall schema determines the individual variables while the latter balances the individual variables that strive for dynamic equilibrium within the whole. The top-down approach dominated Western architectural history; for the classical Greeks and Romans and their Renaissance and neoclassical apologists, the system of proportions, gables and architraves, the columns and bases had their preestablished place and character that was ordered 'from above.' In the bottom-up method, the grand plan does not dictate, but the relation between the elements is primary. For Arnheim, this approach is exemplified in the Gerritt Rietveld house in Amsterdam, where each element derives its character from its unique capacities and requirements: it can serve some purposes, is unsuitable for others, needing certain conditions in order to function, and the pattern of the whole arranges itself on the basis of these characteristics. The sensible whole is achieved through ordering individual relations. This approach weighs the delicate balance and the rhythmic interrelation of elements—the independent integrity of each element leads to the "dissolution of the compact mass."[43] Like musical improvisation, each player contributes her unique sound and disposition to the overall weave in a spirit of collective cooperation rather than hierarchical imposition—a *modus vivendi* rather than an overarching *modus operandi*. This approach is the one that underlies Scarpa's work as well as the organisational method employed in the Japanese garden.

Heir to the legacy of Platonic ideal, the top-down approach has shaped Western culture and determined the approach to design we continue to take for granted, one that haunts us each time we impose a prefixed plan conceived in the pretence of our individual minds. Yet, this is not the only way. The Japanese have nothing that corresponds to the Platonic idea, and they have never developed the dichotomy between the world of matter and the world of ideas.[44] Another often misunderstood characteristic that bears on the difference between the two design approaches is that in Japanese, the word for 'self,' *jibun*, is not an isolated agent but implies a share of something which is both separate and not separate and both individual and shared, which is far more complex than the easy generalisation that Japanese culture does not value the individual. The integrity of individual elements in dynamic equilibrium characteristic of the design approach of the Japanese garden and Scarpa's Brion Cemetery seem to share this polyvalent sense of identity. And in this suppleness, the pressure on the hypertrophic ego to stamp the design with individuality is not an issue. Individualisation is an achievement, but not an end in itself. "Individual self-expression has turned into another social convention," Anton Ehrenzweig complained.

> If we were to formulate a new maxim today that could replace the platitude of free self-expression, it would be the opposite demand. Instead

of straining too hard to discover his inner self, the student should objectively study the outside world.[45]

Compensating for the inevitable use of computer design with embodied methods of discovery, while turning one's attention outward to the concrete variables of the situation, patiently listening to its latent sounds and stories, sensing its currents of feeling, its shifting winds and mutating waters—discerning desires that are not yet spoken, making that place autochthonous through the efforts of sustained attention and patient endurance—these are ways to recover from the dizzying vertigo that has so impoverished our culture.

Notes

1. José Ortega y Gasset, *The Revolt of the Masses*, anonymous translation (New York: W.W. Norton, 1932), 164.
2. See Gebser, page 12 where he insists that Petrarch discovered the landscape as the moment when "the isolated part becomes a piece of land *created* by his perception." The letter is widely considered to be the first evidence of environmental writing.
3. Roland Barthes, *The Eiffel Tower and Other Mythologies*, trans. Richard Howard (Berkeley: University of California Press, 1997), 6.
4. Ibid., 4.
5. Ibid., 9.
6. Marshall Blonsky, ed., *On Signs* (Baltimore: Johns Hopkins, 1985), 124.
7. Geoffrey Hartman, *The Unmediated Vision* (New York: Harcourt, Brace and World, 1966), 112.
8. Maurice Merleau-Ponty, "The Eye and the Mind," in *Maurice Merleau-Ponty Basic Writings*, ed. Thomas Baldwin (London: Routledge, 2004), 312.
9. Paul Valéry, *The Collected Works of Paul Valéry*, Vol. 8, trans. Malcolm Cowley (Princeton: Princeton University Press, 1972), 25–26.
10. Semir Zeki, "Artistic Creativity and the Brain," *Science* 293, no. 5527 (2001), 51–52.
11. Although, as Livingstone insists, this "where" pathway is limited in its capacity to detect more subtle movements.
12. Margaret Livingstone, *Vision and Art: The Biology of Seeing* (New York: Abrahms, 2014), 118–128.
13. Jane Hirshfield, *Nine Gates: Entering the Mind of Poetry* (New York: HarperCollins, 1997), 54.
14. Thinkers such as Anton Ehrenzweig, Alan Watts, Martin Jay and Juhani Pallasmaa have correlated peripheral vision with creativity and the unconscious mind.
15. Ehrenzweig, Anton, *The Psycho-Analysis of Artistic Vision and Hearing* (London: Routledge, 1953), 206.
16. Livingstone, *Vision and Art*, 81–83.
17. Rainer Maria Rilke, *Letters on Cézanne*, trans. Joel Agee (New York: Fromm, 1985), 36.
18. Juhani Pallasmaa, *The Eyes of the Skin* (London: Wiley, 1996).
19. Kevin Rooney, Robert Condia, and Lester Loschky, "Ambient Processing of Built Environments: Intellectual and Atmospheric Experiences of Architecture," *Frontiers in Psychology* 8, no. 326 (2017), 1–20.

20. Anton Ehrenzweig, *The Hidden Order of Art: The Psychology of the Artistic Imagination* (Berkeley: University of California Press, 1971), 129.
21. Jean Starobinski, *L'Oeil Vivant: Essais* (Paris: Gallimard, 1961), 26.
22. Alan Watts, *The Way of Zen* (New York: Pantheon, 1957).
23. Edward T. Hall, *The Hidden Dimension* (New York: Anchor Books, 1969), 62.
24. Ehrenzweig, *Hidden Order*, 29.
25. As quoted in Jean Gebser, *The Ever-Present Origin* (Athens: Ohio University Press, 1984), 411.
26. Gert J. Van Tonder, Michael J. Lyons, and Yoshimichi Ejima, "Visual Structure of a Japanese Zen Garden," *Nature* 419 (2002).
27. David Slawson, *Secret Teachings in the Art of Japanese Gardens* (New York: Kodansha, 1987), 99.
28. Ehrenzweig, *Hidden Order*, 129.
29. Ibid.
30. Walter Benjamin, *The Arcades Project* (Cambridge, MA/London, UK: The Belknap Press of Harvard University Press, 1982/1999), 494.
31. Ibid.
32. Andrea Jelić, Gaetano Tieri, Federico De Matteis, Fabio Babiloni, and Giovanni Vecchiato, "Neurophysiological Perspective on Embodiment, Motivation and Affordances," *Frontiers in Psychology* 31 (2016).
33. Georg Simmel, *The View of Life: Four Metaphysical Essays with Journal Aphorisms*, trans. John A. Y. Andrews and Donald N. Levine (Chicago: University of Chicago Press, 2010), 9.
34. Pablo Neruda, "Towards an Impure Poetry," in *Five Decades: Poems 1925–1970*, trans. Ben Bellitt (New York: Grove, 1977), 7.
35. Marco Frascari, "Architectural Synaesthesia: A Hypothesis on the Makeup of Scarpa's Modernist Architectural Drawings," at: http://art3idea.psu.edu/synesthesia, 7.
36. Ibid., 3.
37. Neruda, "Towards an Impure Poetry," 7.
38. Guy Claxton, *Intelligence in the Flesh* (New Haven: Yale University Press, 2015), 177.
39. S. Catitti, "Michelangelo as Archon of the Tectones: The Laurentian Library: Patronage and Building History," in *San Lorenzo: A Florentine Church*, eds. R. Gaston and L.A. Waldman (Florence: Villa I Tatti, 2017), 389.
40. Alva Noë, *Out of Our Heads* (New York: Hill and Wang, 2009), 124.
41. Ehrenzweig, *The Hidden Order of Art*, 145.
42. As quoted in Hirshfield, *Nine Gates: Entering the Mind of Poetry*, 37.
43. Rudolph Arnheim, *The Dynamics of Architectural Form* (Berkeley: University of California Press, 1977), 197.
44. Iain McGilchrist, *The Master and his Emissary* (New Haven: Yale University Press, 2009), 452.
45. Ehrenzweig, *The Hidden Order of Art*, 142.

The Soil of the Sensible **11**

Rather than looking down at our drawings from above, or straight ahead of us at a screen—let us shift directions and listen to the words of a poet:

> Imagine walking down a city street, distracted, hurrying, hot, and see-ing, in the mass of people about a half a block ahead, a friend. From a glimpse of dark hair and perhaps the dipping motion of a shoulder, how easy it is to recognise a person we know amid the rest.[1]

That all-at-once spontaneous moment of recognition, that sudden wrinkle in an otherwise amorphous sea—and the accompanying sense of affection and delight—completely shifts our mood. This is not a rarified event, but one that happens all the time. The inimitable "dipping motion of a shoulder" that imme-diately individuates the figure from the teeming crowd is a prime example of what Merleau-Ponty called the "the soil of the sensible."[2] That spontaneous gesture is not an abstraction of movement—it is more innocent and more fresh. It communicates wordlessly through a richly woven fabric of shared movement and affection. It is primordial in the sense that it belongs to a primary order, and the word *order*, let us remember, comes from 'to begin to weave.' We recognise our friend because we share a history both as individuals and as humans and that mutuality has woven an invisible tissue between us—if not, how can you explain how the minimal suggestion of a "a glimpse of dark hair" differentiates your friend? That same instantaneous recognition is also sometimes present when we hear a certain voice, or breathe in a particular scent:

> When a sound or a scent once sensed and long inhaled—at once pres-ent and past, real and not just factual, ideal, not yet abstract—come to

life again, the enduring and the hidden essence of things is soon liberated, and our true, seemingly long expired Self awakens reanimated by the heavenly nourishment that infuses it. A minute, free from the order of time, has, so that we may feel it, recreated the human in us free from the order of time.[3]

Proust muses about a kind of recognition which precedes us, the scent or gesture that singularly allows a glimpse into something deeper, something free from the order of time.

Integration

The poets' testimony to the power of gesture and scent to trigger deeper dimensions of consciousness exemplifies poetry's prerogative to reveal multiple layers of reality simultaneously. Poetry transports us in a seemingly effortless way (a feat only achieved with a tremendous amount of effort), to a fullness underlying that which we take for granted every day. Awareness of the integration of multiple layers of consciousness in the present moment was Gebser's ultimate intention: the cohesion of the archaic, the resonance and making of magic, the dreams and memories of myth, the abstraction and systematisation of the mental—functioning together in a shared weave. *Integrate* means 'to make whole' and comes from the root *tangere*, like the words *tangible* and *touch*, and *integer*, a whole number, not a fraction. Integers include both whole numbers and their negative counterparts—which are equally as powerful as their positives. The foundational layers of consciousness operate with the power of the negative numbers, from the other side of the visible ledger. Gebser was gravely concerned that the one-sided rationality that tears apart—imprisoned in its ever-narrowing focus while racing towards an ever-expanding frontier, and dangerously compensated with regression into irrational and anachronistic political structures—could only be overcome with a new kind of consciousness. He was not alone in warning of the implications of these dangerous tendencies, and his strategy for integration had two main features: the first was to stop fighting against time—he called it integrating time as the fourth dimension, and the second was to open to multiple ways of knowing, which he called aperspectivity. Perspective is to see from one point of view, and as we know, our perspective determines what is able to be seen, how we make sense of it, and what our probable actions and valuations might be. By aperspectivity, Gebser did not intend the opposite of perspective, but an envelopment of perspective, a simultaneous awareness of all sides at once.

To finally lose the lens and see with your whole body. This was what Picasso and the Cubists were trying to achieve. And, the contemporary interest in atmospheres is heading in this same inclusive direction. Integration meant the supersession of duality across disciplines, the recognition of the integration of mind and body, space and time, subject and object—and as Dewey said, "integration is an achievement rather than a datum."[4]

In terms of language, integration means that a word is an atmosphere, a gesture, a sound, an image, a concept and a mutating historical artefact—all at once. In literature, integration was apparent in Virginia Woolf's sovereign command of time, in James Joyce's rerooting of language in its archaeological past and in Marcel Proust's bottomless memory. Gebser was also a keen critic of architecture and pointed to the supersession of three-dimensional space in Frank Lloyd Wright's Fallingwater, its embrace of cyclical time and rootedness in place, its integration of the right angles of human experience in a forest setting. He also acknowledged Hans Scharoun's Berlin Philharmonic as an integration of audience and performers in mutual attunement between person and place, as we discussed in Chapter 6.[5] And while the achievements of these works are without question, the occasion to design a philharmonic or launch a luxury residence over a waterfall are increasingly rare. While the distinction of extraordinary belongs obviously to these works, I want to direct our attention back to where we started this chapter—the revelatory richness of the most nonchalant gesture and the time-imploding curvature of a certain sound—to not take for granted that life exists more fully in what is commonly called small. "Only the concrete can be integrated, never the merely abstract,"[6] insisted Gebser. That the concrete particulars of ordinary experience are abundantly available to all should make them no less worthy of our design attention and skill.

Inhabiting

Our habitat—the matrix of our daily habits—does not recognise distinctions between natural and cultural domains. It is a word that evokes a texture of associations that we share with other animals. And we have seen over the course of this study just how we have gradually abstracted ourselves from this living matrix. In its immunity to exclusivity, *habitat* and its verb *inhabit* directly challenge "a thinking which looks on from above and thinks of the object-in-general" and is more able to situate us in the "'there is' which precedes it . . . the soil of the sensible and humanly modified world, this primordial historicity,"[7] as Merleau-Ponty wrote. The coming-to-terms with the primordial historicity is more fittingly captured in the verb *inhabit*. Unlike the verb *dwelling*, inhabiting aligns with the messy processes of becoming, and because it does not pretend to abide in a transcendent being, is unburdened with a hopeless nostalgia. Nostalgia comes from the Greek *nostas*—meaning 'place,' and *algia*, meaning 'pain.' Nostalgia is the pain of being torn from a place. Inhabiting deals with the pain of being torn by constantly weaving—and does not understand the world as something into which we have been thrown, but knows it as one into which we have been born, a world whose constant becoming we join in making and tending. Inhabiting does not see fragments and shards, but torn threads in need of mending, and accepts that mending is an activity that is never-ending.

Eating

Dignifying the ordinary is something available to all. If it is true that "setting determines gestures,"[8] as André-Franck Concord insisted, the shared meal is an elemental starting place. The act of eating is a prime example of what Rudolph Arnheim called the spontaneous symbolism of practical experience[9] and echoes Dewey in his lament that the integrated life of civilisation is torn asunder when practical activities of daily life—walking, eating, bathing, sleeping, cleaning, being bored, gardening, exploring and making things—are shorn of their symbolic connotations and resonances. The mind/body 'problem' that has plagued Western civilisation is irresolvable when the meaning of these daily actions is reduced to their strictly physical function on the one hand and the principles that govern them are reduced to abstract concepts on the other. "The most important cognitive virtue of a civilisation probably consists in the working interrelation between practical physical activity and so-called abstract thought,"[10] wrote Arnheim. The architect can contribute to healing this age-old breach when she succeeds in "reinforcing deep-seated spiritual connotations inherent in all the simple aspects of domesticity."[11] Eating is so thoroughly laden with symbolism that we can approach it as a primal metaphor for architectural experience. The passage of food from the outside to inside through the portal of the mouth, the flesh and fluids shared, the sacrament of bread and wine, commemorates this primal unity. The table around which we sit is already storied with layers of cultural memory. In *A Pattern Language*, Christopher Alexander and his colleagues examine the design features which contribute to the pattern of eating.

"Without communal eating, no human group can hold together,"[12] they insist. The tendency to mark and sanctify important events with a shared meal is prominent across cultures. Thomas Merton points out that

> the feast is of such a nature that it draws people to itself and makes them leave everything else in order to participate in its joys . . . the mere act of eating together, quite apart from a banquet or some other festival occasion, is by its very nature a sign of friendship and of 'communion.'[13]

This sharing and the social bonds strengthened by it are important not only in domestic settings, but in the workplace and larger community as well.

The atmosphere of the meal is as important as the food that is shared. The importance of the emotional ambiance in which eating takes place is further reinforced by the growing body of research on the enteric nervous system. Referred to as a second brain, the enteric nervous system consists of the 500 million neurons embedded in the gastrointestinal system that not only manage digestion but have been correlated with depression, autism and immune response.[14] Alexander highlights the importance of lighting in creating the atmosphere of the meal[15] and the subtle dynamics of the sitting area to create the optimal conditions for conversation and conviviality.[16] In my own experience, I have noticed that because eating is both a social activity, and also an intimate one involving the sensitive area of the mouth, creating a truly congenial setting for the meal involves orchestrating a sense of protection and a sense of openness—and pivots around the tensions of the prospect/refuge polarity. A seating area allows one to completely relax and let one's guard down when it works like an eddy in a stream, a place not isolated from a larger area, but sheltered from its turbulence. Rivers flow and eddies form—an eddy is a "standing-streaming."[17] Guarding the back, particularly its sensitive extremes, the neck and lumbar area offers a calming sense of refuge. Protection at the back and opening in the front is an axis of deep pleasure, a configuration that affords a memorable meal. An archetypal example of this can be found in the ruins of Hadrian's villa for his guests. The dining area is curved and solid at the back while opening out to a long reflecting pool. The meal is a coming together of the elements: fire for cooking, water for drinking, the substance of flesh, the aromas of the atmosphere and their alchemical transformation in making the meal. Paying attention to these intimate particulars need not be viewed as a fall from architecture's metaphysical calling. On the contrary, architecture's highest aspiration is

Image 11.1 Eating area: Sarah Robinson, architect

Source: Courtesy Technical Imagery Studios.

Image 11.2 Student lounge, Porto School of Architecture: Alvaro Siza, architect

Source: Photo Sarah Robinson.

to create a sense of human homecoming as Aldo Van Eyck insisted, and memorably added:

> Space has no room and time has not a moment for man . . . Whatever space and time mean, place and occasion mean more. For space in the image of man is place, and time in the image of man is occasion.[18]

A meal is a necessity that can fill a void or an occasion for creativity and communion. In creating the conditions for this occasion, architects have the opportunity to mend the threads of weakened experience.

Sleeping

Sleeping is necessary to life, and once pondered, is anything but ordinary. Just as every day is followed by a night, waking consciousness is followed by dream consciousness in an interdependence of rhythm. Rituals mark liminal passages. *Limen* means 'threshold,' and crossing the threshold from waking to dreaming is among the most mythical of transformations, and it takes place daily. The ritual of sleep, as Walter Benjamin reminds us, is one of the few rituals left to us. Our cycles of consciousness entrain with the lightness and darkness of our rotating planet. Our entire organism is tuned to this rhythm— and in the time span of human history, it is only recently that we have lost the darkness of night that patterned the cycles of sleeping and waking. The human eye contains a novel photoreceptor that uniquely senses the blue/violet wavelengths of the light spectrum. Our eyes evolved not just for seeing; our retina also contains non-cone, non-rod receptors that absorb twilight, which signal our brain to entrain with the cycling of day and night.[19] Chronobiologists study the physiological, biochemical and behavioural synchronisation to light that we share with all other plants and animals. Circadian timing is an integral feature in the biochemistry of our cells; our endochrine levels delicately tune to the shifting cycles of day and night and their disruption is correlated with sleep disorders, breast and prostate cancer, and infertility.[20]

Prior to industrialisation, humans experienced dark nights and bright, broad-spectrum days. Unlike artificial light, sunlight varies in intensity, spectral content and timing over the course of a day. In contemporary life, we spend most of our time indoors, and consequently receive on average less than two hours of sunlight per day. Yet evidence clearly indicates that the light needed for vision and the light that regulates circadian rhythms are clearly different. Electrical lighting in buildings is designed for visual performance and not for the maintenance of endocrine rhythms. Not enough natural light during the day and too much artificial light during the night disrupts circadian rhythms and sleep cycles. What this entails is that we cannot sleep just anywhere—like plants and other animals, the biochemistry of our cells entrain to the cycles of darkness and light. The neurobiology of sleeping suggests that the nightly ritual of sleep has certain requirements: a quiet and darkened room, a place of refuge for the body and protection for the back,

Image 11.3 Sleeping area: Sarah Robinson, architect

Source: Courtesy Cortili Photo, Milan

head and neck that honours our deeper animal past. The quality and direction of natural light needs to be considered in every situation, but most carefully in terms of where sleeping will take place. Waking to eastern sun has long been considered a fortuitous alignment to greet the day. Proust famously slept and worked in his cork-lined bedroom. Cork is among the most humane materials for its porous resemblance to skin, its capacity to regulate temperature and absorb reverberation, dust and allergens. I prefer to line bedroom ceilings with cork, not only for its ability to soften sound, but also because it is lush to look at while lying down.

Being Bored

The verb *boring* is different from being bored, a distinction that is hidden in the origin of the word itself. The verb *bore*, like the verb *pore*, is rooted in the word for 'opening.' To bore is to drill a hole, to perforate, and is the past tense of *bear*, as in bearing a child. "In the beginning was boredom,"[21] wrote Kierkegaard. How one deals with this openness that is a basic feature of life defines to what extent they are boring. To be boring is to numb the pores of experience with a constant stream of stimulus that stifles the eruption of that ever-present openness. Being bored is allowing the openness at the heart of life to intrude on one's routine in its own due course—to tolerate the sense that nothing is happening, even when it might be, but at a slower pace, in a softer voice or in a form that has not yet fully ripened. Bertrand Russell was also convinced that the capacity to endure boredom was necessary to a happy life and is one of the most basic things that should be taught to the young. And indeed, childhood is the ground in which boredom can, if allowed, truly flourish. Doing nothing necessarily precedes doing something; the most spontaneous invention comes from the condition of boredom. The 'mindless' activities of playing, puttering, whittling, tinkering, weaving, spinning that are the web of storytelling came from an era in which time was not yet equated with money, or understood as a container that needed to be constantly filled. "To ward off boredom at any cost is vulgar,"[22] declared Nietzsche. To fill a child's hands with cell phones and their minds with a constant stream of brightly coloured, fast-action video games is to clog these openings. Rather than whining of boredom as a state from which to escape, it can potentially be a way to rest. Perhaps the "windless calm"[23] or "nondescript cotton wool"[24] of boredom should be regarded as the other face of mental engagement. "If sleep is the apogee of physical relaxation, boredom is the apogee of mental relaxation,"[25] wrote Walter Benjamin. Indeed, one cannot possibly go without sleep, so what makes us think that mental exhaustion does not have its rejuvenating counterpart?

The same distinction between being boring or being bored can equally be applied to architecture. Boring architecture is ubiquitous—ill-proportioned post-war apartment blocks with no surface relief, anodyne suburban plots and glaring glass skyscrapers all have the effect of numbing human experience. Their repetitiveness derives from a shortsighted desire to cut costs or from the pressure to conform, which makes them tedious in the most vulgar sense. There is another kind of repetitiveness that yields a rhythmic sense of continuity, like being bored in its most generative connotation. In the town of Pavia, Italy, where I live, most of the buildings are uniform in their material use. They are mostly brick, worn off over the centuries, and the windows are more or less evenly proportioned and spaced. The difference is that each expression has been allowed to follow its own course, to be bored in its own time and not demolished and made new. This layering imparts a sense of harmony to the whole that respectfully relates to the others. This exercise in restraint tolerates gaps in which life can enter. This milieu seems to obviate the need to deliberately shock, which is another form of warding off boredom at any cost. Too often the insatiable thirst for novelty becomes just another routine dulling the recognition of the extraordinary when it does finally arrive to ruffle the windless calm.

Walking

We know the world through the mind of our feet. The more than 200,000 nerve endings in the soles of our feet act as antennae to proprioceptively attune body and surface. Our feet are ticklish because they are so highly sensitive—it is remarkable that an organ so finely tuned is precisely the one that enables the most rugged and enduring use. If you live until you are 80 years old, you will likely have walked an average of 110,000 miles—four times the circumference of planet Earth. Like eating and sleeping, walking is not only a vital function, but a way of knowing—one that puts us in contact with our surroundings, whether a lush forest, a mountain hike or a pulsating urban street, immersively and omni-directionally. Walking engages six dimensions of awareness—the four directions, plus up and down. The pace of walking is regulated by the length of our legs, the topography of surfaces, the air that we breathe into our lungs—and this thickened tempo has long been the basis of aesthetic, spiritual, environmental, urban and political practices. Michel de Certeau dedicated a significant part of his study of everyday life to the practice of walking. "History begins at the ground level with footsteps,"[26] he wrote. The history we know through the mind of our feet is one that can only be practiced—it is a kind of knowing which has "fallen silent."[27] For de Certeau, walking was a form of resistance to totalising planning solutions. For Guy Debord and the Situationists, walking was a method to discover and create an alternative city, one not composed of axes and frames, but topographies of texture and mood. Walking was key to their practice of psychogeography—an empirical method that studied "the precise laws and specific effects of the geographical environment, consciously organised or not, on the emotions and behaviours of individuals."[28] J. J. Gibson emphasised that we not only perceive, but proprioceive and lamented the fact that architects pay so little attention to proprioception in their work. The architectural practice of the London-based Public Works counter this deficit in their public projects that involve walking bodies, both human and constructed. When invited to design a pavilion for the Serpentine Gallery, instead of designing a static object, they proposed a roaming stall that would

Image 11.4 Street tree-life in Cartagena de Indias, Colombia

Source: Photo Sarah Robinson.

create relations with the diverse users of Kensington Park. This practice in movement explored alternative ways to engage design in human experience beyond showcasing vanity icons, while questioning the role of architects in their seemingly endless production.

An Architecture of Moments

While inhabiting refers to the structure of behaviour that we call 'habit,' it also includes those interruptions of habit that awaken and instil new ways of experiencing—the wrinkles and knots and delights that occasionally protrude from the fabric of the ordinary. As we have seen with memory, time is not only duration, it is qualitatively textured. Habit is more than routine—habitual practices are the texture through which the new enters. "Habit is the routine assimilation of newness,"[29] Bachelard wrote. And further, "to seize habit in its essence, it is therefore necessary to seize it in its growth. Thus, by incremental successes, habit becomes the synthesis of novelty and routine, and that synthesis is fertilised through creative instants."[30] Walking down a crowded street and suddenly recognising a friend is a creative instant. The revelry unleashed by a certain tone of voice is an instant as well. Virginia Woolf called these intensifications of experience *moments of being* and over the course of her life categorised time in two different ways—a "nondescript cotton wool" and exquisitely specific "moments of being" which were not the result of extraordinary actions or events, but intensifications of consciousness that emerged, unbidden, from the stream of the ordinary. She was convinced that

> behind the cotton wool is hidden a pattern; that we—I mean all human beings—are connected to this; that we are parts of the work of art . . . we are the words, we are the music, we are the thing itself.[31]

These creative instants rend the veil of the ordinary, yet the ordinary is the very ground for their entry. She wondered why these moments could be vividly recalled, while many events are easily forgotten and did not offer an explanation, but furnished many rich examples. One of her earliest memories was from infancy—lying safe in her cradle, lulled by the rhythms of the sea outside her window, the flutter of linen curtains gently awakened by the soft breeze. She felt as if she were "lying in a grape and seeing through a film of semi-transparent yellow."[32] Cesare Pavese also wrote that we do not remember days, we remember *attimi*—which can be translated as moments or instants. Both writers were dedicated to expressing this luminous quality of awareness that crests differently from the other waves.

Henri Lefebvre also developed a theory of moments in his critique of everyday life. He understood moments to be differentiations in lived time—a recognition that "grasps the fabric of the lived on the loom of continuity."[33] Like Virginia Woolf's moments of being, Lefebvre's moments offered glimpses into a deeper order within the ordinary. Moments were not only personal but are shared by and with others in a mutual communicative fabric of social consciousness. His theory of moments "excludes the boundary between nature and society (or nature and culture); it also includes the idea of a reciprocal immanence between the sociological and the individual. There is no separation between them."[34] He saw the potential for moments to add another dimension to everyday life, and suggested that an intervention be made to distribute "its elements and instances into 'moments' in such a way as to intensify the vital performance of the everyday, its capacity for communication . . . for enjoyment, by defining new modes of enjoyment in natural and social life."[35] Guy Debord took up this proposition and spatialised

Lefebvre's moments to create his place-generated 'situations.' He wanted to find a way to integrate the distinct quality of moments into designed situations while acknowledging their ephemeral passage. Situations were "sums of possibilities,"[36] provocations that were lived but also lived beyond. The new beauty would be the "beauty of situation"[37] designed to transform context through participatory interventions.

Both Lefebvre and Debord's moments were indebted to Bachelard's theory of instants. Bachelard understood that psychic continuity is not a given, but is constructed of "concantenated rhythmic patterns"[38] he called instants. He anticipated what we are now learning about consciousness—that although it appears to us as a steady stream, it is perhaps more the nature of quanta. Where quanta appear as discrete packets of energy within a field, instants were a "flashing forth from time" and "a creative source of time itself."[39] For Bachelard, "real time exists only through the isolated instant, which is to be found wholly in the act, in what is actual, in the present."[40] What would it mean to enact an instant? As designers, how can we create the conditions for instants to happen? In his study of Bachelard, Edward Casey identifies two features which qualify instants—the sudden and the surprising. "Suddenness is a primary dimension of the instant," Casey explains, and says that "in the sudden we are already in the arms of the surprising."[41] *Surprise* literally means to 'take us over' and this seizure takes place 'in an instant.' Casey asks:

> What else but an instant can reveal to us the ever-new manifestations of the same depthless novel or the same person we love? And what but an instant can render us susceptible to the newly presented, to the unfamiliar that is drawn in the orbit of the habitual?[42]

The most memorable experiences of architecture have the quality of instants, awakening us because they happen suddenly, upsetting our expectations and recalibrating our consciousness. The element of surprise can be orchestrated in the manipulation of expectations. Years of living in Frank Lloyd Wright's buildings never dulled the sense of delight they continually yielded. Taliesin West seems to have grown from the Sonoran desert like an indigenous plant, and possesses the same powers of regeneration. It is Rilke's "mature star of soon,"[43] eternally old *and* eternally new. Just when you think you have seen it all, the place continues to draw from its treasure of moments, one after another, like pearls on the necklace of time. In Herzog and de Meuron's Dominus winery, the thick glass door into the tasting room catches light on its edge as it opens. Green light very literally flashes forth, intensifying the faint light that makes its way through the rubble of the gabion walls.

The evocation of a green glass bottle of wine is revealed in that instant. The surprise of a leaden door that floats lightly on its pivot, a handrail already warm to the touch, the occasion to walk on water, the searing touch of the charred wood weave of an urban carpet—we can call these an architecture of moments. And building these storehouses of moments requires thought, care and most of all *time*—time in the making and time in the tending. The vocabulary of rhythms, fabric, looms, hidden patterns common to Woolf, Lefebvre and Bachelard's descriptions offer more compelling clues. The new makes its entrance through the weave of the ordinary. Gracing the cycles of daily life invites its entry. Repetition is key. The poet Wendell Berry speaks not of the routine of a long marriage but of an old love made new through many sleeps. The rhythm of waves Virginia Woolf heard through an open window and the flutter of linen cannot be sensed in an air-conditioned, hermetically sealed room. The serenity of a cradle withers under fluorescent lights and pockmarked ceilings. Proust's aromas lose their hallucinatory power if they have been bleached.

In addition to the sudden and the surprising, another quality of an architecture of moments is the recognition of the embodiment of care and courtesy. This approach, again, does not abide in an overarching scheme, but in linked decentralised relationships in which the whole emerges inductively from attention to concrete particulars, and is motivated by a sense of empathy and care for the experience of the other. Just as moments of being enter through the weave of the ordinary, an architecture of moments concentrates on honouring and supporting gestures and experiences with acts of courtesy. The compact mass of the building is thus transformed into a field of care.[44] An example of this approach can be found in Alvar Aalto's Viipuri Library. Set at the periphery of an urban pine forest, its white and angular form is a direct contrast to the surrounding textures. Its decentralisation continues with its three separate entrances, each one dignified according to the experience it is intended to afford, and each treated with an equal amount of care. The side entrance located near the street is a newspaper reading room, in which papers can be read from a standing position, as that was the customary posture of the time. The children's library has its own entrance aligning with the playground in front; the children are greeted by brass doors that have the same level of detail and quality as those at the main entrance. Water fountains to quench thirst and sinks for washing sandy hands are located openly at the entrance; satisfying these bodily needs is announced and celebrated, not hidden away. This library is proportioned according to the changing shape of a child's growing body and lit with pendants made of waxed paper. Reading is warmed in the glow of this directed yet softened light. This library shares no direct link with the main library, giving children a sense of propriety in their own space.

Image 11.5 Architecture of Moments, Viipuri Library: Alvar Aalto, architect
Source: Photo Sarah Robinson.

Image 11.6 Viipuri Library: Alvar Aalto, architect

Source: Photo Sarah Robinson.

The main library is lit from above through a series of circles, whose aesthetic appeal is simultaneous with what they *do*: evenly illuminating the space and protecting the books from direct light. The ventilation system is also designed to keep the bookshelves dust-free. The sunken reading area provides the sense of protection that naturally lends itself to abandoning oneself to the book. The whole sequence of checking out books is choreographed with a curvature of movements in which the hand is greeted and guided by the sinuous curves of warm wood. The stairs, too, are designed with low risers and wide treads covered seamlessly in linoleum; footsteps are slowed and sound is absorbed. The community meeting room is crowned with undulating wood slats designed to carry the voice of the speaker evenly to all parts of the room, in another decentralisation befitting a democratic society. Each detail is treated with the utmost consideration for the experience of those who inhabit the library, and the overall balance of the whole emerges from the condensation of courtesy in each detail. These compounded condensations of care are both the substance and setting for an architecture of moments.

Playing

Playing—its very mention evokes an image of children, an open field, lightness. The root of the word *play* means 'to fully engage, to fix one's attention'—and indeed, one plays with a sense of abandon or not at all. Playing is loose and light while being completely absorbing; if we are worried when we play, we are not really playing. And if we are hurried, we cannot play either; the sense of spontaneity is completely lost. In this sense, play is truly a flight from the grind, and perhaps for this reason it is a state we allow unreservedly only to our children and our pets. But musicians play and athletes also play. In these latter two cases, the other dimension of play, to fully engage and fix one's attention, comes to the fore. Why do musicians and athletes play when they are doing their jobs, while the rest of us merely work—what is the difference? Both musicians and athletes practice incessantly; repetition is the only way to coordinate their nervous systems, postures, gestures and muscles with their instruments—whether those instruments are violins, balls or golf clubs. An extraordinary amount of work goes into this coordination, yet we still call it play. Perhaps we use this verb because the performance of their work is a source of pleasure, in a zone out of the ordinary. During their performances, their childlike absorption and sense of abandon is something in which we all get to participate. A musician practices so they can be heard; an athlete plays with and for others. Like other expressions of art, mirroring and empathy is integral to the work, and in their playing, they perform a function for all of society.

Play is dependent on a field for its playing, which is configured according to the possibilities of the game and in turn constrains what can be played on it. A soccer player internalises the distance to the goal, the width of the sidelines and the ambient positions of fellow players in terms of the strategies rehearsed in innumerable iterations. The dynamics and coordinates of the game are in this sense inscribed in her nerves and tissues. The violin is an extension of the violinist's body who coordinates his skill with that of the other musicians, modulated according to the gestures and facial expressions of the conductor and the acoustic possibilities of the space in which the performance takes place. "What the playing field is to the game, architecture is to culture in the broadest sense,"[45] wrote Dalibor Vesely. In an analogous way, he wanted to bring to light this complex interaction in architectural terms.

Counterforms

Understanding this formative interaction requires that we rethink form; this was a central preoccupation for Aldo Van Eyck, who also was concerned not so much with how things look, but with what they *do*. For him, architecture was not a search for forms, but a configurative discipline whose task was to "get closer to the center of human reality and build its counterform."[46] According to Van Eyck, design elements should be configured to support the shapes and rituals of everyday life:

> A wall, a seat or some steps on which to repose, talk, wait or watch; a table around which people gather for an occasion; a balustrade, wall or lamppost against which one can lean and smoke a pipe, a door that allows one to tarry with dignity. All these things are not spaces as such but they constitute place in the most physical sense.[47]

He understood architecture's capacity to structure movements and to modulate thought and feeling and was convinced that design had its most potent effect not in grand schemes as much as it did in the intimate topography of ordinary gestures and movements.

> Large structures (infrastructures) must not only be comprehensible in their own right, they must above all—this is the crucial point—assist the overall comprehensibility of the *minutely configured intimate fabric* which constitutes the immediate counterform of each and every citizen's everyday life . . . Each citizen would thus 'inhabit' the entire city in space and time.[48]

The architect's task, therefore, was to "provide the urban 'interiors' society needs; the built counterform of its dwindling identity."[49]

A contemporary example illustrating what it might mean to build life-promoting counterforms comes again from child development. As early as the second week after birth, babies are able to anticipate the shapes of the objects they wish to grasp. By five months of age, they have developed the neuromusculature enabling them to shape their hands into different grasping positions—the baby's hand can already mirror the precise curvature of the ball for which she reaches.[50] In Van Eyck's lexicon, her desire for the ball and the shaping her hand to reach for it is the form, and the ball is the counter-form. The embodied knowledge manifest in this intertwining of shape and intention is apparent in the way we use the term *to grasp*. We grasp with our hands, and we grasp an idea or concept. Both idea and object are embedded in this fabric of habitual gesture and expectation. The technical term for this interaction is *prehension*,[51] the capacity to anticipate and act in advance of the sensory phenomena towards which one's intentions are directed. Anticipating the shape of the ball comes from experiencing the ball; the baby does not draw upon a genetically programmed routine but develops a repertoire of expectation/shape/fulfilment through open play. Through the direct experience of playing with the tensions and resistances, the roughness and smoothness and couplings with the objects, her bodily capacities, her personal repertoire of 'I cans,' is gradually forged. This formative process is what makes a richly textured play environment so very crucial.

The groundwork laid in the early explorations with the hands are the basis for further amplifications of prehension, such as when we move through streets and already anticipate the height and width of walkways and shape our body accordingly. Prehension is closely tied with the body schema, the set of bodily expectations correlated with one's repertoire of movements allowing us to navigate the world with ease and is interrupted if the built form does not match those embodied expectations—just as we saw in the case of Scarpa's syncopated stair. Van Eyck clearly stated that the crucial role of design is to *minutely configure the intimate fabric* that constitutes the counterform of everyday life. Prehension entails desire, intention, expectation—actions generally attributed to the mind—outwardly expressed as the shape of a hand, the arch of a spine, the swerve of the torso—actions of the body. Van Eyck's call for human homecoming is realised when the form of desire finds its counterform constructed in the world. Homecoming happens when habits find their support and completion *in* the place of the city.

Play was thought to be an activity exhibited only by higher mammals, but is now understood to have evolved repeatedly across different taxonomic orders. Play can therefore be considered fundamental to inhabiting, a method of adapting to and coming to know our habitats. Play may also be considered in terms of mental rehearsal, and as some researchers suggest, "may be tied in with mirror neurons and social imitation and learning in ways that we cannot yet fathom, but may have played a crucial role in evolution in many different levels."[52] The baseline prevalence of play suggests that the interaction between the field and the playing it affords has still broader implications. Van Eyck's counterforms and Vesely's analogy can be fleshed out further when we consider the relatively recent cultural phenomena of board sports. The evolution of skateboarding and snowboarding can be traced back to surfing. And a brief study of the surfboard illustrates the body/mind/culture coupling that physical form affords. While the surfboard is obviously an instrument that affords surfing, the surfboard—unlike a musical instrument which is designed to allow certain sounds, yet is flexible enough to be played in different ways— is nonspecific. Its nonspecificity has spawned many other sports and subcultures to go along with them. The film *Dogtown and the Z Boys* documents how on days when the waves were not big enough to surf, surfers put wheels on their surfboards and rode around Los Angeles, eventually creating smaller boards and using them to cruise around inside empty swimming pools. This of course is the origin of skateboarding, and even today, skateboard parks are designed with the features that emulate the old lima-bean-shaped swimming pools with concrete rims that populated Los Angeles in the 1970s. When the practice moved to colder climes, they invented snowboarding. You could trace all of these developments back to the open shape of the surfboard, which affords a certain flow that goes beyond waves caused by water.[53]

The evolution of board sports has changed both the topography of our cities and the possibilities for movement they afford—where one sees a bench, another sees a curvature that could generate a possible trick. The tool of the board opens a way of perceiving the environment through one's repertoire of possible movements, and those flowing movements seek out contours that will allow and promote that particular gesture. Each *topos*—the Greek word for 'place'—suggests movements that go along with it and, understood in this way, forms *form*. It is not just that skateboards move some ways and not others that causes the skateboarder to favour certain shapes and contours over others. Skateboarding has generated its own subculture—a meshwork of postures, gestures, movements, linguistic expressions, clothing and attitudes in rhythm with the flowing movements afforded by the board. Board sports require loose-fitting clothing to accommodate the movements, the general outlook is open, experimental and antiauthoritarian and the role of performance is more akin to dance as an artistic expression and spectacle. The tool of the skateboard generates behaviour as well as a culture and local topography that supports it. This is yet another illustration that 'we feel because we do,' our affective dispositions are calibrated by our movements, actions and gestures, and those dispositions in turn trigger a cascade of further consequences.

The architect and skateboarder Iain Borden details the ways that skateboarders extend their body into the board, coupling terrain and movement in a dynamic whose pivot is the boarder's own centre of gravity. "You must get the feeling that your mind is located in your centre of gravity. The rest of your body moves around this centre point as a wheel moves around a hub,"[54] he writes. And from that centre of gravity radiates the envelope of 'I cans' directly resulting from the integration of the possibilities of the skateboard into one's motor repertoire—one moves not on, but *with* the skateboard. Some skateboarders feel that "their skateboard takes on their personality, and becomes almost 'an actual part' of themselves."[55] This dynamic amalgam of body, tool, situation in movement is what Borden calls "super architectural space."[56] This highly plastic, concentrated space of play avails new experience that seeks out concrete means for its expression.

The uses of the terms *space* and *terrain* in this context recall the differentiation between the two Greek terms for space—*topos* and *choros*. *Topos* is the root of *topography*, while *choros*, the root of *choreography*, means both 'the place of the dance' and 'the dance' itself. The experimental attitude of the culture of skateboarding is constantly open to new exploratory terrain. They reinhabit neglected, peripheral zones of urban areas with their bodies in an act of reclamation in which the place of the dance becomes the dance itself. Understanding the limits of their bodily possibilities therefore empowers on multiple levels. The marginal discards of conventional urbanism, rather than sites "fraught with boredom and frustration . . . in a bland culture governed by the sacred principle of convenience" become instead "laboratories of the possible."[57] Their skilled movements have attuned their perception to recognise infinite possibilities in gaps, blocks and slopes that even trained designers miss. "Street skateboarding creates unexpected eruptions of meaning, retranslating the objects of the city," transforming "these elements into sites of energetic pleasure. Skateboarding is a critique of the emptiness of meaning in zero-degree architecture,"[58] Borden writes. And their anthem is all the more powerful because it operates on the visceral "soil of the sensible" that is prior to words.

Visceral Urbanism

Understanding cities in terms of their success or failure in *minutely configuring the intimate fabric* resonates with Richard Sennett's approach to urbanism that proposes *modest making* rather than grand schemes. "A more vigorous urbanism has to be a visceral urbanism, since space and place come alive in the body," he insists.[59] It would be difficult to find a more poignant embodiment of this sort of modesty and attention than in the hundreds of playgrounds that Aldo Van Eyck built in postwar Amsterdam. The playgrounds reinvigorated the empty pockets and sites of demolished buildings, and Van Eyck was among the very few architects to recognise not only the developmental needs of children, but the value of integrating the old with new not only in terms of architecture, but in terms of creating situations that would invite intergenerational encounters. His playgrounds were inclusive places welcoming young and old together, in a mutually enriching way and his intention was for them "to become part of the city's everyday fabric . . to respond to the child's elementary inclinations and movements and activate his imagination."[60] The playgrounds would accomplish this because they were

> conceived of these simple vital things—only then will imaginative non-abstract constructions and forms be evolved. As long as attention is directed not to aesthetic effects, but to experience value, archetypal ideas valid for different parts of the world in varied form will soon ensue.[61]

Image 11.7 Aldo Van Eyck Zeedijk playground, Amsterdam 1955

Source: Photo Har Oudejans.

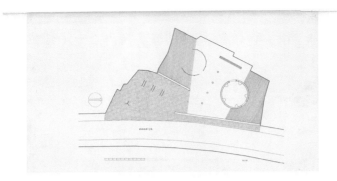

Image 11.8 Aldo Van Eyck Zeedijk playground plan, Amsterdam 1955

Image 11.9 Aldo Van Eyck playground, Zaanhof, Amsterdam 1948
Source: Courtesy Hannie and Aldo Van Eyck.

The playgrounds are configurations of simple structures that are open-ended, in the sense that they invite multiple ways to respond and play with them. The benches are arranged judiciously so that caretakers could keep an eye on the children without encroaching on their activities and they succeeded in becoming part of the urban fabric because they are not fenced in.

The careful analysis[62] that they have since received can help us understand why they have worked so well and are so beloved. The playground equipment

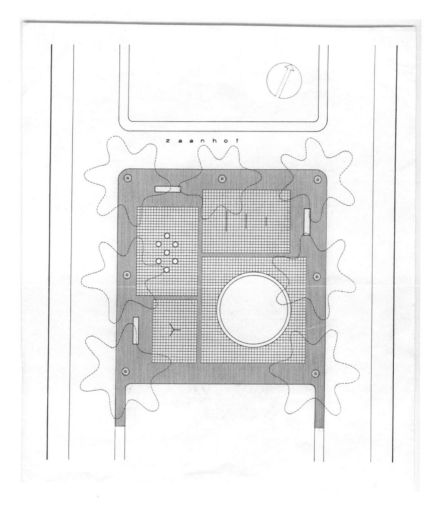

Image 11.10 Aldo Van Eyck playground plan, Zaanhof Amsterdam 1948
Source: Courtesy Hannie and Aldo Van Eyck.

was nonspecific like a surfboard that does not suggest an exclusive mode of use. Van Eyck was explicitly against 'abstract forms,' yet his critics have praised this playground equipment for being so abstract. Van Eyck succeeded in creating 'vital forms' that generated improvisation because they were open to individual interpretation. The most striking feature, however, and the most unusual at the time, was the fact that the playgrounds were not fenced in. Rather than playgrounds, they more closely resembled furniture arrangements, with toys for kids and benches for grown-ups. And this is exactly how they functioned: the lack of a hard boundary turned the invisible boundary into a living edge, a porous membrane which contained the young and old together, as if they were inhabiting a protected precinct much like a room. Certain etiquette developed around these nodes of activity; a shared code of conduct naturally emerged which created its own self-organising circle of behaviour. The absence of a fixed boundary exemplifies the import of Shunryū Suzuki's cryptic remark, "If you want to keep your cow close to you, give him a big pasture."[63] Indeed, the absence of an outward restraint causes one to create an inner boundary; the lack of an outward structure of control forces one to generate one's own with the resources at hand. Children can learn to become self-regulating when given the opportunity to exercise their limits and receive feedback from their environment. Yet this can only happen when they have been given 'a large pasture,' as the Zen saying goes.

Healing

"It is only in the burning house that the fundamental architectural problem becomes visible for the first time,"[64] wrote Giorgio Agamben. The destructive force of fire is the antithesis of the call to shelter, yet our relationship with fire is at the heart of human becoming. Every home in ancient Greece had two things—a hearth and a loom. Humanising the destructive force of fire, channeling its heat to warm and to cook, the hearth sheltered the never-ending occupations of weaving and mending. The act of tending fire reenacts the story of human becoming that is architecture's very origin. This tending or its miscarriage is also at the heart of one of the original experiments that founded the environmental movement. The year before Henry David Thoreau built his cabin on Walden Pond, he accidentally set fire to the 200-acre forest on its border. Thoreau never admitted a causal connection between his experience of the destructive force of fire and the genesis of his grand experiment, but the timing of the events suggests one nonetheless. It has been scarcely mentioned that the most famous celebration of the woods was conceived so near the charred remains of another forest. Perhaps building himself a hut and "devouring himself alive"[65] within its walls was a way for Thoreau to heal the wound that he himself had inflicted.

Tied to the words *holy* and *whole*, healing is a process comprised of distinctly overlapping phases. Describing the less acknowledged aspects of this process, in her book *Regeneration*, the writer Pat Barker refers to a physician who

> knew only too well how often the early stages of change or cure may mimic deterioration. Cut a chrysalis open, and you will find a rotting

caterpillar. What you will never find is that mythical creature, half caterpillar, half butterfly . . . No, the process of transformation consists almost entirely of decay.[66]

We tend to focus on the form of the chrysalis, unaware of the messy process that it shelters. Rites of passage make potentially traumatic changes tolerable by framing them with appropriate actions—the process of healing also unfolds according to certain stages and is in need of vessels to support its passage. The chrysalis is the counterform of the process of healing. Perhaps Thoreau was moulding his own chrysalis, the shell that would allow his transformation. In his cabin on the shore of Walden Pond, all the attractions of the house were concentrated in one room: his sources of heat were a fireplace and a stove, his accoutrements a bed, a desk, a table and three chairs—the functions of living pared to their essence. This simplicity created a space for him to focus on his most pressing work.

> I went to the woods because I wished to live deliberately, to front only the essential facts of life, and see if I could not learn what it had to teach, and not, when I came to die, discover that I had not lived . . . I wanted to live deep and suck out all the marrow of life, to live so sturdily and Spartan-like as to put to rout all that was not life, to cut a broad swath and shave close, to drive life into a corner, and reduce it to its lowest terms.[67]

The corner was not something to be abolished or transcended—but inhabited. He spoke tenderly of domesticity: the fire was his companion; the daily tasks took on a concentrated meaning. The frame of his shelter did not cut him out of the landscape but allowed him to meaningfully enter into it. "This frame," writes Thoreau, "so slightly clad, was a sort of crystallisation around me."[68] This crystalline husk, built from the trees of the very same forest, allowed his communion with nature so essential to his process of healing. Just as the body responds to the trauma of being torn by slowing weaving new tissues, so do we heal through creative actions. Creation compensates for deterioration. If we understand another layer of *Walden* as a narrative of healing, three agents of transformation come to the fore: the first is the vessel—the shelter for vulnerability; the second is immersion in natural processes; the third is creative engagement.

The regenerative power of nature simply cannot be overstated. Countless studies have shown that contact with nature improves healing. Oliver Sacks

Image 11.11 Trees, Varallo, Italy

Source: Photo Sarah Robinson.

finds gardens both essential to his own creative process and also indispensable in his treatments for patients.

> All of us have had the experience of wandering through a lush garden or a timeless desert, walking by a river or an ocean, or climbing a mountain and finding ourselves simultaneously calmed and reinvigorated, engaged in mind, refreshed in body and spirit. The importance of these physiological states on individual and community health is fundamental and wide-ranging. In forty years of medical practice, I have found only two types of non-pharmaceutical 'therapy' to be vitally important for patients with chronic neurological diseases: music and gardens.[69]

Admitting that he cannot say exactly how nature reorganises and calms our brains, he has witnessed that even for his most neurologically disturbed patients, gardens and nature are more powerful than any medication. "The effects of nature's qualities on health are not only spiritual and emotional but physical and neurological. I have no doubt that they reflect deep changes in the brain's physiology, and perhaps even its structure."[70] He insists that the healing effects of nature have to do not only with our innate *biophilia*—love of nature—but also what he calls *hortophilia*: the desire to interact, manage and tend nature, which is also deeply instilled. Viewing nature from a hospital bed has enormous benefits, but engaging with nature in creating and tending gardens allows us to actively join in healing processes that envelop our own efforts. The phytochemicals secreted by plants and trees have beneficial effects on the immune and central nervous system. The higher level of negative ions in settings with rich vegetation has been shown to beneficially treat depression. Touching a genuine versus a synthetic leaf produced cerebral blood flow changes indicative of relaxation. Another study found that hands-on working with plants decreased muscular tension and relaxed wakefulness. The exposure to microorganisms in the soil has been shown to be a powerful indicator of health, and has been suggested in the treatment of depression, fatigue and cognition.[71] With so many beneficial influences at so many levels of health and well-being, integrating plants into healing environments is perhaps the easiest way that architecture can enhance and promote life.

An exemplary work of an architecture of healing is Alvar Aalto's Paimio Sanatorium. Immersed in a Finnish forest, the building was designed for patients recovering from tuberculosis and was informed by Aalto's own personal experience. When Aalto himself was hospitalised, he realised that hospitals are rarely designed from the patient's point of view, who is almost always lying down. Instead, at Paimio:

> The room design is determined by the depleted strength of the patient reclining in his bed. The color of the ceiling is chosen for its quiet, the light sources are outside the patient's field of vision, the heating is oriented towards the patient's feet and the water runs soundlessly from the taps to make sure that no patient disturbs his neighbour.[72]

Windows and the placement of beds were based on solar considerations and daylighting, balconies were colorful and located to optimise resting in the sunshine, and common spaces were designed to promote interaction. Aalto and his wife Aino carefully designed the furniture, fixtures and door hardware to afford comfort and aesthetic delight. Because the rooms were intended to be shared by two people, sinks were designed to be noiseless so as not to disturb one's fellow patient, handles were designed to be easily and silently opened. The iconic Paimio armchair's sensuous curves were not designed purely for visual delight but were shaped according to the patient's spine to facilitate easier breathing. Aalto acknowledged the precedent in Marcel Breuer's Wassily chair, but intentionally used wood instead of metal because metal conducts heat away from the body. For this reason, the handrails on the stairs are made of wood, a material that is porous, because it once too breathed. Being porous, it is more responsive to the ambient environment. We tend to see this chair in isolation, as an object, but the original context of the chairs is that they were arrayed in a communal room, situated in a sunlit ensemble.

Color was a critical element in the healing process that Aalto orchestrated. The floors were covered in yellow linoleum, a material which gains its name from the linseed oil with which it is produced. This naturally pliant substance affords fluid surfaces; linoleum can be unfurled like a rug without pronounced joints or interruptions, and it is soft enough to absorb sound and durable enough to sustain heavy traffic. Cheerful yellow is a refreshing contrast to the cliché of hospital gray. "The element of color—it is another world," wrote Frank Lloyd Wright. "That probably is the most mysterious world of all—even more mysterious than form."[73] Color is energy that we resonate with like sound and we perceive color not only with our eyes, but through our skin. Babies are treated for jaundice with blue light; the excess of yellow is corrected with its opposite wavelength on the light spectrum. And conversely, yellow compensates for the melancholy 'blues.' Colours directly impact our emotional processes. This resonance has given rise to rich cultural symbolism and connotations: the word *gray,* for example, refers to a color, a mood and ambiguous suggestions of meaning. The tuning of emotions with color choices is one of the most accessible ways to create humane environments. Prisons have painted rooms pink to calm down inmates without the use of force, drugs or social isolation. The green that Aalto used on the ceilings has a calming effect on the sympathetic nervous system due to its medium frequency in the electromagnetic spectrum.[74] Surgeons wear green uniforms to restore the visual fatigue caused by the color red. It is of course no accident that green, the ubiquitous color of nature, possesses these calming effects.[75] The selection of colors, the affordances of handles, faucets, sinks, windows, the handrails, the symphony of chairs in the communal rooms—every detail was considered with attention to the healing process. Aalto explicitly stated that his aim for the building was for it to function as a "medical instrument."[76] And I don't think he intended *instrument* in the mechanistic sense, but rather in the sense of a musical instrument, one that in concert with the human breath and movement is animated to make music. The building was a field of care, outfitted and detailed to invite and organise actions, calibrate moods, postures and gestures, coloured and lit to attune person and place in a total atmosphere of well-being.

Notes

1. Jane Hirshfield, *Nine Gates: Entering the Mind of Poetry* (New York: Harper, 1998), 33.
2. Maurice Merleau-Ponty, "The Eye and the Mind," in *Merleau-Ponty Reader*, eds. Ted Toadvine and Leonard Lawlor (Evanston: Northwestern, 2007), 312.
3. Paul C. Berger, "Marcel Proust," *Das Buch* 3, no. 2 (Mainz, 1951), 19.
4. John Dewey, *Human Nature and Conduct* (New York: Henry Holt, 1922), 32.
5. Peter Blundell Jones has written about Gebser's influence on Scharoun. See "From the Neo-Classical Axis to Aperspective Space," *The Architectural Review* 1093 (Mar 1988), 19.
6. Jean Gebser, *The Ever-Present Origin*, trans. Noel Barstad and Algis Mickunas (Athens: Ohio University Press, 1985), 99.
7. Merleau-Ponty, "The Eye and Mind," in *Merleau-Ponty: Basic Writings*, ed. Thomas Baldwin (London: Routledge, 2004), 312.
8. André-Franck Concord, "Slum Construction," *Potlatch* no. 3 (July 6, 1954).
9. Rudolph Arnheim, *The Dynamics of Architectural Form* (Berkeley: University of California Press, 1977), 210.
10. Ibid.
11. Ibid.
12. Christopher Alexander et al., *A Pattern Language* (New York: Oxford University Press, 1977), 697.
13. Ibid.
14. Adam Hadhazy, "Think Twice: How the Gut's 'Second Brain' Influences Mood and Well-Being," *Scientific American*, February 12, 2010.
15. Christopher Alexander et al., *A Pattern Language*, 845.
16. Ibid., 858.
17. Evan Thompson, *Mind in Life: Biology, Phenomenology, and the Sciences of Mind* (Cambridge, MA: Harvard University Press, 2007), 346.
18. Ibid.
19. Russell N. Van Gelder, "Non-Visual Photoreception: Sensing Light Without Sight," *Current Biology* 18 (2008), 38–39.
20. Wei Shung Chung and Cheng-Li Lin, "Sleep Disorders Associated with the Risk of Prostate Cancer," *BMC Cancer* 19 (2019), 146.
21. Soren Kierkegaard, *Either/Or: A Fragment of a Life*, trans. Swenson (Princeton: Princeton University Press, 1944), 77.
22. Friedrich Nietzsche, *The Gay Science: With a Prelude in Rhymes and an Appendix of Songs*, trans. Walter Kaufmann (New York: Knopf Doubleday, 2010), 108.
23. Ibid.
24. Virginia Woolf, "A Sketch of the Past," in *Moments of Being*, 2nd ed. (New York: Harcourt Brace, 1985), 72.
25. Walter Benjamin, *Illuminations*, trans. Harry Zohn (New York: Schocken Books, 2007), 91.
26. Michel de Certeau, *The Practice of Everyday Life*, trans. Steven Rendall (Berkeley: University of California Press, 2011), 129.
27. Ibid.
28. Guy Debord, "Introduction to a Critique of Urban Geography," in *The Situationists and the City*, ed. Tom McDonough (London: Verso, 2009), 62.
29. As quoted in Eileen Rizo-Patron et al., *Adventures in Phenomenology: Gaston Bachelard* (Albany: SUNY Press, 2019), 25.
30. Ibid.
31. Woolf, "A Sketch of the Past," 72.
32. Ibid., 70.

33. Stuart Elden, *Understanding Henri Lefebvre* (London: Bloomsbury, 2004), 173.

34. Ibid.

35. Ibid.

36. DeBord, "Introduction to a Critique of Urban Geography," 62.

37. Ibid.

38. Edward Casey, "The Difference an Instant Makes," in *Adventures in Phenomenology Gaston Bachelard*, ed. Eileen Rizo-Patron (Albany: SUNY Press, 2019), 20.

39. Ibid.

40. Ibid., 27.

41. Ibid.

42. Ibid.

43. As quoted in Gebser, *The Ever-Present Origin*, 497.

44. The phenomenologist John Wild first used the term 'field of care' to describe the way we inhabit the world. "When I think of myself or some other person as being in the world. I mean something more than mere spatial inclusion, as a cup in a cupboard or a shoe in a box. I am in the world rather as in a field of care." in his *Existence and the World of Freedom* (Englewood Cliffs, NJ: Prentice-Hall, 1963), 47.

45. Dalibor Vesely, *Architecture in the Age of Divided Representation* (Cambridge, MA: MIT Press, 2006), 106.

46. As quoted in Robert McCarter, *Aldo Van Eyck* (New Haven: Yale University Press, 2015), 118.

47. Ibid., 117.

48. Ibid.

49. Ibid.

50. Frank R. Wilson, *The Hand: How Its Use Shapes the Brain, Language and Human Culture* (New York: Pantheon, 1998), 99.

51. Colin McGinn, *Prehension: The Hand and the Emergence of Humanity* (Cambridge, MA: MIT Press, 2015).

52. Kerrie Lewis Graham and Gordon Burghardt, "Current Perspectives on the Biological Study of Play: Signs of Progress," *The Quarterly Review of Biology* (2010), 393–418.

53. I originally addressed this subject in my essay, "Articulating Affordances," in *Meaning in Architecture* (Manhattan, KS: New Prairie Press, 2019).

54. Iain Borden, *Skateboarding and the City* (London: Bloomsbury, 2019), 177.

55. Ibid., 178.

56. Ibid., 176.

57. Ibid., 201.

58. Ibid., 216.

59. .Richard Sennett, *Building and Dwelling* (New York: Penguin, 2019), 16.

60. Ibid.

61. Ibid.

62. Rob Withagen and Simone R. Caljouw, "Aldo Van Eyck's Playgrounds: Aesthetics, Affordances and Creativity," *Frontiers in Psychology* 8 (2017).

63. Shunryū Suzuki, *Zen Mind, Beginner's Mind* (New York: Weatherhill, 1970), 14.

64. As quoted in Leland de la Durantaye, *Giorgio Agamben: A Critical Introduction* (Palo Alto: Stanford University Press, 2009), 51.

65. Ellery Channing wrote Henry David Thoreau a letter on March 5, 1845 suggesting that he go out to Walden Pond, build himself a hut and begin the grand process of devouring himself alive.

66. Pat Barker, *Regeneration* (New York: Penguin, 1992), 246.

67. Henry David Thoreau, *Walden: Or, Life in the Woods* (New York: Dover, 1995), 59.

68. Ibid., 56.

69. Oliver Sacks, *Everything in its Place: First Loves and Last Tales*(New York: Picador, 2019), 59.
70. Ibid.
71. The Natural Environments Initiative: Illustrative Review and Workshop Statement. J. Africa, A. Logan, R. Mitchell, K. Korpela, D. Allen, L. Tyrväinen, E. Nisbet, Q. Li, Y. Tsunetsugu, Y. Miyazaki, and J. Spengler; on behalf of the NEI Working Group, *The Natural Environments Initiative: Illustrative Review and Workshop Statement* (Boston, MA: Harvard School of Public Health, 2014).
72. Goran Schildt, *Alvar Aalto, A Life's Work: Architecture, Design and Art* (Helsinki: Otava Publishing, 1994), 69.
73. *Frank Lloyd Wright Collected Writings, 1949–1959*, ed. Bruce Brooks Pfeiffer (New York: Rizzoli, 1992), 77.
74. These references are thanks to the architect and color consultant Laura Sangiorgi. For further reading see Frank Mahnke, *Color, Environment and Human Response* (New York: Wiley, 1996).
75. For more on restorative environments see Rachel Kaplan and Stephen Kaplan, *The Experience of Nature: A Psychological Perspective* (Cambridge: Cambridge University Press, 1989).
76. Schildt, *Alvar Aalto*, 69.

Fields of Care: Concluding Thoughts

12

The reader who has made it this far in this study of interactions between our bodies and our habitats has surely noticed that several themes keep recurring. The first is openness: the irreducible fact of the human condition is that we are open. The bodies we house are open bodies, dependent on interchange and communion with surrounding life. There really is an inhalation and an exhalation of being,[1] as Merleau-Ponty said. What is outside eventually comes inside. Surfaces are two-sided like the skin—we cannot touch without being touched in return. And because we are open, we need boundaries strong and flexible enough to also close. Complementarity and interdependence belong to this openness. We not only breathe in and out, we breathe in a certain rhythm, our heart beats in rhythm, our perceptual experience oscillates in rhythms. "Life is waves,"[2] declared Gaston Bachelard. Every crest is followed by a trough in unceasing movement. Our experience of color, once again, lays bare the facts of this unending balancing act. In his Ganzfeld installation at the Villa Panza in Varese, Italy, James Turrell created an all-white room without corners. Where there would normally be a 90-degree angle at the meeting of a vertical wall with a horizontal ceiling, he fused the surfaces with a bend. He wanted to recreate the conditions of a blizzard in which all surfaces disappear into the whiteness of snow and the lines where you begin and end dissolve along with these otherwise trustworthy coordinates. The three sides of the room opened to a field of pure color. The whiteout was the precondition for entering into the wavelengths of red. Red radiated from nowhere and everywhere, and was no longer color—it was pure experience. But it didn't take long to feel completely exhausted by the intensity demanded of red. And when you turned around for some relief, what you saw on the opposite wall was the most luscious green. Yet, what appeared to be green was not actually green; it was the white wall of the room from which you entered. Your eyes created green where there was white, to compensate for the overwhelming power of red. Life is waves and continually seeks equilibrium within movement.

The body compensates for what it lacks. The dialectic of prospect and refuge is a basic characteristic of human experience. We need both the cave and the panorama, but cannot have one without the balancing of the other. The primacy of breathing is the vital oscillation between that which is open, and that which can close. We have seen this again and again through the course of this study. The spatial art of music evolved differently in different places depending on the character of topography and materials and their relative porosities and the nature of their boundaries. "There are two fundamental kinds of spatial sensation that are compatible with man's primordial nature," wrote Aldo Van Eyck.

> They must always be present somehow in what we make—both at once . . . There is the spatial sensation that makes us envy birds in flight, there is also the kind that recalls the sheltered enclosure of our origin. Architecture will defeat its own end if it discards either the one or the other of these great human aspects.[3]

The in-between elements of architecture must embody this tension: every stair is a possibility of flight; every corridor a mysterious journey, a gallery of delights; every passage an enticement of light and shadow. And these places of transition must eventually lead to a feeling of arrival—a sense of homecoming.

The very fact that when we touch, we are touched in return speaks to the way we truly inhabit our worlds. Our habitats are not containers; they are fields of care that support us in a mutual mesh. We do not stand against the world to survey it from above and are unable to dissect consciousness because we can never step outside of it. Whether we touch with our eyes, our tongues, our skin—we are always touching another. We are enveloped in the world and cannot transcend it. The verb *envelop*, at its root, means 'to be involved.' It is also the origin of the word *warp*, the ordering threads of weaving. We are woven into our worlds, and woven of them. *Weaving* is another verb that has reverberated through this text: Merleau-Ponty speaks of the way his body is threaded into his Paris apartment; Aldo Van Eyck was dedicated to weaving the intimate fabric of Amsterdam; the key to understanding urban patterns for Lefebvre was to study their rhythms on the loom of continuity; Vitruvius and Semper both referred to early architecture as the weaving of walls; Indra Kagis McEwen has stressed how the ancient Greeks wove their boats and their city and imagined the protector of Athens as the goddess of the loom. Our bodies heal by weaving new nerves and tissues. Cities and bodies that are woven—when torn—can be mended. In cloth, warp becomes weave, structure is skin, form and meaning are immanent with one another. The elasticity of thread, the fact that it is not an object but a verb of connection and binding makes it more than a metaphor for reimagining the possibilities of building.

The metaphor of the container and the contained that has guided Western thought with its vocabulary of inert matter, fragmentation, and frozen and petrified movement has crippled the architectural imagination for over two millennia. It is helpful to remember that the word *paradigm*, understood today as the set of ideas that guide thinking, derives from the Greek *paradiegma*, a word that described a tool used in building. The *paradiegma* was a pattern used in the process of building that served as both model and measure. There are two ways to understand *paradiegma*—one is Plato's immutable template and the other is the mutable rhythm that patterns movement, a dynamic order like a dance that becomes internalised and reinforced with every new tracing of gesture. The successes in neuroscience have come not from approaching the body as an immutable template, but in discerning patterns in its magnetic resonances, electrical currents and blood flows. We are resonant bodies patterned by our interactions in the mediums in which we are immersed. Together with the language of weaving, we have spoken of resonance, reverberation, orientating force fields and atmospheres. "Whether people are fully conscious of this or not, they actually derive countenance and sustenance from the atmosphere of things they live in and with,"[4] wrote Frank Lloyd Wright. This statement reveals the atmospheric educational philosophy he shared with Dewey—we learn by doing and we learn through immersion. The only way to learn to swim is to jump into the water, and it is well known that the only way to truly learn a language is through immersion into its mother tongue. One learns to swim by experiencing the differential gravity of water firsthand. And no matter how much one may study its vocabulary and grammar, one does not become fluent in a language unless one enters the body of its rhythms and flows.

This is why I insist that architecture cannot be read. To read is to stand outside, to digitise from a distance in the private bubble demanded of eye and word. Experience, by its very nature is immersive: we are in a building as a fish is in water. And because we are immersed in them, every building moves us with its vibrations, reverberations and resonances for better or for worse. What Merleau-Ponty discovered in Cezanne's paintings can equally be applied to architecture: "If a work is successful, it has the strange power of being self-teaching."[5] To learn architecture, there is no substitute for spending as much time as possible in masterpieces. Atmospheric learning comes at us in all directions, through all the senses and capacities—in due time. Architecture is inherently slow, and demands time to impart its teachings, which in turn are preserved and unfold over a longer period of time. You are probably tired of hearing me speak about Taliesin, but I simply cannot overstate how deeply that place worked its way into my consciousness and shaped my perception—it was the most silent, steadfast and patient teacher.

The other irreducible fact of the human condition is our plasticity. Plastic comes from plasma—'to mould.' Our seemingly infinite adaptability is bounded only by its compensating fact: whatever we do not use, we lose—practicing, repeating, rehearsing, caring, tending and loving are the verbs that stabilise form. *Homo fabers* who make tools and are made by them, we easily forget that all technology is a declension of the body. All of our tools are extensions and applications of our capacities for action. We tend to forget too that our sensitivities have been eons in the making, a colossal head start with which we cannot possibly compete. Our own bodies are our most sensitive tools for knowing our world, and developing and refining these hard-won capacities and aptitudes would seem to be the true calling of our innate plasticity. So, before donning an EEG helmet or some other device, let us first pay attention to the world around us and not rely on technology to tell us how we feel. Such tools are helpful aids but no substitute for firsthand experience. Experience has been debased and distrusted so thoroughly that to gain legitimacy, we must now validate it with mechanical methods. With deep respect for the finely tuned marvel of our bodies, the approach outlined here values the authenticity of firsthand experience, honours openness while respecting its limits and prefers modest making over totalising schemes. Building with threads that can be sewn and mended, situated poetics is the skill to cultivate meanings that are already there, in acts of humane courtesy and an attitude of tenderness and exquisite care.

Notes

1. Maurice Merleau-Ponty wrote "We speak of 'inspiration,' and the word should be taken literally, there really is an inspiration and expiration of Being . . ." in the "Eye and the Mind."
2. Gaston Bachelard, *The Dialectics of Duration* (Manchester: Clinamen Press, 2000), 130.

3. Aldo Van Eyck, *Aldo Van Eyck Writings, Volume 1: The Child, the City and the Artist*, eds. Vincent Ligtelin and Francis Strauven (Amsterdam: SUN, 2008), 117.
4. Frank Lloyd Wright, *The Natural House* (New York: Horizon Press, 1958), 135.
5. Maurice Merleau-Ponty, "Cezanne's Doubt," in *The Merleau-Ponty Aesthetics Reader: Philosophy and Painting*, ed. Micheal Smith (Evanston: Northwestern University Press, 1993), 186.

Taxonomy of Interactions Appendix

Archaic

1. Breathing

    1. Affirming the Breath

        a. Rhythms
        b. Visibility
        c. Poetics

    2. Empathy

        a. Actual movement
        b. Traces of movement
        c. Motor resonance

    3. Entrainment

        a. Synchrony
        b. Eurhythmy
        c. Proportioning

    4. Epistemology of the Skin

        a. Sensorimotor communicative
        b. Layered porosity
        c. Inner/outer

5. Cultures of Breathing
   a. Bio-cultural thermal devices
   b. Integrated vernacular strategies
   c. Minimise or eliminate refrigerants

2. Resistance

   1. Strength in Vulnerability
      a. Openings
      b. Sensitivity to pain
      c. Density of connections

   2. Interconnection
      a. Forests, wetlands, mangroves
      b. Adaptive not mitigative
      c. Social/interpersonal

   3. Lungs of the City
      a. Green roofs, walls, towers
      b. Urban forests and gardens at multiple scales
      c. Restore migration corridors

   4. Mindful Physical Presence
      a. Touching
      b. Friction
      c. Slowing down

3. Touching

   1. Sensory Training
      a. Sensory symphonies
      b. Touching / being touched
      c. Carnal hermeneutics

   2. Haptic Perception
      a. Mediated by vibrations
      b. Role of past experience
      c. Feedback of resistance

Magical

1. Resonating

    1. Origins of Music

        a. Coextensive with emotions
        b. Restorative of psychic balance
        c. Technology of bonding

    2. Buildings as Musical Instruments

        a. Context dependency of sound/tone
        b. Acoustic acumen of ancients
        c. Situated music

    3. Sound as a Building Material

        a. Space interpenetrates the body
        b. Acoustic capacities of materials
        c. Multimedia performance work

2. Dancing

    1. Choros

        a. Identity of place and dance
        b. Tone made visible
        c. Unthawing frozen music

    2. Kinaestethic Awareness

        a. Historic precedents
        b. Situated dance
        c. Healing and social bonding

    3. Mechanisms of Mutuality
        a. Mimic processes of ritualisation
        b. Formalization, repetition, exaggeration
        c. Elaborating, manipulation and delay

3. Making

    1. Homo Faber
        a. Making as a way of knowing
        b. Listening to materials
        c. Weaving architecture

2. Bodying Forth Form
    a. Demolish hylomorphic model
    b. Intervening in fields of force
    c. Itinerant, improvisational, rhythmic

Mythical

1. Imagining

    1. Animistic
        a. Nowhere is there a dead thing
        b. Threshold between inner and outer
        c. Nonlinear dreamtime

    2. Physiology of the Imagination

        a. Organ is the psyche
        b. Negative capability
        c. Open-ended

    3. Complementarity

        a. Interdependent opposites
        b. Ambivalence/polyvalence
        c. Reciprocal meanings

    4. Suspension

        a. Tension/delay
        b. Mirroring/epiphany
        c. Subtle bodies

    5. Metaphor

        a. Archetypes / patterning fields
        b. Symbolic complexes
        c. Primal metaphors

2. Remembering

    1. Spatial and Practiced

        a. Architecture built the mind
        b. Memories are situated
        c. Cities as mnemonic devices

   2.   Physiology of Memory

       a.   Hippocampus / place cells
       b.   Rehearsal/plasticity
       c.   Amnesia disables imagination

3.   Storytelling

   1.   Oral Culture

       a.   Knowledge is external
       b.   Rhythmic mnemonics
       c.   Primal words

   2.   In Praise of Slowness

       a.   Repetition
       b.   Visceral presence
       c.   Wisdom

   3.   Empathy and Story

       a.   Capacity to imagine life situations
       b.   Autobiography of places
       c.   Looking through eyes of another

Mental

1.   Abstracting

   1.   Vision is Constructive and Dynamic

       a.   Physiology of vision
       b.   Ecologically situated
       c.   Peripheral vision

   2.   Japanese Garden Design

       a.   *Fuzei*: breeze, feeling
       b.   *Shakkei*: capture alive
       c.   Tuning perception

   3.   Natural History of Perception

       a.   Primacy of movement
       b.   Sifting process
       c.   Patterns of recognition

2. Framing

    1. Limits/Thresholds

        a. Reenactment
        b. Rites of passage
        c. Transition/transformation

    2. Decentralied / dissolution of the mass

        a. Counterform to support cathartic acts
        b. Multisensory evocation
        c. Affirms / gently emphasises instability

3. Thinking

    1. Layering

        a. Perceiving is also thinking
        b. Reasoning is also intuition
        c. Observation is also invention

    2. Improvisation

        a. Thinking through making
        b. Rules implicit in structure
        c. Freedom within constraints

    3. Nature of the Medium

        a. Flexibility to process
        b. Proximity to body
        c. Directness of consequence

    4. Omnidirectional Weaving

        a. Inductive/indicative
        b. Relationships between
        c. Form is meaning

Integral

1. Inhabiting

    1. Concrete not abstract

        a. Primordial historicity

   b.   Aperspectival
   c.   Inclusion of time

2.   Gracing the Cycles of Daily Life

   a.   Primal metaphors
   b.   Eddies
   c.   Atmosphere

3.   Architecture of Moments

   a.   Qualitatively textured
   b.   Surprise / suddenness
   c.   Condensations of care

2.   Playing

   1.   Counterforms

   a.   Affordances
   b.   Prehension
   c.   Intimate fabric

   2.   Visceral Urbanism

   a.   Dynamic engagement
   b.   Moving / feeling coextension
   c.   Porous boundaries

   3.   Healing

   1.   Chrysalis

   a.   Protective shell
   b.   Time out of time
   c.   Honoring process

   2.   Immersion in Nature

   a.   Biophilia
   b.   Hortophilia
   c.   Phytochemicals / microorganisms

   3.   Creative Engagement

   a.   Plants / gardening
   b.   Arts
   c.   Nurturing relations

4. Instrument for Healing

    a. Colors
    b. Acoustic privacy
    c. Postures

Index

Note: Page numbers in *italics* indicate a figure on the corresponding page.